The *Manhattan Tutors* Guide to the

Lower Level ISEE®

Quantitative Reasoning and Mathematics Achievement

Manhattan Tutors
217 East 70th Street #2291
New York, NY 10021
office@manhattan-tutors.com

Acknowledgements

Special thanks to:

Meghan Flanigan
Andrea Gottstein
Alex Polizzotti
Meredith Willis
Richard Wu

Copyright © 2023 by Manhattan Tutors, LLC. All rights reserved. No part of this book may be reproduced or retransmitted in any form or by any means, electronic or mechanical, including photocopying, recording, or by any information storage and retrieval system, without the written permission of the Publisher, except where permitted by law.

ISEE is a registered trademark of the Educational Records Bureau, which does not sponsor or endorse this product.

Manufactured in the USA

Contents

Part I
Introduction

How to Use This Book

This book is designed to help students in grades 4 and 5 master the Quantitative Reasoning and Mathematics Achievement sections of the Lower Level *Independent School Entrance Exam* (ISEE).

Over the years, the team at Manhattan Tutors has found that students are understandably overwhelmed by the enormous amount of information contained in most test prep books. The math sections tend to be particularly intimidating for students who are preparing for the test.

The Manhattan Tutors Guide to the Lower Level ISEE: Quantitative Reasoning and Mathematics Achievement was written with students in mind. Our streamlined guide is designed to provide students with a tailored study plan that they can use to focus their preparation and minimize the amount of time they need to get ready for the ISEE.

Here's your step-by-step guide for using this book:

1. With your student, read through the ISEE Math Strategies in Part II and complete the practice problems.

2. Have your student take the first practice test in Part V. Review the questions he or she answered incorrectly, and focus your remaining time on studying those question types and math fundamentals.

3. Six weeks before the real test, take the second practice test in Part V. Compare your student's results with those from the first practice test, and identify areas of improvement and areas he or she still needs to work on.

4. Four weeks before the real test, take the diagnostic test provided by the ERB. This test, *What to Expect on the Lower Level ISEE*, can be found at www.ERBLearn.org/parents/isee-preparation.

5. Remember: the ISEE is just one component of a comprehensive application. Schools consider a student's grades, extracurriculars, teacher recommendations, and personal essays, so try not to stress too much over the test!

Warmest regards,

The Staff of Manhattan Tutors

The Lower Level ISEE: What You Need to Know

The ISEE is a standardized admissions test administered by the Educational Records Bureau (ERB). Many of the independent elementary, middle, and high schools that are members of the ERB require the ISEE, or another standardized test such as the SSAT, as part of their admissions processes.

Test Structure
The ISEE is offered at four levels (primary, lower, middle, and upper), based on the grade to which the student is applying. The Lower Level ISEE is for students in grades 4 and 5 who are applying for admission to grades 5 and 6. The number of questions and the time allotted for each section can be found in the table below. The free-response essay is not scored, but it is sent to the schools to which you apply.

Section	Number of Questions	Time Allotted (in minutes)
Verbal Reasoning	34	20
Quantitative Reasoning	38	35
Reading Comprehension	25	25
Mathematics Achievement	30	30
Essay	1 prompt	30

Quantitative Reasoning and Mathematics Achievement
Both sections conform to standards set by the National Council of Teachers of Mathematics. *You cannot use a calculator on either math section, and scratch paper is not allowed.* You should plan on performing all of your calculations directly on the test booklet.

Quantitative Reasoning (QR), as the name would suggest, is designed to test your reasoning abilities. QR questions ask you to apply your knowledge of math concepts to word problems and real-world situations. You usually aren't expected to memorize equations or math terminology for this section; instead, you may need to estimate numerical values, compare and contrast quantities, use your reasoning abilities to calculate the probability of certain events, and analyze and interpret data. This section is split into two parts: word problems and quantitative comparisons.

Mathematics Achievement (MA) is a more "traditional" math test. You should expect to perform calculations, demonstrate knowledge of math terminology, and convert common metric units, among many other tasks.

Test Logistics

Registering for the ISEE

Students can take the ISEE *once per season*. The Fall, Winter, and Spring / Summer seasons run from August through November, December through March, and April through July, respectively. Most students now take the test once in October or November, and again in December, which gives them two shots at the test before the standard January application deadline. You should double-check the website of every school to which you are applying; some schools prefer that students apply earlier in the fall.

The test is offered in both paper-pencil and online formats and can be taken at local participating schools, ProMetric Test Centers, or ISEE Testing Offices. The most current test dates and locations are found at www.iseetest.org.

Accommodations

The ISEE offers a wide range of testing accommodations to students with documented learning differences or physical challenges. Your parent or guardian must set up an account at https://iseeonline.erblearn.org/ and submit documentation for ERB review. The process can take up to three weeks, so be sure to submit everything far in advance of when you plan to take the test.

The Day Before the Test

Don't plan on cramming the day before the test. You can spend a little time reviewing vocab flashcards and going over key math equations, but you should focus on being as calm and relaxed as possible. Most importantly, you should get all of the necessary items packed up the day before the test so that you don't forget anything as you're headed out the door!

What to Expect on the Day of the Test

When you arrive at your test site, you will need to show a hard copy of your verification letter in order to check in. You must also present an approved form of identification, such as your library card, birth certificate, social security card, school report card, school ID, passport, or green card. Photocopies of these forms of identification are accepted at school testing centers and ISEE testing offices; *hard copies of your ID must be presented at ProMetric Testing Centers.* Your parent or guardian must also have an original copy of his or her own ID if you are testing at a ProMetric Center. The Lower Level ISEE lasts 140 minutes. There is a 5 to 10 minute break after both the Quantitative Reasoning and the Mathematics Achievement sections.

What to Bring to the Test

Students taking the paper test should bring #2 pencils, as well as pens with blue or black ink. These items are not allowed if you are taking the test on a computer. We recommend you also bring an analog watch in case there is not a clock in the testing room. The following items are prohibited at all testing centers: cell phones and other electronic devices, scratch paper, calculators, calculator watches, rulers, protractors, compasses, dictionaries, and thesauruses.

Understanding Your Scores

The ISEE provides perhaps the most baffling score report of any standardized test. Your results will show four scores for each of the four multiple-choice sections of the test: a scaled score, percentile rank, stanine, and stanine analysis. When friends tell you what they scored on the ISEE, they're almost always talking about the stanines. Schools care most about your stanine and percentile rank.

Scaled Score: ranges from 760 to 940 for each section and is derived from your raw score. Your raw score is how many questions you answered correctly on each section.

Percentile Rank: compares your score in each section to other students in the same grade who have taken the test within the last three years. A percentile rank of 75, for example, means that you did as well as or better than 75 percent of students in your grade who have taken the ISEE within the last three years.

Stanine: ranges from 1 to 9 for each section. A score of 1 to 3 is considered below average, 4 to 6 average, and 7 to 9 above average.

Stanine Analysis: compares your Verbal Reasoning and Reading Comprehension scores and compares your Quantitative Reasoning and Mathematics Achievement scores.

Keep in mind that your score compares you only to students in your grade who have taken the test. Since students from grades 4 and 5 take the Lower Level ISEE, it wouldn't be fair for 4th graders to be scored on the same scale as 5th graders. That also means that the younger you are, the more likely you are to encounter unfamiliar material on the test.

Part II
Mathematics Strategies

Chapter 1
Strategies for Quantitative Reasoning and Mathematics Achievement

Mathematics Strategies

As with all standardized tests, you'll often hear that you must possess a thorough understanding of all the topics on the ISEE in order to do well. While this is what the ERB would like you to believe, it simply isn't true. Learning the math fundamentals tested on the ISEE should of course be one of your top priorities. However, mastering the strategies in this section can help boost your score even higher, and you should always be thinking of them as you move through the math section on the test.

Strategies are listed in order from least difficult to master to most difficult to master. There is a mini quiz after each section to help you practice implementing the strategies.

1. Fill in an answer for every question

There is no penalty for guessing on the ISEE, so you have a 25% chance of getting a question correct by randomly choosing A, B, C, or D. If you're able to eliminate one incorrect answer, your odds increase to 33%, and if you can eliminate two answers, then you have a 50% chance of guessing the correct answer!

You should review your answer key before time is up to make sure you've filled in every single bubble on the answer key. *Make sure you circle your answers in the test booklet, as well.* If you make a mistake when bubbling the answer key, it will be much easier to fix if you can compare the answer key and the circled answers in the test booklet.

Mini Quiz - Strategy #1
Questions: 6
Time Limit: 3 minutes

1. Meredith was trying to calculate the mean of her test scores. She did not know what she had scored on each of the first 3 tests but knew that the sum of her scores was 240. If Meredith scored a 90 on her fourth test, then what was the mean score for all four tests?

   (A)   79.25
   (B)   82.50
   (C)   85.75
   (D)   100.00

2. What is the value of x in the math equation $16 = 3x + 4$?

   (A)   1
   (B)   2
   (C)   3
   (D)   4

3. Jessie spent 30% of her 9-hour workday in meetings. How many minutes of her workday did she spend in meetings?

   (A)   2.7
   (B)   3
   (C)   162
   (D)   378

4. What is the value of n in the expression $\frac{20(25+35)}{4} = n$?

   (A)   200
   (B)   300
   (C)   400
   (D)   600

5. If the length of the base of a triangle is increased by 20 percent and the height is decreased by 40 percent, what is the percent decrease in the area of the triangle?

   (A)   8%
   (B)   20%
   (C)   28%
   (D)   30%

6. What is the sum of $1.9 + 3.7$?

   (A) $4\frac{3}{5}$

   (B) $5\frac{1}{5}$

   (C) $5\frac{2}{5}$

   (D) $5\frac{3}{5}$

Did you find those questions difficult? That's because several of them were Upper Level ISEE math questions! The time limit was also deliberately decreased on this quiz to force you to select answers quickly. If you applied Strategy #1, you should have still circled an answer for each question. Check the answer key to see how many you guessed correctly!

2. Pay close attention to what the question asks

Some answers might seem correct but don't address what the question asks. The writers of the ISEE are deliberately trying to trick you - don't fall for it! Pay close attention to key words in the questions so that you don't miss terms such as *positive*, *negative*, *sum*, etc. Reading comprehension still plays a huge role in the ISEE math section.

Example #1
Which positive value of x satisfies the equation $(x + 3)(x - 5) = 0$?

(A)   -5
(B)   -3
(C)   3
(D)   5

This question is more difficult than what you will see on the Lower Level ISEE. However, by using your reading comprehension skills you can still eliminate two wrong answer choices. The question specifically asks for a *positive* value. Therefore, you should immediately cross off (A) and (B). **Choice (D) is the only correct answer.**

In the Mini Quiz on the next page, key words are in bold. You should get in the habit of circling similar terms on every Lower Level ISEE math question.

Mini Quiz - Strategy #2
Questions: 3
Time Limit: 3 minutes

1. If $x + 4 = 6$, then $\mathbf{2x} = ?$

   (A)   2
   (B)   3
   (C)   4
   (D)   6

2. If Nicole walks 1 **mile** in 20 **minutes**, how many **miles** does she walk in 2 **hours**?

   (A)   1
   (B)   6
   (C)   12
   (D)   18

3. The width of a square is 8 inches. What is the square's **area**?

   (A)   8 in^2
   (B)   16 in^2
   (C)   32 in^2
   (D)   64 in^2

These questions weren't overly difficult, but you might have accidentally selected the wrong answer if you didn't confirm what the question was asking.

3. Be efficient with your time

You have just over one minute to complete each of the questions on the math sections. If you've been working on a question for 20 seconds and feel like you're stuck, it's time to move on. You can always go back to it later if you have time.

Each question is worth 1 point, regardless of difficulty. If you spend 15 minutes working on 10 impossible questions at the beginning of a section and you end up not having time to do 10 super easy questions at the end of a section, you just got 20 questions wrong! If you'd had time to work on those last 10 questions, at least you would have gotten 10 correct overall.

Mini Quiz - Strategy #3
Questions: 7
Time Limit: 7 minutes

1. If $4x + 3 = 15$, what is the value of $3x$?

   (A)   3
   (B)   6
   (C)   9
   (D)   12

2. If x can be divided by both 4 and 5 without leaving a remainder, then x can also be divided by which number without leaving a remainder?

   (A)   8
   (B)   12
   (C)   15
   (D)   20

3. Use the set of numbers shown to answer the question.

   $$\{2, 6, 10, 18, 24...\}$$

   Which describes this set of numbers?

   (A)   prime numbers
   (B)   composite numbers
   (C)   even numbers
   (D)   odd numbers

4. $2 + 20 =$

   (A)   2
   (B)   10
   (C)   20
   (D)   22

5. Use the pattern to help answer the question.

   $$1 + 3 = 2^2$$
   $$1 + 3 + 5 = 3^2$$
   $$1 + 3 + 5 + 7 = 4^2$$

   What is the solution to
   $1 + 3 + 5 + 7 + 9 + 11 + 13$?

   (A) 5^2
   (B) 7^2
   (C) 13^2
   (D) 15^2

6. Which of the following is the greatest?

   (A) $6.7 + 4.2$
   (B) $6.7 - 4.2$
   (C) $\frac{6.7}{4.2}$
   (D) 6.7×4.2

7. Which improper fraction is equivalent to $10\frac{1}{2}$?

   (A) $\frac{1}{2}$
   (B) $\frac{5}{2}$
   (C) $\frac{20}{2}$
   (D) $\frac{21}{2}$

Questions 3, 4, 6, and 7 should have been a bit easier than the others. If you spent too much time on 1, 2, and 5, you may not have had time to answer the easier questions.

4. Don't fall for trick answers

The ERB claims it doesn't include answers that are intended to trick students, but that's misleading. The ERB acknowledges that it includes *common mistakes or misconceptions* in its answer choices. Although there are some genuinely easy questions on the ISEE, be very careful when choosing your answer.

Example #1
Kayla draws a path on the coordinate grid. She begins at point (1,2) and moves 3 spaces to the right and 4 spaces up.

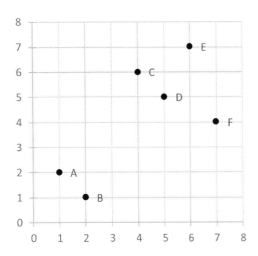

What is the point where Kayla lands?
(A)   C
(B)   D
(C)   E
(D)   F

Remember that on the coordinate grid, the first number in a pair of points refers to horizontal movement, and the second number refers to vertical movement. To find (1,2), start at (0,0) – also known as the origin – and then move right 1 and up 2. This lands at point *A*. Then, move 3 spaces to the right and 4 spaces up to land at point *C*. **Choice (A) is the correct answer**. If you got mixed up, you might have first gone 2 spaces to the right and 1 space up and landed on point *B* as your starting point. From there, if you went 3 spaces to the right and 4 spaces up, you would have landed on point *D*.

Mini Quiz - Strategy #4
Questions: 4
Time Limit: 4 minutes

1. What fraction of the largest triangle below is shaded in?

(A)　$\frac{4}{5}$

(B)　$\frac{5}{4}$

(C)　$\frac{4}{9}$

(D)　$\frac{9}{4}$

2. Which of the following fractions is equivalent to 0.3?

(A)　$\frac{3}{10}$

(B)　$\frac{3}{100}$

(C)　$\frac{30}{30}$

(D)　$\frac{30}{50}$

3. Brooks draws a path on the coordinate grid. He begins at point (3,1) and moves 3 spaces to the right and 4 spaces up.

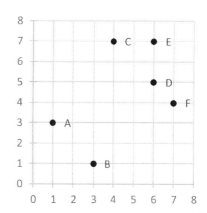

What is the point where Brooks lands?

(A)　C
(B)　D
(C)　E
(D)　F

4. Which of the following is equivalent to 8?

(A)　$12 \times 4 \div 2$
(B)　$16 \div 4 \times 2$
(C)　$48 \div 3 \times 2$
(D)　$4 \times 5 \div 2$

5. Work backwards

There is one major, helpful difference between the ISEE and the tests you take in school: it's entirely multiple choice. There is exactly one correct answer to each question, and you can use this to your advantage. If you encounter a question you don't know how to solve, try using the answer choices provided by the ISEE to work backwards.

Example #1
If $x + 2 = 10$, what is the value of x?

(A)   5
(B)   6
(C)   7
(D)   8

$5 + 2 = 7$, so (A) is incorrect. $6 + 2 = 8$, so (B) is also incorrect. It's probably pretty obvious to you that (C) doesn't work, either. $8 + 2 = 10$, so you know **(D) is the correct answer.**

Example #2
Dorothy recorded the number of grasshoppers on her front porch each day for 5 days. She spotted 4 more grasshoppers on Thursday than she did on Tuesday and Wednesday combined.

GRASSHOPPERS SPOTTED EACH DAY

Monday	🦗 🦗 🦗 🦗
Tuesday	🦗 🦗
Wednesday	🦗
Thursday	🦗 🦗 🦗 🦗 🦗
Friday	🦗 🦗

Based on the data, how many grasshoppers are represented by the 🦗?

(A)   1
(B)   2
(C)   3
(D)   4

This question is tricky. You can make it easier by using the given answer choices and working backwards. If (A) is correct, then Dorothy spotted a total of 3 grasshoppers on Tuesday and Wednesday combined and 5 grasshoppers on Thursday. But, 5 is only 2 greater than 3, so this doesn't match what the question says. Now, let's look at (B). If this answer is correct, then Dorothy spotted 6 grasshoppers on Tuesday and Wednesday combined, and 10 grasshoppers on Thursday. 10 is 4 greater than 6, **so (B) is the correct answer!**

Mini Quiz - Strategy #5
Questions: 4
Time Limit: none

1. Isaac recorded the number of hummingbirds at the feeder each day for 5 days. He spotted 5 more hummingbirds on Friday than he did on Monday and Thursday combined.

HUMMINGBIRDS SPOTTED EACH DAY

Monday	🐦 🐦
Tuesday	🐦 🐦 🐦
Wednesday	🐦
Thursday	🐦 🐦
Friday	🐦 🐦 🐦 🐦 🐦

Based on the data, how many hummingbirds are represented by the ?

(A)   1
(B)   3
(C)   5
(D)   7

2. If $2x + 1 = 7$, what is the value of x?

(A)   1
(B)   2
(C)   3
(D)   4

3. Lynelle solves a problem using the clue table.

Clue Table

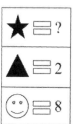

In the equation $☺ + (▲ \times ★) = 16$, what is the value of $★$?

(A)   1
(B)   2
(C)   3
(D)   4

4. If $4x - 1 = 19$, what is the value of x?

(A)   5
(B)   6
(C)   7
(D)   8

Working backwards is an advanced strategy that requires a lot of practice, but it's an extremely powerful tool once it's mastered. You can only work backwards when each answer choice is a number.

Answer Key - ISEE Math Strategies

Strategy #1

1. B
2. D
3. C
4. B
5. C
6. D

Strategy #2

1. C
2. B
3. D

Strategy #3

1. C
2. D
3. C
4. D
5. B
6. D
7. D

Strategy #4

1. C
2. A
3. B
4. B

Strategy #5

1. C
2. C
3. D
4. A

Part III
Mathematics Fundamentals

Chapter 2
Applied Arithmetic

Math Definitions

You should memorize the following definitions before taking the Lower Level ISEE.

Vocab Word	Definition	Examples
Integer	A number that does not contain fractions or decimals Integers can be positive, negative, or zero	-100, -5, 0, 2, 50
Even number	A number that is divisible by two. Zero is even	-34, -10, 0, 8, 92
Odd number	A number that is not divisible by two	-7, 1, 9, 99
Positive number	A number greater than zero	1, 4, 45, 100
Negative number	A number less than zero	-34, -16, -9, -5
Whole number	Positive integers and zero	0, 1, 5, 50, 75
Prime number	A number divisible only by 1 and itself. 1 is not prime. 2 is the only even prime number	2, 3, 5, 7, 11, 13, 17
Composite Number	A positive integer which is not prime	4, 10, 25, 50, 100
Consecutive numbers	A series of integers that appear in the same order as they do on the number line	5, 6, 7 -6, -5, -4
Distinct numbers	Numbers that are different from one another	1, 2, 3, 4, 5
Consecutive even integers	A series of even integers that appear in the same order as they do on the number line	-2, 0, 2, 4 34, 36, 38
Consecutive odd integers	A series of odd integers that appear in the same order as they do on the number line	-9, -7, -5 3, 5, 7
Sum	The result of addition	The sum of 5 and 7 is 12
Difference	The result of subtraction	The difference of 20 and 5 is 15
Product	The result of multiplication	The product of 3 and 9 is 27
Quotient	The result of division	The quotient of 12 and 4 is 3
Divisible by	A number is divisible by another if there is no remainder	10 is divisible by 2 7 is not divisible by 2
Remainder	The amount that is left over after performing division	When 9 is divided by 2, the remainder is 1
Inclusive	Includes all integers in a range	There are 5 integers, inclusive, from 7 to 11 (7, 8, 9, 10, & 11)

Digits	The integers from 0 to 9	123 has three digits
Factor	All of the integers that a certain integer is divisible by Each integer has limited factors	The factors of 20 are 1, 2, 4, 5, 10, and 20
Multiple	The result of multiplying an integer by another integer Each integer has infinite multiples	Multiples of 5 include 5, 10, 15, 20, 25, etc
Numerator	The top part of a fraction	The numerator of $\frac{4}{5}$ is 4
Denominator	The bottom part of a fraction	The denominator of $\frac{10}{13}$ is 13

Practice Problems

1. List 5 integers
2. List 5 prime numbers
3. Is 1 prime?
4. Is 2 prime?
5. List 4 consecutive odd integers
6. What is the quotient of 100 and 5?
7. List 5 multiples of 4
8. How many digits does 109,805 have?
9. When 100 is divided by 30, what is the remainder?
10. List 5 composite numbers
11. A student picked a number greater than 12 but less than 17. If the number is prime, what number did the student pick?
12. A student picked a number greater than 30 but less than 36. If the number is prime, what number did the student pick?
13. A student picked a number greater than 24 but less than 30. If the number is prime, what number did the student pick?
14. A student picked a number greater than 37 but less than 43. If the number is prime, what number did the student pick?
15. How many multiples of 3 are there between 20 and 50?
16. How many multiples of 6 are there between 10 and 40?
17. How many multiples of 4 are there between 0 and 21?
18. How many multiples of 3 are there between 1 and 34?

Intro to Exponents

Exponents are used to tell you how many times a certain number should be multiplied by itself. Exponents are composed of a *base*, which is written as a large number, and an *exponent*, which is the small number that indicates how many times the base should be multiplied times itself.

$$5^3 = 5 \times 5 \times 5 = 125 \qquad\qquad 2^5 = 2 \times 2 \times 2 \times 2 \times 2 = 32$$

2^2 is referred to as "two squared" or "two to the second," 2^3 is "two to the third," etc.

Exponents may show up in some of the PEMDAS questions on the test, so it's a good idea to have a basic understanding of how they work. Remember, exponents are the second operation, after parentheses, that should be completed in PEMDAS.

Practice Problems

1. $3^2 =$ _____

2. $6^2 =$ _____

3. $9^2 =$ _____

4. $2^6 =$ _____

5. $4^3 =$ _____

6. $2^4 =$ _____

Order of Operations / PEMDAS

The order of operations (PEMDAS) tells you what order to solve equations. You may already be familiar with the trick for remembering PEMDAS:

Please Excuse My Dear Aunt Sally

This means that you should always complete **p**arentheses first, then **e**xponents. **M**ultiplication and **d**ivision are then completed from left to right; finally, **a**ddition and **s**ubtraction are completed from left to right.

Correct: $12 - 5 + 3 = 7 + 3 = 10$ ✓

Incorrect: $12 - 5 + 3 = 12 - 8 = 4$ ✗

Correct: $14 \div 7 + 10 \times 4 - 6 + 5 = 2 + 40 - 6 + 5 = 42 - 6 + 5 = 36 + 5 = 41$ ✓

Incorrect: $14 \div 7 + 10 \times 4 - 6 + 5 = 2 + 40 - 6 + 5 = 42 - 6 + 5 = 42 - 11 = 31$ ✗

It is very easy to make careless mistakes when working with PEMDAS. To minimize the risk of errors, you can use the inverted pyramid method of solving PEMDAS problems: only simplify one type of operation per line, and then rewrite the simplified equation on the next line. Repeat as necessary until you have simplified the expression.

Example #1	Example #2
What is the value of	What is the value of
$(2^3 - 4) + (5 + 23) + 33 - 6$?	$10 \div 2 + 3 \times 3 - 4 + 1$?
(A) 59	(A) 11
(B) 60	(B) 18
(C) 63	(C) 21
(D) 66	(D) 30

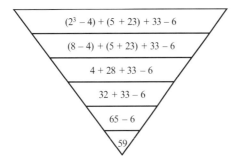

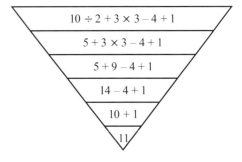

The correct answer is (A).

The correct answer is (A)

Practice Problems

1. $15 - 5 + 8 = $ _____
2. $14 + 12 - 6 + 2 = $ _____
3. $2 + (5 - 3) + 4 = $ _____
4. $5 + (9 - 4) + 7 = $ _____
5. $(6 + 2) + (6 - 3) + 1 = $ _____
6. $4 \times 4 - 6 \times 2 = $ _____

7. $3 \times (5 - 2) \div 9 = $ _____
8. $100 \div (20 \div 4 \times 2) = $ _____
9. $6 \times (2 + 7) \div (3 \times 3) = $ _____
10. $4 + (2 \times 3) \div (4 \div 2) = $ _____
11. $2 + (2^2 \times 3) \div (4 \div 2) = $ _____
12. $(2^3 \times 3^2) \div (6 \div 2) = $ _____

13.   Which expression is equivalent to 21?
      (A) $(3 + 3) \times 4 + 2$
      (B) $3 + (3 \times 4) + 2$
      (C) $3 + 3 \times (4 + 2)$
      (D) $3 + (3 \times 4 + 2)$

14.   Which expression is equivalent to 2?
      (A) $(2 \times 5) + 3 - 7$
      (B) $2 \times (5 + 3) - 7$
      (C) $2 \times 5 + (3 - 7)$
      (D) $2 \times (5 + 3 - 7)$

15.   Which expression is equivalent to 14?
      (A) $(3 + 1) \times 2 + 6$
      (B) $3 + (1 \times 2) + 6$
      (C) $3 + 1 \times (2 + 6)$
      (D) $3 + (1 \times 2 + 6)$

16.   Which expression is equivalent to 11?
      (A) $(4 \times 1) + 2 - 1$
      (B) $4 \times (1 + 2) - 1$
      (C) $4 \times 1 + (2 - 1)$
      (D) $4 \times (1 + 2 - 1)$

17.   Which expression is equivalent to 2?
      (A) $(6 - 2) + 2 \times 1$
      (B) $6 - (2 + 2) \times 1$
      (C) $6 - 2 + (2 \times 1)$
      (D) $6 - 2 + 2 \times 1$

18.   Which expression is equivalent to 7?
      (A) $(5 + 2) \times 3 - 2$
      (B) $5 + (2 \times 3) - 2$
      (C) $5 + 2 \times (3 - 2)$
      (D) $5 + (2 \times 3 - 2)$

Introduction to Fractions

Fractions are numerical quantities that are not whole numbers. They are represented in two parts: the numerator (the top) and the denominator (the bottom). Fractions indicate "part out of whole." Examples of fractions include $\frac{1}{2}$ and $\frac{16}{5}$. Fractions also indicate division. $\frac{1}{2}$, for example, means "one divided by two."

Visualizing Fractions
When first learning fractions, it is easiest to use shaded shapes to visualize them.

Example
What fraction is represented by the shaded section of the shape below?

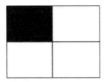

The square is divided into 4 equal sections, and 1 section is shaded in. Remember, fractions indicate "part out of whole." What *part* of the *whole* shape is shaded in? 1 part out of 4. You can represent this fraction as $\frac{1}{4}$

Something very important to note about the shape above is that *it was divided into 4 sections of equal size.* You cannot make a fraction out of one shape that has been divided into sections of different sizes. However, it is possible to say what fraction of a total number of shapes are shaded in, even if they are not all the same size.

Example
What fraction is represented by the unshaded section of the shape below?

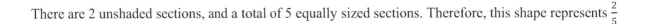

There are 2 unshaded sections, and a total of 5 equally sized sections. Therefore, this shape represents $\frac{2}{5}$

Visualizing Equivalent Fractions

Fractions that look different, like $\frac{1}{2}$ and $\frac{2}{4}$, can mean the same thing.

Example

   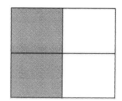   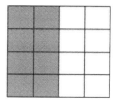

Above, you can see three large squares of equal size that have all been divided into a different number of equally sized smaller pieces. The first square is divided into 2 pieces, the second square is divided into 4 pieces, and the third square is divided into 16 pieces. Furthermore, an equally sized section of each of the larger squares has been shaded in.

The first square represents the fraction $\frac{1}{2}$: one piece out of two pieces has been shaded in. The second square represents the fraction $\frac{2}{4}$: two pieces out of four pieces have been shaded in. Finally, the third square represents $\frac{8}{16}$: eight pieces out of sixteen pieces have been shaded in.

Visually, you can see that the same total amount of each square has been shaded. That means that

$$\frac{1}{2} = \frac{2}{4} = \frac{8}{16}$$

Example

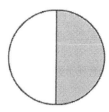   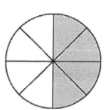

Above, you can see two circles of equal size that have been divided into a different number of equally sized pieces. The circle on the left represents the fraction $\frac{1}{2}$. The circle on the right represents the fraction $\frac{4}{8}$. When you look at the circles, you can see that the same portion of each one has been shaded in.

Therefore, $\frac{1}{2} = \frac{4}{8}$.

Reducing Fractions

To reduce a fraction, figure out a number that goes into both numbers in the fraction. For example, if both numbers in the fraction are even, you can start by dividing by 2.

Example

Reduce the fraction $\frac{8}{10}$

8 and 10 are both even, so you can divide both of them by 2. $\frac{8 \div 2}{10 \div 2} = \frac{4}{5}$. This fraction can't be reduced any further. $\frac{8}{10} = \frac{4}{5}$. Both will result in 0.8 if you plug them into a calculator.

If the numbers on the top and the bottom of the fraction are not both even, you'll have to think of a number other than 2 that they are both divisible by.

Example

Reduce the fraction $\frac{15}{25}$

2 does not go into 15 or 25, but 5 does. Divide both numbers by 5.

$\frac{15 \div 5}{25 \div 5} = \frac{3}{5}$. There are no numbers that go into both 3 and 5, so this fraction has been reduced as much as possible.

Example

Reduce the fraction $\frac{27}{81}$

Although 27 and 81 are not even, you might notice that they are both divisible by 9.

$\frac{27 \div 9}{81 \div 9} = \frac{3}{9}$. You're not finished just yet: 3 and 9 are both divisible by 3.

$\frac{3 \div 3}{9 \div 3} = \frac{1}{3}$. This fraction is now fully reduced.

Practice Problems

Fully Reduce

1. $\dfrac{10}{20}$

2. $\dfrac{6}{10}$

3. $\dfrac{15}{45}$

4. $\dfrac{999}{999}$

5. $\dfrac{232}{444}$

6. $\dfrac{55}{99}$

7. $\dfrac{100}{300}$

8. $\dfrac{126}{94}$

9. $\dfrac{12}{9}$

10. $\dfrac{20}{10}$

11. $\dfrac{32}{34}$

12. $\dfrac{7}{35}$

13. $\dfrac{10}{100}$

14. $\dfrac{8}{24}$

15. $\dfrac{15}{30}$

16. $\dfrac{5}{40}$

17. $\dfrac{20}{60}$

18. $\dfrac{40}{50}$

19. $\dfrac{18}{45}$

20. $\dfrac{12}{18}$

Improper Fractions and Mixed Numbers

So far we have dealt only with fractions in which the numerator is smaller than the denominator. In many instances, however, the numerator will be larger than the denominator. This type of fraction is known as an improper fraction. Because fractions indicate division, this means that improper fractions represent numbers larger than 1. $\frac{9}{4}$ means "9 divided by 4." While you might not know the exact value off the top of your head, you do know that 4 goes into 9 more than one time.

You will need to know how to convert between improper fractions and mixed numbers. Mixed numbers are another way of representing improper fractions. To convert an improper fraction into a mixed number, see how many times the denominator of the fraction goes evenly into the numerator of the fraction. That result goes on the left. Then, take whatever is left over (the remainder) and put it over what was originally the denominator of the fraction. This fraction goes on the right.

Example

Convert $\frac{9}{7}$ to a mixed number

7 goes into 9 one time, with a remainder of 2. Place the 1 on the left, then take the remaining 2 and put it on top of your original denominator, which gives you $1\frac{2}{7}$

Example

Convert $\frac{30}{11}$ to a mixed number

11 goes into 30 two times, with a remainder of 8. Put the 2 on the left and the 8 on top of the original denominator. The final answer is $2\frac{8}{11}$

To convert from a mixed number to an improper fraction, multiply the denominator of the fraction by the big number on the left. Then, add the numerator of the fraction to this number. This sum becomes the new numerator, while the original denominator remains the same.

Example

Convert $3\frac{4}{9}$ to an improper fraction

$9 \times 3 = 27$, and $27 + 4 = 31$. 31 is the new numerator, and the denominator is 9. The improper fraction is $\frac{31}{9}$

Representing Fractions as Whole Numbers

Fractions represent division. Therefore, $\frac{15}{1} = 15$, $\frac{40}{1} = 40$, etc.

Example
What fraction of the circle below is shaded in?

You can see that the whole fraction is shaded in, so in most cases 1 would be an acceptable answer. However, this question asks you to represent your answer as a fraction. There are 4 pieces, and all 4 pieces are shaded in, so the fraction is $\frac{4}{4}$

Example
What fraction of the circles below is shaded in?

In most cases, 2 would be an acceptable answer. Once again, you've been asked to give your answer as a fraction. Each circle has been divided into 2 pieces, and 4 pieces total have been shaded in, so the answer is $\frac{4}{2}$

Practice Problems

Convert to Mixed Numbers

1. $\frac{9}{4}$

2. $\frac{12}{5}$

3. $\frac{99}{80}$

4. $\frac{50}{40}$

5. $\frac{27}{4}$

6. $\frac{17}{16}$

7. $\frac{3}{2}$

8. $\frac{88}{45}$

Convert to Improper Fractions

9. $1\frac{2}{7}$

10. $2\frac{3}{4}$

11. $1\frac{5}{12}$

12. $4\frac{3}{8}$

13. $3\frac{4}{9}$

14. $5\frac{1}{5}$

15. $4\frac{2}{3}$

16. $8\frac{8}{9}$

Convert to Whole Numbers

17. $\frac{4}{2}$

18. $\frac{100}{10}$

19. $\frac{12}{3}$

20. $\frac{5}{5}$

21. $\frac{27}{9}$

Operations with Fractions

In this section, you will learn to add, subtract, multiply, divide, and compare fractions. You will also learn strategies for questions that involve adding or subtracting mixed numbers.

Adding and Subtracting Fractions

Adding and subtracting fractions requires a common denominator. That means the denominator of both fractions must be the same number. When you add or subtract the fractions, only the numerators will change.

Example

$$\frac{6}{11} + \frac{4}{11} = \frac{10}{11}$$

If the bottoms of the fractions are not the same, you have to do more work. You must ask yourself what number both of the denominators go into.

Example

$$\frac{3}{7} + \frac{1}{2} = ?$$

7 and 2 both go into 14. For $\frac{3}{7}$, $7 \times 2 = 14$, so you'll also need to multiply the numerator by 2, giving you $\frac{3 \times 2}{7 \times 2} = \frac{6}{14}$. For $\frac{1}{2}$, $2 \times 7 = 14$, so you'll also need to multiply 1 by 7, giving you $\frac{1 \times 7}{2 \times 7} = \frac{7}{14}$. Now that you've found a common denominator, you can add like you did in the first example. $\frac{3}{7} + \frac{1}{2} = \frac{6}{14} + \frac{7}{14} = \frac{13}{14}$

Sometimes, it can be tricky to find a common denominator. Using the *bow tie method* will help you easily find a common denominator in any pair of fractions!

Example

$$\frac{1}{7} + \frac{4}{9} = ?$$

Although you might have a hard time finding the common multiple of 7 and 9, you can easily solve this equation by using the bow tie method. $9 \times 1 = 9$, $7 \times 4 = 28$, and $7 \times 9 = 63$. You can rewrite this equation as $\frac{9}{63} + \frac{28}{63} = \frac{37}{63}$

Multiplying and Dividing Fractions
Multiplying and dividing fractions is much easier than adding and subtracting fractions! When multiplying, simply multiply straight across the numerator and straight across the denominator.

Example
$$\frac{6}{11} \times \frac{4}{11} = ?$$

$$\frac{6}{11} \times \frac{4}{11} = \frac{6 \times 4}{11 \times 11} = \frac{24}{121}$$

Dividing fractions requires two more steps than multiplying fractions. First, flip the second fraction. Then, change the division sign to multiplication and multiply like you did in the previous example. This method is called "keep, switch, flip," because you "keep" the first fraction, "switch" the division sign, and "flip" the second fraction.

Example
$$\frac{6}{11} \div \frac{4}{11} = ?$$

$$\frac{6}{11} \div \frac{4}{11} = \frac{6}{11} \times \frac{11}{4} = \frac{6 \times 11}{11 \times 4} = \frac{66}{44} = \frac{33}{22} = \frac{3}{2}$$

Finally, you should know that any fraction that has a 0 in the denominator is *undefined*. Fractions like $\frac{0}{0}$ or $\frac{19}{0}$ cannot be solved. Fractions with 0 in the numerator and any number but 0 in the denominator equal 0. For example, $\frac{0}{10} = 0$.

Comparing Fractions
You may be asked to compare fractions. Using a partial bowtie method makes this a piece of cake!

Example
Which is larger: $\frac{2}{11}$ or $\frac{3}{20}$?

$$\frac{2}{11} + \frac{3}{20} = \overset{40}{\underset{11}{2}} \times \overset{33}{\underset{20}{3}}$$

Multiply the denominator of one fraction by the numerator of the other fraction, and then write the product above the numerator. Whichever fraction has the larger number above it is the larger fraction. In this case, $\frac{2}{11} > \frac{3}{20}$ because 40 > 33.

You might be asked which fraction is the least of four fractions like $\frac{6}{10}, \frac{9}{20}, \frac{21}{40}$, and $\frac{25}{50}$. You may be able to see that only one of the fractions, $\frac{9}{20}$, is less than $\frac{1}{2}$, so you do not need to use the method shown above.

Comparing Multiple Fractions

You'll need to compare as many as four fractions on the Lower Level ISEE.

Example

Which fraction is the smallest?

(A) $\frac{4}{10}$

(B) $\frac{11}{20}$

(C) $\frac{6}{10}$

(D) $\frac{15}{30}$

You may be tempted to do something like this: first, compare $\frac{4}{10}$ and $\frac{11}{20}$. Using the method we learned in the previous section, you'll find that $\frac{4}{10}$ is smaller. Eliminate (B) since you are looking for the smallest fraction. Then, compare $\frac{4}{10}$ and $\frac{6}{10}$, etc. You'll notice that this method is quite time consuming. There is another strategy that will work better on this question. Notice that of the four fractions, only (A) represents a fraction less than $\frac{1}{2}$. The other three fractions are either greater than or equal to $\frac{1}{2}$. If you're comfortable enough eyeballing fractions like this, you'll be able to save yourself a lot of time! **(A) is the correct answer.**

Finding Intermediate Fractions

You may be asked to find a fraction that is between two other fractions.

Example

Which fraction is between $\frac{7}{10}$ and $\frac{18}{20}$?

(A) $\frac{1}{4}$

(B) $\frac{1}{3}$

(C) $\frac{4}{5}$

(D) $\frac{9}{10}$

There's a strategy for these questions, as well. If possible, change all the fractions so they have the same denominator. $\frac{7}{10} = \frac{14}{20}, \frac{1}{4} = \frac{5}{20}, \frac{4}{5} = \frac{16}{20}$, and $\frac{9}{10} = \frac{18}{20}$. The only fraction you can't convert is $\frac{1}{3}$, but that doesn't matter because you can already see that **(C) is the correct answer.** $\frac{14}{20} < \frac{16}{20} < \frac{18}{20}$

Adding, Subtracting, Multiplying, and Dividing Mixed Numbers

Finally, you will need to know how to manipulate mixed numbers using all of the basic operations. In most instances, it is easiest to first convert the mixed numbers to improper fractions, complete the operation as you normally would, and then convert back to a mixed number.

Example

$$2\frac{1}{4} + 3\frac{1}{2} = ?$$

$$2\frac{1}{4} + 3\frac{1}{2} = \frac{9}{4} + \frac{7}{2} = \frac{9}{4} + \frac{14}{4} = \frac{23}{4} = 5\frac{3}{4}$$

Example

$$5\frac{1}{6} - 3\frac{2}{3} = ?$$

$$5\frac{1}{6} - 3\frac{2}{3} = \frac{31}{6} - \frac{11}{3} = \frac{31}{6} - \frac{22}{6} = \frac{9}{6} = 1\frac{3}{6} = 1\frac{1}{2}$$

Example

$$1\frac{1}{4} \times 4\frac{4}{5} = ?$$

$$1\frac{1}{4} \times 4\frac{4}{5} = \frac{5}{4} \times \frac{24}{5} = \frac{5 \times 24}{4 \times 5} = \frac{120}{20} = 6$$

Example

$$2\frac{5}{8} \div 1\frac{1}{8} = ?$$

$$2\frac{5}{8} \div 1\frac{1}{8} = \frac{21}{8} \div \frac{9}{8} = \frac{21}{8} \times \frac{8}{9} = \frac{21 \times 8}{8 \times 9} = \frac{168}{72} = 2\frac{24}{72} = 2\frac{1}{3}$$

Practice Problems

Add, subtract, multiply, or divide

1. $\frac{5}{9} + \frac{2}{9} = $ _____

2. $\frac{5}{11} \div \frac{4}{9} = $ _____

3. $\frac{3}{7} \times \frac{6}{7} = $ _____

4. $\frac{11}{12} - \frac{3}{4} = $ _____

5. $\frac{19}{20} \div \frac{2}{3} = $ _____

6. $\frac{23}{25} + \frac{1}{5} = $ _____

7. $\frac{8}{13} - \frac{4}{13} = $ _____

8. $\frac{7}{8} - \frac{1}{2} = $ _____

9. $\frac{9}{11} \div \frac{3}{4} = $ _____

10. $\frac{2}{9} \times \frac{3}{7} = $ _____

Which fraction is larger?

11. $\frac{2}{7}$ or $\frac{3}{8}$

12. $\frac{3}{4}$ or $\frac{7}{10}$

13. $\frac{1}{6}$ or $\frac{1}{7}$

14. $\frac{4}{5}$ or $\frac{8}{10}$

15. $\frac{7}{12}$ or $\frac{6}{8}$

Which fraction is the largest?

16. $\frac{6}{12}$, $\frac{3}{7}$, $\frac{8}{14}$, or $\frac{1}{2}$

(A) $\frac{6}{12}$

(B) $\frac{3}{7}$

(C) $\frac{8}{14}$

(D) $\frac{1}{2}$

17. $\frac{12}{25}$, $\frac{14}{26}$, $\frac{3}{7}$, or $\frac{25}{50}$

(A) $\frac{12}{25}$

(B) $\frac{14}{26}$

(C) $\frac{3}{7}$

(D) $\frac{25}{50}$

18. $\frac{4}{9}$, $\frac{15}{33}$, $\frac{6}{13}$, or $\frac{45}{89}$

(A) $\frac{4}{9}$

(B) $\frac{15}{33}$

(C) $\frac{6}{13}$

(D) $\frac{45}{89}$

Which fraction is between the two fractions?

19. $\frac{1}{8}$ and $\frac{1}{2}$

    (A) $\frac{3}{8}$

    (B) $\frac{1}{10}$

    (C) $\frac{1}{16}$

    (D) $\frac{5}{9}$

22. $\frac{1}{2}$ and $\frac{9}{10}$

    (A) $\frac{3}{8}$

    (B) $\frac{3}{4}$

    (C) $\frac{6}{13}$

    (D) $\frac{19}{20}$

20. $\frac{1}{5}$ and $\frac{6}{10}$

    (A) $\frac{7}{10}$

    (B) $\frac{1}{2}$

    (C) $\frac{1}{6}$

    (D) $\frac{2}{10}$

Solve

23. $1\frac{3}{7} + 2\frac{2}{14}$

24. $3\frac{4}{5} \times 2\frac{1}{7}$

25. $5\frac{5}{6} \div 2\frac{1}{4}$

26. $7\frac{1}{3} - 4\frac{2}{3}$

27. $1\frac{7}{8} + 2\frac{1}{4}$

21. $\frac{3}{5}$ and $\frac{11}{15}$

    (A) $\frac{11}{20}$

    (B) $\frac{1}{4}$

    (C) $\frac{1}{2}$

    (D) $\frac{2}{3}$

28. $6\frac{2}{5} - 3\frac{1}{10}$

Decimals

You will need to be able to add, subtract, and convert decimals on the Lower Level ISEE.

Adding and Subtracting Decimals

To add and subtract decimals, line up the decimal points and then add or subtract as you normally would.

$$
\begin{array}{r}
17.670 \\
+\ \ 4.321 \\
\hline
21.991
\end{array}
\qquad\qquad
\begin{array}{r}
9.0100 \\
-\ \ .0221 \\
\hline
8.9879
\end{array}
$$

Converting Fractions to Decimals

It's easiest to convert fractions to decimals when the denominator of the fraction is 100.

$$\frac{50}{100} = 0.50 \qquad \frac{99}{100} = 0.99 \qquad \frac{36}{100} = 0.36 \qquad \frac{8}{100} = 0.08$$

Notice that all you need to do is move the decimal place in the numerator of the fraction two spaces to the left in order to create a decimal.

What do you do if the number in the bottom of the fraction is not 100? Use multiplication to change it into 100!

$$\frac{4}{25} = \frac{4 \times 4}{25 \times 4} = \frac{16}{100} = 0.16 \qquad \frac{9}{10} = \frac{9 \times 10}{10 \times 10} = \frac{90}{100} = 0.90 \qquad \frac{1}{50} = \frac{1 \times 2}{50 \times 2} = \frac{2}{100} = 0.02$$

Converting Decimals to Fractions

This is pretty easy: when you are given a decimal, move the decimal two places to the right, put that number in a fraction over 100, and reduce if necessary.

$$0.73 = \frac{73}{100} \qquad 0.42 = \frac{42}{100} = \frac{21}{50} \qquad 0.01 = \frac{1}{100} \qquad 0.12 = \frac{12}{100} = \frac{3}{25}$$

Multiplying

To multiply decimals, remove all of the decimals from the equation and then multiply as you normally would. When you're finished, add back in the total number of decimal places that were in the original numbers.

Example

$1.5 \times 2.5 = 15 \times 25 = 375 = 3.75$

There were 2 decimal places in the original equation (0.5 and 0.5), so 2 decimal places must be added in at the end.

Converting Decimals to Mixed Numbers

Finally, you'll need to be comfortable converting decimals to mixed numbers.

Example

What is the sum of 2.9 + 1.7?

(A) $3\frac{3}{5}$

(B) $4\frac{1}{5}$

(C) $4\frac{2}{5}$

(D) $4\frac{3}{5}$

First, add the decimals to get 4.6. You can eliminate (A) because it starts with a 3. Then, convert 0.6 to a mixed number:

$$0.6 = \frac{60}{100} = \frac{6}{10} = \frac{3}{5}$$

(D) is the correct answer.

Practice Problems

1. $4.954 - 2.91 = $ _____
2. $3.21 + 0.1202 = $ _____
3. $11.43 - 5.921 = $ _____
4. $12.5 + 6.34 = $ _____
5. $0.491 - 0.199 = $ _____
6. $10.9 + 0.04 = $ _____
7. $4.09 + 6.112 = $ _____
8. $1.2304 - .503 = $ _____
9. $3.2 \times 1.1 = $ _____
10. $4.5 \times 2.5 = $ _____
11. $3.75 \times 1.25 = $ _____
12. $2.4 \times 3.1 = $ _____
13. $5.25 \times 3.75 = $ _____
14.   Convert .55 to a fraction
15.   Convert .09 to a fraction
16.   Convert .40 to a fraction
17.   Convert .12 to a fraction
18.   Convert .95 to a fraction

19.   Convert $\frac{43}{100}$ to a decimal

20.   Convert $\frac{6}{100}$ to a decimal

21.   Convert $\frac{93}{100}$ to a decimal

22.   Convert $\frac{1}{100}$ to a decimal

23.   Convert $\frac{55}{100}$ to a decimal

24.   Convert 1.1 + 2.3 to a mixed number
25.   Convert 2.5 + 1.3 to a mixed number
26.   Convert 1.9 + 6.7 to a mixed number
27.   Convert 4.4 + 2.3 to a mixed number

Negative Numbers

Adding, subtracting, multiplying, and dividing negative numbers are key skills that you must be able to perform quickly and accurately on the ISEE.

Adding and Subtracting Negative Numbers
You should always think of the number line when you have to add or subtract negative numbers.

Example
$10 + (-5) = ?$

Imagine 10 on the number line. If you add 5 to 10, it would move 5 units to the right, giving you 15. By adding *negative* five, you are adding "negativeness" to the 10, which drags it left on the number line by 5 units. The answer is 5.

Example
$-5 + (-2) = ?$

Imagine -5 on the number line. If you added +2, you would move two units to the right, resulting in -3. However, adding -2 means you move two units to the left. The answer is -7.

Example
$13 - (-7) = ?$

Imagine 13 on the number line. You can think of subtracting negative 7 as "taking away negativeness," which will result in an answer that is more positive than the original number. The answer is 20.

Students generally become confused when they start dealing with subtracting positive numbers from negative numbers. However, the concept is exactly the same!

Example
$-3 - 5 = ?$
First, imagine -3 on the number line. If you subtract 5 from +3, you would move to the left. You should do the same thing when starting with a negative number. Start at -3, and move 5 units to the left. The answer is -8.

Example
$-9 - (-6) = ?$

Any time you have to "minus a negative," you can instead change it to "plus a positive." You can also think of this as "taking away negativeness," making the final answer more positive. $-9 - (-6) = -9 + (+6) = -3$.

Practice Questions

1. $5 + 27 = $ _____
2. $4 + 8 = $ _____
3. $101 - 21 = $ _____
4. $45 - 17 = $ _____
5. $10 - 15 = $ _____
6. $0 - 47 = $ _____
7. $10 + (-8) = $ _____
8. $28 + (-11) = $ _____

9. $-18 + (-10) = $ _____
10. $-29 + 15 = $ _____
11. $-36 + 12 = $ _____
12. $-100 + (-200) = $ _____
13. $0 + (-10) = $ _____
14. $10 - (-4) = $ _____
15. $27 - (-8) = $ _____
16. $0 - (-11) = $ _____

Percents

Percent means "out of 100." When you are asked to find a percent, it's the same thing as finding how many times out of 100 times something happens. Once you've mastered fractions and decimals, dealing with percents is easy.

Converting Fractions into Percents
It's easiest to convert fractions into percents when the denominator of the fraction is 100.

$$\frac{50}{100} = 0.50 = 50\% \qquad\qquad \frac{97}{100} = 0.97 = 97\% \qquad\qquad \frac{1}{100} = 0.01 = 1\%$$

If the denominator is 100, you can skip the middle step and convert directly from a fraction to a percent by adding a percent sign to the numerator.

If the denominator of the fraction is not 100, you'll need to multiply in order to change it to 100.

$$\frac{10}{25} = \frac{10 \times 4}{25 \times 4} = \frac{40}{100} = 0.40 = 40\% \qquad\qquad \frac{7}{10} = \frac{7 \times 10}{10 \times 10} = \frac{70}{100} = 0.70 = 70\%$$

Converting Percents into Fractions
Converting percents into fractions is also very easy. Drop the percent sign and put the number on the top of a fraction. The denominator of the fraction will always be 100. Then, reduce the fraction if necessary.

$$35\% = \frac{35}{100} = \frac{7}{20} \qquad\qquad 8\% = \frac{8}{100} = \frac{2}{25} \qquad\qquad 99\% = \frac{99}{100}$$

Practice Problems

Convert the Fractions to Percents

1. $\frac{14}{100}$

2. $\frac{65}{100}$

3. $\frac{1}{2}$

4. $\frac{45}{50}$

5. $\frac{8}{10}$

6. $\frac{3}{4}$

Convert the Percents to Decimals

7. 90%
8. 65%
9. 3%
10. 12%

Convert the Percents to Fractions

11. 15%
12. 28%
13. 63%
14. 44%

Units of Measurement

You should memorize the following units of measurement before taking the Lower Level ISEE. Related questions on the test most often ask for the appropriate units of measurement for a specific item.

Length

Standard unit of measure:

meter

1 meter is approximately 3 feet.

Related units:

Millimeter - the thickness of a credit card
Centimeter - a bit less than half an inch
Kilometer - a bit more than half a mile

Mass

Standard unit of measure:

gram

1 gram is approximately the weight of a sugar packet

Related units:

Milligram - about the weight of a snowflake
Kilogram - a little more than two pounds

Volume

Standard unit of measure:

liter

Large bottles of soda are 2 liters

Related units:

Milliliter: there are about 5 milliliters in a teaspoon

Prefixes

You may have noticed that the related units above all use the same prefixes.

Milli: one thousandth
Centi: one hundredth
Kilo: one thousand

Memorizing these prefixes will help you recognize any units of measurement that appear on the ISEE.

Practice Questions

1. What units are most appropriate for measuring the length of a leaf?
2. What units are most appropriate for measuring the weight of a basketball?
3. What units are most appropriate for measuring the volume of a small bottle of medicine?
4. What units are most appropriate for measuring the volume of a bathtub?
5. What units are most appropriate for measuring the weight of a car?
6. What units are most appropriate for measuring the length of a basketball court?
7. What units are most appropriate for measuring the weight of a person?
8. What units are most appropriate for measuring the length of a credit card?

Perimeter and Area

Perimeter measures the length of the outside of a shape, while area measure the space inside of a shape.

Perimeter

To find perimeter, add up the lengths of all of a shape's sides.

<table>
<tr>
<td>

The easiest questions will provide you with all the lengths.

Example
What is the perimeter of the triangle shown below?

(A)   4 cm
(B)   5 cm
(C)   9 cm
(D)   14 cm

$5 + 5 + 4 = 14$, so **the correct answer is (D).**

</td>
<td>

Harder questions will only provide some of the side lengths.

Example
What is the perimeter of the rectangle shown below?

(A)   3 ft
(B)   6 ft
(C)   9 ft
(D)   18 ft

The side across from 3 ft is also equal to 3 ft. The side across from 6 ft is also equal to 6 ft.
$3 + 3 + 6 + 6 = 18$. **The correct answer is (D).**

</td>
</tr>
</table>

Area

On the Lower Level ISEE, you will only be asked to find the area of squares and rectangles. To find the area of a square or rectangle, multiply the length by the width. Area is labeled in "square units."

<table>
<tr>
<td>

Example
What is the area of the rectangle shown below?

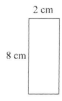

(A)   10 square centimeters
(B)   14 square centimeters
(C)   16 square centimeters
(D)   20 square centimeters

$8 \times 2 = 16$. **The correct answer is (C).**

</td>
<td>

Example
What is the area of a square with a side length of 5 inches?

(A)   5 square inches
(B)   10 square inches
(C)   20 square inches
(D)   25 square inches

The lengths of all four sides of a square are equal. $5 \times 5 = 25$. **The correct answer is (D).**

</td>
</tr>
</table>

Triangle Area

The equation to find the area of a triangle is "one half base times height," which can be written as $\frac{1}{2}bh$ or $\frac{bh}{2}$. The base and height of the triangle must be perpendicular to each other.

Example
What is the area of the triangle below?

8 in

6 in

(A)   8 square inches
(B)   14 square inches
(C)   24 square inches
(D)   48 square inches

The base of the triangle is 6, and the height of the triangle is 8. $\frac{(6)(8)}{2} = 24$. **The correct answer is (C).**

Example
A triangle has an area of 25 square centimeters. If the triangle's base is 10 centimeters long, what is the triangle's height?
(A)   5 cm
(B)   10 cm
(C)   15 cm
(D)   20 cm

Set up the equation and fill in the missing information:

$$\frac{1}{2}bh = A$$

$$\frac{1}{2}(10)h = 25$$

$$5h = 25$$

$$h = 5$$

The correct answer is (A)

Applied Area

Some questions will combine multiple shapes and ask you to find the area. In these questions, you should find the area of each individual shape and then add the areas together to find the total area.

Example
What is the area of the figure shown below?

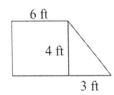

6 ft

4 ft

3 ft

(A)   6 square feet
(B)   12 square feet
(C)   24 square feet
(D)   30 square feet

Find the area of each shape individually. The rectangle is 24 square feet (6×4). The triangle is 6 square feet ($\frac{1}{2} \times 4 \times 3$). $24 + 6 = 30$. **The correct answer is (D).**

Example

The perimeter of a square is 16 inches. If a rectangle with a width of 2 inches has the same area as the square, what is the length of the rectangle in inches?

(A)   6
(B)   8
(C)   10
(D)   12

First, find the area of the square. All four sides of a square are the same length, so divide the perimeter by 4 to find the length of one side. Each side of this square is 4 inches. Then, multiple the lengths of adjacent sides to find the area: 4 × 4 = 16. The area of this square is 16 square inches. Finally, ask yourself "what times 2 equals 16?" **The correct answer is (B).**

Practice Problems

1.   What is the area of a square with a side length of 6 centimeters?

2.   What is the perimeter of the regular pentagon shown below?

4 in

3.   What is the area of a rectangle with a width of 4 feet and a length of 12 feet?

4.   The perimeter of a square is 20 inches. If a rectangle with a width of 1 inch has the same area as the square, what is the length of the rectangle in inches?

5.   What is the area of the figure shown below?

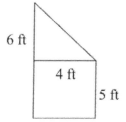

6.   What is the area of the triangle shown below?

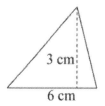

3 cm

6 cm

7.   What is the perimeter of the trapezoid shown below?

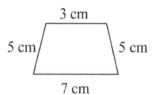

8.   What is the perimeter of a rectangle with a width of 6 feet and a length of 4 feet?

9.   What is the area of the shaded region in the figure shown below?

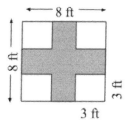

10. What is the area of the figure shown below?

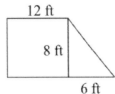

11. What is the area of the triangle shown below?

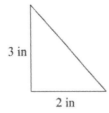

12. Each square in the shape shown below has an area of 4 square centimeters. What is the shape's total area?

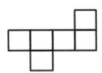

13. What is the perimeter of a regular hexagon with side lengths equal to 5 meters each?

14. The perimeter of a square is 40 inches. If a rectangle with a width of 25 inches has the same area as the square, what is the length of the rectangle in inches?

15. What is the area of the unshaded region in the figure below?

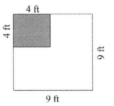

16. What is the area of the triangle shown below?

17. The perimeter of a square is 32 inches. If a rectangle with a width of 16 inches has the same area as the square, what is the length of the rectangle in inches?

18. Each square in the figure below has a perimeter of 12 inches. What is the total perimeter of the 5 shaded shapes in the figure?

19. What is the perimeter of a triangle with three equal sides of 3 inches each?

20. What is the area of the shaded region in the figure below?

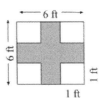

21. What is the width of a rectangle with an area of 45 square feet and a length of 5 feet?

22. What is the area of the figure shown below?

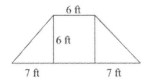

Mathematical Properties

There are four mathematical properties you should memorize for the Lower Level ISEE.

Associative Property

The *associative property* states that when adding or multiplying, the sum or product will be the same regardless of how the numbers are grouped.

Examples

$$2 + 7 + 5 = 2 + 7 + 5$$
$$(2 + 7) + 5 = 2 + (7 + 5)$$
$$9 + 5 = 2 + 12$$
$$14 = 14$$

$$3 \times 4 \times 2 = 3 \times 4 \times 2$$
$$(3 \times 4) \times 2 = 3 \times (4 \times 2)$$
$$12 \times 2 = 3 \times 8$$
$$24 = 24$$

The associative property does not work with subtraction or division.

Commutative Property

The *commutative property* states that you can reverse the order of numbers in addition and multiplication and still get the same answer.

Examples

$$3 + 6 = 6 + 3$$
$$9 = 9$$

$$3 \times 6 = 6 \times 3$$
$$18 = 18$$

The commutative property does not work with subtraction or division.

Distributive Property

The *distributive property* states that you get the same answer when you multiply by a group of numbers added together as you do when you multiply each number separately and then add the products together.

Examples

$$3 \times (2 + 4) = 3 \times 2 + 3 \times 4$$
$$3 \times 6 = 6 + 12$$
$$18 = 18$$

$$(4 + 5) \times 3 = 4 \times 3 + 5 \times 3$$
$$9 \times 3 = 12 + 15$$
$$27 = 27$$

Identity Property

The *identity property* states that any number multiplied by 1 is itself.

Examples

$$6 \times 1 = 6$$

$$99 \times 1 = 99$$

Practice Problems

Identify the Property

1. $10 \times 1 = 10$

2. $6 \times 2 = 2 \times 6$

3. $1 \times 1 = 1$

4. $(4 \times 8) \times 6 = 4 \times (8 \times 6)$

5. $(8 \times 10) + (8 \times 2) = 8 \times (10 + 2)$

6. $1 \times 7 = 7$

7. $(9 \times 6) \times 7 = 9 \times (6 \times 7)$

8. $3 + 9 = 9 + 3$

9. $4 \times (5 + 7) = 4 \times 5 + 4 \times 7$

10. $12 + 4 + 2 = 2 + 4 + 12$

Select the Best Answer

11. Which diagram best represents the distributive property?
    (A) $\bullet \times 1 = \bullet$
    (B) $(\blacktriangle + \blacksquare) + \bullet = \blacktriangle + (\blacksquare + \bullet)$
    (C) $\blacktriangle \times \blacksquare = \blacksquare \times \blacktriangle$
    (D) $\blacksquare \times (\blacktriangle + \bullet) = (\blacksquare \times \blacktriangle) + (\blacksquare \times \bullet)$

12. Which diagram best represents the identity property?
    (A) $\blacktriangle \times (\blacksquare + \bullet) = (\blacktriangle \times \blacksquare) + (\blacktriangle \times \bullet)$
    (B) $\blacktriangle \times 1 = \blacktriangle$
    (C) $\blacktriangle + \bullet = \bullet + \blacktriangle$
    (D) $(\blacktriangle + \bullet) + \blacksquare = \blacktriangle + (\bullet + \blacksquare)$

13. Which expression correctly uses the distributive property to solve $3 \times (2 + 4)$?
    (A) $(3 \times 2) + 4$
    (B) $(3 \times 4) + 2$
    (C) $(3 + 2) \times (3 + 4)$
    (D) $(3 \times 2) + (3 \times 4)$

14. Which diagram best represents the distributive property?
    (A) $\blacktriangle \times (\blacksquare + \bullet) = (\blacktriangle \times \blacksquare) + (\blacktriangle \times \bullet)$
    (B) $\blacktriangle \times 1 = \blacktriangle$
    (C) $\blacktriangle + \bullet = \bullet + \blacktriangle$
    (D) $(\blacktriangle + \bullet) + \blacksquare = \blacktriangle + (\bullet + \blacksquare)$

15. Which diagram best represents the commutative property?
    (A) $\bullet \times 1 = \bullet$
    (B) $(\blacktriangle + \blacksquare) + \bullet = \blacktriangle + (\blacksquare + \bullet)$
    (C) $\blacktriangle \times \blacksquare = \blacksquare \times \blacktriangle$
    (D) $\blacksquare \times (\blacktriangle + \bullet) = (\blacksquare \times \blacktriangle) + (\blacksquare \times \bullet)$

16. Which diagram best represents the commutative property?
    (A) $\blacktriangle \times (\blacksquare + \bullet) = (\blacktriangle \times \blacksquare) + (\blacktriangle \times \bullet)$
    (B) $\blacktriangle \times 1 = \blacktriangle$
    (C) $\blacktriangle + \bullet = \bullet + \blacktriangle$
    (D) $(\blacktriangle + \bullet) + \blacksquare = \blacktriangle + (\bullet + \blacksquare)$

17. Which expression correctly uses the distributive property to solve $(3 + 5) \times 7$?
    (A) $(3 \times 7) + 5$
    (B) $(3 \times 7) + (5 \times 7)$
    (C) $(3 \times 5) + 7$
    (D) $(3 + 5) \times (3 + 7)$

Clocks and Telling Time

You need to know how to read analog clocks and how to tell time on the Lower Level ISEE.

There are a few things you must memorize in order to tell time:

1. There are 24 hours in a day

2. There are 60 minutes in 1 hour

3. The short hand on the clock points to the hour

4. The long hand on the clock points to the minute

5. Each number on a clock represents 1 hour. Each number on a clock *also* represents 5 minutes

Telling Time on an Analog Clock
Let's see what this looks like in practice. The clocks below have been divided into sections to make telling time easier. The faces of the clocks have been divided into 12 equally sized sections, each of which has a number inside of it. If the hour hand falls on 6 or anywhere inside the section labeled 6, for example, then the hour is 6. It doesn't matter what part of the section the hour hand lands in.

On the clock above, the short hand is pointing at 8, and the long hand is pointing at 12. That means the hour is 8, and the minutes are 00, so the time is 8:00. On analog clocks, you can't tell if it's A.M. or P.M.

This clock is also divided into 12 sections, but it shows a different time. The hour hand falls into the section labeled 2. The minute hand is pointing at 11. Each number that circles the outside of the clock represents 5 minutes. $11 \times 5 = 55$, so 11 represents 55 minutes. The time on this clock is 2:55.

The hour hand on this clock falls into the 4 section, and the minute hand points to 6. 6 × 5 = 30, so the 6 represents 30 minutes. The time is 4:30.

Finding Elapsed, Starting, and Ending Times

There are 60 minutes in 1 hour. 1 minute after 1:59, for example, is 2:00. It is *not* 1:60! Finding elapsed time is easiest when you work in increments of 1 hour.

Example
It is 1:20 P.M. What time will it be in 2 hours?

In 1 hour, it will be 2:20 P.M. In 2 hours, it will be 3:20 P.M.

Example
It is 3:15 A.M. What time will it be in 3 hours and 10 minutes?

In 3 hours it will be 6:15 A.M. Add on an additional 10 minutes to get 6:25 A.M.

Example
A student started looking for his watch at 4:25 P.M. How much time had elapsed if he found his watch at 6:00 P.M.?

4:25 to 5:25 is 1 hour. 25 to 60 is 35 minutes. 1 hour and 35 minutes had elapsed.

Example
A girl walked her dog for 1 hour and 15 minutes. If she finished walking her dog at 3:25 P.M., what time did she start?

3:25 P.M. minus 1 hour is 2:25 P.M. 2:25 P.M. minus 15 minutes is 2:10 P.M.

Converting Times

To convert minutes to hours, remember that there are 60 minutes in 1 hour.

Example
120 minutes equals how many hours?

120 ÷ 60 = 2. Therefore, 120 minutes equals 2 hours exactly.

Example
186 minutes equals how many hours?

186 ÷ 60 = 3 remainder 6. Therefore, 186 minutes equals 3 hours and 6 minutes.

Practice Problems

Determine the Elapsed Time

1. 2:10 + _____ = 3:10

2. 4:15 + _____ = 7:40

3. 1:35 + _____ = 4:15

4. 10:15 + _____ = 11:55

5. Joey finished his homework at 6:15 P.M. If he started at 4:00 P.M., how long did it take him to finish?

6. An infant woke up from a nap at 3:40 P.M. If she originally went to sleep at 1:20 P.M., how long was her nap?

7. A boy helped his father cook dinner. They finished cooking at 7:05 P.M. If they started cooking at 6:20 P.M., how long did it take them?

8. Paige went for a bike ride at 5:40 P.M. If she got home at 8:10 P.M., how long was her bike ride?

Determine the Ending Time

9. 2:00 + 3:00 = _____

10. 4:15 + 6:20 = _____

11. 1:25 + 6:30 = _____

12. 11:10 + 0:50 = _____

13. Jessica started jogging at 2:50 P.M. If she jogged for 3 hours and 30 minutes, what time did she finish?

14. Vanessa spent 1 hour and 5 minutes reading a book. If she started reading at 4:05 P.M., what time was it when she finished?

15. Victor went to the movies at 3:30 P.M. If the movie was 2 hours and 40 minutes long, what time was it when Victor finished?

Convert Minutes to Hours

16. 145 minutes equals _____

17. 68 minutes equals _____

18. 230 minutes equals _____

19. 170 minutes equals _____

20. 310 minutes equals _____

Determine the Time Shown

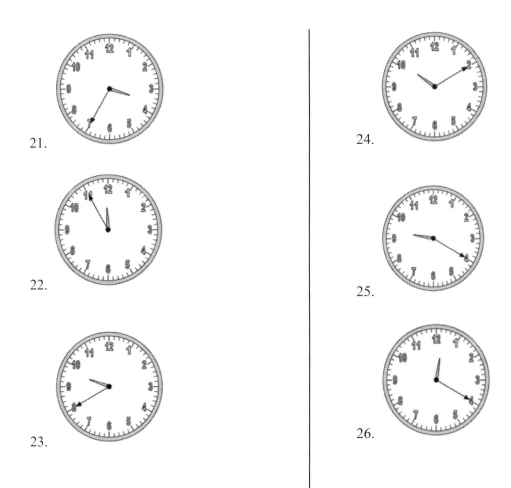

21.

22.

23.

24.

25.

26.

Number Lines

Writing numbers down on a number line makes it easy to tell which numbers are larger and which numbers are smaller.

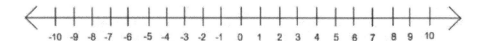

The number line above demonstrates this concept. The numbers grow larger as you move to the right on the number line. Number lines always go in order from left to right.

On the Lower Level ISEE, you may be asked questions about number lines with integers or fractions. These questions could test your ability to fill in an empty number line or find equivalent fractions on a number line.

When each tick mark on the number line indicates an increase or decrease of 1, filling in the number line is easy.

Example
Each tick mark on the number line below indicates 1. Fill in the missing tick marks on the number line.

17

If you know how to add and subtract, you can complete this question without any problems. 1 greater than 17 is 18, so the tick mark to the right of 17 indicates 18. 1 less than 17 is 16, so the tick mark to the left of 17 indicates 16, and so on. You can see the filled in number line below:

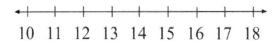

10 11 12 13 14 15 16 17 18

Finding Missing Values on Number Lines

The tick marks on number lines *do not always indicate 1*, and this is where things get more difficult.

If each tick mark represented 1, then the number line would look like this when you fill it in:

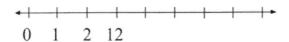

That's obviously incorrect. To determine the value of each tick mark, count the number of equal spaces between 0 and 12. The number line is divided into 3 equally sized sections.

Find the difference between the labeled points on the number line: $12 - 0 = 12$. Then, divide the difference by the number of equally sized spaces between the two tick marks: $12 \div 3 = 4$. Each tick mark represents an increase of 4.

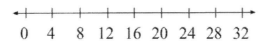

This method works regardless of what the two given numbers on the number line are.

Example

Find the value of the tick mark labeled x.

There are 4 equally sized spaces between 6 and 38. $38 - 6 = 32$. $32 \div 4 = 8$. Therefore, each tick mark represents an increase of 8. The completed number line would look like this:

$x = 46$.

Fractions and Number Lines

Finding fractions on number lines works exactly the same way as finding integers.

Example

On the number line below, find the value of each tick mark and fill in the missing tick marks.

There are 6 equally sized spaces between 0 and 1. $1 - 0 = 1$. $1 \div 6 = \frac{1}{6}$. Each tick mark represents an increase of $\frac{1}{6}$

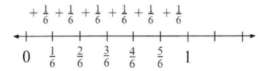

Example

Find the values of x, y, and z on the number line below.

There are 3 equally sized spaces between 1 and 2. $2 - 1 = 1$. $1 \div 3 = \frac{1}{3}$. Each tick mark represents a increase of $\frac{1}{3}$

The value of x is $\frac{2}{3}$, the value of y is $1\frac{1}{3}$, and the value of z is $2\frac{1}{3}$

Equivalent Fractions on Number Lines

You may be asked to find equivalent fractions on number lines.

Example

Using the number lines shown below, what is the equivalent fraction to $\frac{1}{2}$?

On the top number line, there are 2 equally sized spaces between 0 and 1. $1 - 0 = 1$. $1 \div 2 = \frac{1}{2}$. Therefore, each tick mark represents an increase of $\frac{1}{2}$. On the bottom number line, there are 8 equally sized spaces between 0 and 1. $1 - 0 = 1$. $1 \div 8 = \frac{1}{8}$. Therefore, each tick mark represents and increase of $\frac{1}{8}$

The completed number lines will look like this:

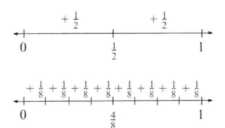

The fraction that is equivalent to $\frac{1}{2}$ is $\frac{4}{8}$

Example

Using the number lines shown below, what is the equivalent fraction to $\frac{4}{6}$?

On the top number line, there are 6 equally sized spaces between 0 and 1. $1 - 0 = 1$. $1 \div 6 = \frac{1}{6}$. Therefore, each tick mark represents an increase of $\frac{1}{6}$. On the bottom number line, there are 3 equally sized spaces between 0 and 1. $1 - 0 = 1$. $1 \div 3 = \frac{1}{3}$. Therefore, each tick mark represents an increase of $\frac{1}{3}$

The completed number lines will look like this:

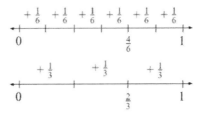

The fraction that is equivalent to $\frac{4}{6}$ is $\frac{2}{3}$

Decimals on Number Lines
Decimals on number lines work the same way as fractions.

Example
On the number line below, find the decimal value of each tick mark and fill in the missing tick marks.

There are 4 equally sized spaces between 1 and 2. $2 - 1 = 1$. $1 \div 4 = \frac{1}{4} = \frac{25}{100} = 0.25$. Each tick mark represents an increase of 0.25

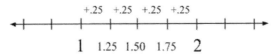

Practice Problems

Find the value of x, y, and z on the number lines below.

1.
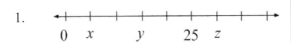

2.
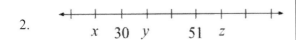

3.
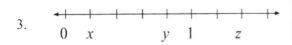

4.
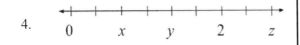

5. What is the equivalent fraction to $\frac{3}{4}$?

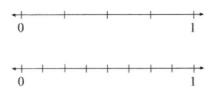

6. What is the equivalent fraction to 1?

7. What is the equivalent fraction to $\frac{3}{8}$?

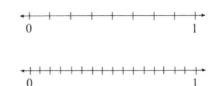

Mean, Median, Mode, and Range

Mean, median, mode, and range are statistical measures.

Mean is the same as an average. To find the mean of a data sct, add up all the numbers and divide by the total number of numbers.

Example: the mean of 3, 7, 4, 5, 9, and 2 is

$$\frac{3 + 7 + 4 + 5 + 9 + 2}{6} = 5$$

Median is the middle number in a data set when you line all the numbers up in order from smallest to largest. If there are an even number of numbers, then the median is the average of the two numbers in the middle.

Example: the median of 2, 1, 7, 5, and 10 is 5. When you line the numbers up, you get 1, 2, 5, 7, 10, and 5 is in the middle.

Mode is the number that shows up most often in a data set. You can commit this to memory by noting that **mo**de and **mo**st both start with **mo-**.

Example: the mode of 4, 7, 100, 3, 7, 5, and 8 is 7, because this number appears twice, while every other number only appears once.

Range is the largest number minus the smallest number in a data set.

Example: the range of 60, 78, 3, 9, 44, and 57 is 75, because $78 - 3 = 75$.

Practice Problems

1. Four friends have the following number of chocolate bars: {15, 13, 20, and 24}. What is the mean number of chocolate bars?
2. In the following data set, which is the greatest: mean, median, mode, or range? {2, 2, 7, 11, 19, 55}
3. Find the mean, median, mode, and range of the data set: {15, 8, 7, 21, 5, 21, 22, 17, 10}
4. Find the mean, median, mode, and range of the data set: {29, 22, 22, 17, 33, 32, 27}
5. What is the median of the following data set? {4.2, 2.4, 5.1, 6.3, 2.8}
6. What is the mode of the following data set? {3.75, 2.53, 3.77, 2.88, 2.53, 3.33}
7. What is the range of the following data set? {1.1, 8.4, 7.9, 2.3, 0.85, 4.2, 8.38}

Probability

Probability tells you the likelihood of something happening. It is expressed as a number between 0 (event never occurs) and 1 (event always occurs). Probability can be expressed as a fraction, decimal, or percent.

$$\text{Probability} = \frac{number\ of\ favorable\ outcomes}{total\ possible\ number\ of\ outcomes}$$

Example #1

What is the probability of flipping heads on a coin?

This one is easy. There are two possible outcomes: heads or tails. Heads is a "favorable outcome," so it goes in the numerator. The probability of flipping heads is $\frac{1}{2}$

Example #2

What is the probability of rolling a 3 or a 4 on a die?

Another easy one! There are six possible outcomes, and two of them are "favorable." The probability of rolling a 3 or a 4 on a die is $\frac{2}{6} = \frac{1}{3}$

Example #3

A box of 32 colored pencils contains 3 red, 5 yellow, 8 green, 6 purple, 4 pink, and 6 blue pencils. If a student randomly selects a colored pencil without looking, which color has a 1 out of 8 chance of being selected?
(A)   red
(B)   blue
(C)   green
(D)   pink

To answer this question, find the probability of selecting each of the colored pencils given in the answer choices. Red = 3 out of 32; blue = 6 out of 32; green = 8 out of 32; and pink = 4 out of 32. Then, reduce the probabilities to their simplest form until you find a match. This works the same way as reducing a fraction: you must find a number that both the numerator and denominator are divisible by. Red = 3 out of 32; blue = 3 out of 16; green = 1 out of 4; and pink = 1 out of 8. **The correct answer is (D).**

Example #4
A student selected four cards, without looking, from a stack of letter cards labeled A through M. If none of the cards in the stack repeat, what is the probability that the first card selected is the letter D?

(A) $\frac{9}{13}$

(B) $\frac{4}{9}$

(C) $\frac{4}{36}$

(D) $\frac{1}{13}$

First, determine how many total cards are in the stack: 13. There is extra information in this question that is designed to trick you; it doesn't really matter that four cards are selected! All that matters is that there is only 1 card labeled D in the stack, so the chances of it being selected first are 1 out of 13. **(D) is the correct answer.**

Practice Problems

1. There is a 0.4 probability that it will rain tomorrow. What is the probability that it will not rain tomorrow?

2. A bag of 100 gumballs contains 30 red, 25 yellow, 5 blue, 20 green, 10 purple, and 10 pink gumballs. If a gumball is selected at random, which color has a 1 out of 4 chance of being selected?
   (A)   red
   (B)   yellow
   (C)   green
   (D)   purple

3. There are 10 boys and 15 girls in a class. If a teacher selects a student at random, what is the probability that the student will be a girl?

4. A bag holds 3 red marbles, 2 blue marbles, and 4 yellow marbles. If a marble is selected at random, what is the probability it will be yellow?

5. A bag of change contains 6 quarters, 10 dimes, 12 nickels, and 22 pennies. If a coin is selected at random, which coin has a 6 out of 25 chance of being selected?
   (A)   quarter
   (B)   dime
   (C)   nickel
   (D)   penny

6. A student selected two cards, without looking, from a stack of letter cards labeled A through G. If none of the cards in the stack repeat, what is the probability that the first card selected is the letter B?

   (A) $\frac{1}{7}$

   (B) $\frac{2}{7}$

   (C) $\frac{1}{6}$

   (D) $\frac{6}{7}$

7. A box of 22 markers has 2 blue, 10 green, 4 black, and 6 red markers. If a marker is selected at random, which color has a 1 out of 11 chance of being selected?
    (A)   blue
    (B)   green
    (C)   black
    (D)   red

8. A bag holds 2 red marbles, 5 blue marbles, and 6 yellow marbles. If a marble is selected at random, what is the probability it will be red or blue?

9. A student selected three cards, without looking, from a stack of letter cards labeled A through J. If none of the cards in the stack repeat, what is the probability that the first card selected is either the letter C or the letter J?

    (A) $\frac{1}{10}$

    (B) $\frac{4}{5}$

    (C) $\frac{1}{5}$

    (D) $\frac{9}{10}$

10. A box of 32 colored pencils contains 3 red, 5 yellow, 8 green, 6 purple, 4 pink, and 6 blue pencils. If a student randomly selects a colored pencil without looking, which color has a 1 out of 8 chance of being selected?
    (A)   red
    (B)   blue
    (C)   green
    (D)   pink

11. What is the probability of rolling an even number on a 6-sided die?

12. A student selected one card, without looking, from a stack of letter cards labeled A through Z. If none of the cards in the stack repeat, what is the probability that the first card selected is a vowel? (A, E, I, O, or U)

    (A) $\frac{21}{26}$

    (B) $\frac{5}{26}$

    (C) $\frac{1}{26}$

    (D) $\frac{5}{21}$

13. A bag of 20 gumballs contains 4 red, 6 yellow, 2 blue, and 8 green gumballs. If a gumball is selected at random, which color has a 1 out of 10 chance of being selected?
    (A)   red
    (B)   yellow
    (C)   blue
    (D)   green

14. A box of 25 Legos contains 5 red, 7 yellow, 10 blue, and 3 green Legos. If a Lego is selected at random, which color has a 1 out of 5 chance of being selected?
    (A)   red
    (B)   yellow
    (C)   blue
    (D)   green

Rates

A rate is a measure, quantity, or frequency, and it is usually expressed in terms of one measurement compared to some other measurement. A classic example of a rate is "miles per hour." This phrase indicates how many miles an object travels in one hour. You can also measure "miles per minute," "kilometers per second," or "cost per unit," etc.

Rates can be expressed as fractions:

$$\frac{miles}{hour} \qquad \frac{dollars}{apple}$$

Example #1

A car drives 60 miles in 2 hours. How many miles does the car travel in 6 hours?

There are multiple ways of doing this question. First, we'll solve mathematically. Set up your fractions, making sure that corresponding pieces of information go in the same place in each fraction, and then cross multiply to solve.

$$\frac{60\ miles}{2\ hours} = \frac{x\ miles}{6\ hours}$$

$$(60)(6) = (2)(x)$$

$$360 = 2x$$

$$180 = x$$

The car travels 180 miles in 6 hours. On multiple choice questions, think about whether your answer choice makes sense. In this example, if your answer was 45 miles, would that make sense? Of course not - the car won't travel a shorter distance over a longer period of time! Likewise, if you found an answer of 500 miles, that would be way too big.

You can also think about this question in another way. The car drives 60 miles in 2 hours. 6 hours is 3 times as long as 2 hours. Therefore, the car will travel 3 times as far in this amount of time. $60 \times 3 = 180$.

Example #2

A boy and a girl were riding their bikes at the same speed on a bike path. It took the boy 40 minutes to ride 5 miles. How long did it take the girl to ride 15 miles?

15 miles is 3 times as far as 5 miles, so it will take 3 times as long to travel that distance. $40 \times 3 = 120$. It will take the girl 120 minutes to ride 15 miles.

Practice Questions

1.   If you can buy 7 pens for 30 cents, how pens can you buy with $1.20?

2.   A chef can bake 5 cakes every 2 hours. How many cakes will the chef bake in 12 hours?

3.   Your friend drives 40 miles in 30 minutes. How many minutes will it take your friend to drive 220 miles?

4.   You can write 2 pages of an essay in 3 hours. How many hours does it take to write 12 pages?

5.   A cheetah runs 80 miles per hour. If it always runs at this rate, how far does a cheetah travel in 30 minutes?

6.   On a map, 2.5 cm equals 125 miles. If two cities are 10 cm apart on the map, what is the actual distance between them?

Ratios

Ratios show a relationship between two amounts. You're familiar with ratios, even if you haven't formally studied them before. For example, if there are 8 girls and 9 boys in your class, you would say the ratio of girls to boys is 8 to 9. This information can be represented in several ways:

$$8 \text{ to } 9 \qquad\qquad 8:9 \qquad\qquad \frac{8}{9}$$

Ratios should be written in their most reduced form. Also note that a ratio of 8 to 9 is different than a ratio of 9 to 8! Misleading answer choices will definitely be included on the ISEE.

Example #1
There are 5 pencils and 4 pens in your bookbag. What is the ratio of pens to writing utensils?

There are 4 pens and 9 writing utensils total. Therefore, the ratio is 4 : 9.

Example #2
There are 6 drummers and 12 trombonists in the school band. What is the ratio of trombonists to drummers?

There are 12 trombonists for every 6 drummers, so the ratio is 12 : 6. This reduces to 2 : 1.

Harder questions involving ratios will give you a ratio and one actual number and then ask you to solve for the rest of the missing information. In order to do this, you will need to find what is known as a *multiplier*. For example, if the ratio of girls to boys in a classroom is 2 : 1 and there are 16 girls in the classroom, that means the multiplier is 8, because $2 \times 8 = 16$. Therefore, there are 8 boys in the classroom, because $8 \times 1 = 8$.

Example #3
There are 25 students in a classroom. If the ratio of boys to girls is 3 : 2, how many boys are in the classroom?

There are 5 total "pieces" of this ratio, because $3 + 2 = 5$. There are 25 total students, so that means the multiplier in this example is 5, because $5 \times 5 = 25$. Multiply each piece of the ratio by 5 in order to find the actual number of boys and girls in the classroom. $3 \times 5 = 15$, and $2 \times 5 = 10$, so there are 15 boys and 10 girls.

Example #4
If the ratio of first graders to second graders is 1 : 3, could there be 16 first and second graders in total?

Once again, add up the "pieces" of the ratio. $1 + 3 = 4$, so the real number of students in the classroom will always be a multiple of 4. There could be 1 first grader and 3 second graders, 2 first graders and 6 second graders, etc. 16 is a multiple of 4, so there *can* be 16 total students. There would be 4 first graders and 12 second graders.

Practice Problems

1. There are 13 boys and 15 girls in a classroom. What is the ratio of boys to the total number of students?

2. If the ratio of fourth graders to fifth graders is 3 : 4, could there be 14 total students?

3. The ratio of strawberries to blueberries is 3 : 7. If there are 15 strawberries, how many blueberries are there?

4. There are 40 students in a classroom. If the ratio of girls to boys is 3 : 1, how many girls are in the classroom?

5. The ratio of yellow marbles to blue marbles is 3 : 2. If there are 14 blue marbles, how many yellow marbles are there?

6. There are 30 students in a classroom. If the ratio of girls to boys is 3 : 2, how many boys are in the classroom?

7. If the ratio of sixth graders to seventh graders is 4 : 5, could there be 26 total students?

8. There are six violinists and seven cellists in the school orchestra. What is the ratio of cellists to violinists?

9. The ratio of lions to tigers at a zoo is 4 : 3. If there are 20 lions at the zoo, how many tigers are there?

10. If the ratio of second graders to fourth graders is 2 : 5, could there be 28 total students?

11. The ratio of blue pens to red pens is 4 : 5. If there are 25 red pens, how many pens are there in total?

Place Value and Standard Form

Place value tells you the value of any digit in a number.

Hundred thousands	Ten thousands	Thousands	Hundreds	Tens	Ones
2	1	0	4	2	5

The number in the table above is 210,425. Place value tells us the value of each digit.

The digit 2 is in the hundred thousands place. Its value is 200,000 (2 × 100,000)
The digit 1 is in the ten thousands place. Its value is 10,000 (1 × 10,000)
The digit 0 is in the thousands place. Its value is 0 (0 × 1,000)
The digit 4 is in the hundreds place. Its value is 400 (4 × 100)
The digit 2 is in the tens place. Its value is 20 (2 × 10)
The digit 5 is in the ones place. Its value is 5 (5 × 1)

Therefore, the value of 210,425 is equal to 200,000 + 10,000 + 0 + 400 + 20 + 5

Writing a number in digits is called *standard form*. Some questions on the Lower Level ISEE may ask you to convert a number from word form into standard form, or vice versa.

Example
Write "three hundred fourteen thousand six hundred four" in standard form.

Use the chart from above and fill in the correct numbers.

Hundred thousands	Ten thousands	Thousands	Hundreds	Tens	Ones
3	1	4	6	0	4

The number is equivalent to 300,000 + 10,000 + 4,000 + 600 + 0 + 4 = 314,604

Practice Problems

Write the Value of the Underlined Digit

1. 4,902
2. 940
3. 864
4. 9,261
5. 12,254
6. 82,369
7. 104,001

Write in Standard Form

8. Nine hundred three
9. Fourteen thousand two hundred twenty one
10. Three hundred one thousand four hundred sixty five
11. Sixty seven thousand twelve
12. One hundred fifteen

Write in Word Form

13. 12,052
14. 901
15. 101,010
16. 670,025
17. 202,120
18. 14,231

Translating English into Math

Many algebra word problems will require that you create your own equation. You should memorize the terms on the chart below.

English	Math	Example	Translation
What, a number	Any variable (x, y, etc)	A number is equal to three divided by four	$n = \dfrac{3}{4}$
Equals, is, was, has, costs, are	$=$	x equals 10 An apple costs 4 dollars	$x = 10$ $a = \$4$
Sum, greater than, more, added to, increased by, total	$+$	Ben is four years older than Steve Ben and Steve have a total of $16	$b = s + 4$ $b + s = \$16$
Decreased by, difference, less than, fewer	$-$	Mary has four fewer toys than Cain x is 9 less than y	$m = c - 4$ $x = y - 9$
Product, times, of, twice, triple, half of	$\times$	An apple costs twice as much as a pear x is the product of y and 7	$a = 2p$ $x = 7y$
Per, for, out of, divided by, ratio	$\div$	The ratio of apples to oranges is 4 to 7 Harry drives 40 miles per hour	$\dfrac{a}{o} = \dfrac{4}{7}$ $h = \dfrac{40\ miles}{hour}$

Example #1

Which equation can be read as "3 more than 4 times a number is equal to 4 less than the number?" Let n represent the unknown number.

(A) $3 \times (4 \times n) = n - 4$
(B) $3 \times (4 \times n) = 4 - n$
(C) $3 + (4 \times n) = n - 4$
(D) $3 + (4 \times n) = 4 - n$

First, notice that every answer choice includes $(4 \times n)$, which means you don't really need to take this part of the answer into consideration. It must be correct if it's included in every answer choice! "More" means "+," so "3 more than $(4 \times n)$" = $3 + (4 \times n)$. Eliminate (A) and (B). 4 less than a number can be rewritten as $n - 4$. **(C) is the correct answer.**

Example #2
At the hardware store, Ryan bought 3 boxes of nails that cost $4 each and a shovel. His total before tax was $33. Which equation could be used to find the cost of the shovel (s)?
(A) $4 + s = \$33$
(B) $4 + 3s = \$33$
(C) $3(4) + s = \$33$
(D) $3(4) + 3s = \$33$

First, recognize the information given: (3 boxes of nails at $4 each) + a shovel = $33. Then, turn this information into a math sentence / equation: $(3 \times 4) + s = \$33$. **The correct answer is (C)**. You could also figure out the cost of the shovel. If Ryan spent $3 \times 4 = \$12$ on nails, and he spent $33 total, then he must have spent $33 - 12 = \$21$ on the shovel. Then, go through the answer choices one by one. $4 + 21 \neq 33$; $4 + 3(21) \neq 33$; and $3(4) + 3(21) \neq 33$. Therefore, (A), (B), and (D) are incorrect.

Practice Problems

1. Which equation can be read as "2 less than 6 times a number is equal to 5 more than the number?" Let n represent the unknown number.

    (A) $(6 \times n) - 2 = n + 5$
    (B) $(6 \times n) + 2 = n + 5$
    (C) $2 - (6 \times n) = n + 5$
    (D) $2 + (6 \times n) = n - 5$

2. Which equation can be read as "1 less than a number divided by 4 is equal to the product of the number and 6?" Let n represent the unknown number.

    (A) $\frac{n}{4} - 1 = \frac{n}{6}$
    (B) $\frac{n}{4} - 1 = 6n$
    (C) $\frac{4}{n} - 1 = 6n$
    (D) $1 - \frac{4}{n} = 6n$

3. At the hardware store, Javi bought 2 hammers that cost $10 each and 3 chainsaws. His total before tax was $1,082. Which equation could be used to find the cost of the chainsaws (c)?

    (A) $2(10) + 3c = \$1,082$
    (B) $2 + c = \$1,082$
    (C) $2(10) + c = \$1,082$
    (D) $2 + 3c = \$1,082$

4. Which equation can be read as "3 more than the product of a number and 6 equals the number divided by 5?" Let n represent the unknown number.

    (A) $3 - (6 \times n) = \frac{n}{5}$
    (B) $3 - (6 \times n) = \frac{5}{n}$
    (C) $3 + (6 \times n) = \frac{n}{5}$
    (D) $3 + (6 \times n) = \frac{5}{n}$

5. Which equation can be read as "10 more than a number is equal to 3 less than 7 times the number?" Let n represent the unknown number.

    (A) $10 + n = (7 \times n) + 3$
    (B) $10 + n = (7 \times n) - 3$
    (C) $10 - n = (7 \times n) - 3$
    (D) $10 - n = (7 \times n) + 3$

6. At a school bake sale, Kaitlyn bought 4 chocolate chip cookies that cost $2 each and 5 brownies. Her total before tax was $15. Which equation could be used to find the cost of the brownies (b)?

    (A) $4(2) + b = \$15$
    (B) $4 + 5b = \$15$
    (C) $4(2) + 5b = \$15$
    (D) $8 + b = \$15$

7. Which equation can be read as "a number decreased by 6 is equal to the product of 4 and the number?" Let n represent the unknown number.

    (A) $6 - n = 4 + n$
    (B) $6 - n = 4n$
    (C) $n - 6 = 4 + n$
    (D) $n - 6 = 4n$

8. At the grocery store, a man bought 2 boxes of cereal that cost $3 each and a gallon of milk. His total before tax was $12. Which equation could be used to find the cost of the gallon of milk (m)?

    (A) $2(3) + 3m = \$12$
    (B) $2 + 3m = \$12$
    (C) $2 + m = \$12$
    (D) $2(3) + m = \$12$

9. Which equation can be read as "2 less than a number is equal to 5 more than the number divided by 7?" Let n represent the unknown number.

    (A) $2 - n = \frac{n}{7} + 5$
    (B) $n - 2 = \frac{n}{7} + 5$
    (C) $2 - n = \frac{n}{5} + 7$
    (D) $n - 2 = \frac{n}{5} + 7$

10. At a state fair, a girl bought 1 container of popcorn that cost $7 and 2 ice cream cones. Her total before tax was $21. Which equation could be used to find the cost of the ice cream cones (i)?

    (A) $7 + i = \$21$
    (B) $7 + 2i = \$21$
    (C) $7(2) + i = \$21$
    (D) $7(2) + 2i = \$21$

11. Which equation can be read as "a number increased by 4 is equal to the product of the number and 8?" Let n represent the unknown number.

    (A) $n - 4 = 8n$
    (B) $n + 4 = 4 + n$
    (C) $n + 4 = 8n$
    (D) $n - 4 = 4 + n$

12. Which equation can be read as "2 more than the product of a number and 3 is equal to 5 greater than the number?" Let n represent the unknown number.

    (A) $3n + 2 = n - 5$
    (B) $3n - 2 = n - 5$
    (C) $3n - 2 = n + 5$
    (D) $3n + 2 = n + 5$

Rules of Divisibility

You should memorize the rules of divisibility in the table below. Remember, *divisibility* means one number can be divided by another without leaving a remainder.

A number is divisible by	
2	If the last digit is 0, 2, 4, 6, or 8
3	If the sum of the digits is divisible by 3
4	If the last two digits are divisible by 4
5	If the last digit is 0 or 5
6	If the number is divisible by both 2 and 3
9	If the sum of the digits is divisible by 9
10	If the last digit is 0

You are likely already familiar with the divisibility rules for 2, 5, and 10. The divisibility rules for 7 and 8 are not included in the table because they are very unlikely to show up on the Lower Level ISEE. The divisibility rules for 3 and 9 require a bit more explanation. Take 123 as an example. $1 + 2 + 3 = 6$, and 6 is divisible by 3, which means 123 is divisible by 3. Another example is 999: $9 + 9 + 9 = 27$. 27 is divisible by both 3 and 9, which means 999 is divisible by 3 and 9. Memorizing the rules of divisibility will save you a lot of time, since you won't have to spend time actually doing $999 \div 9$ in order to see if there is a remainder. In the event that you are asked whether a number is divisible by 7 or 8, you can just use long division!

Practice Problems

1. Which whole number is divisible by 9 without a remainder?
   (A)   403
   (B)   405
   (C)   407
   (D)   409

2. Which whole number is divisible by 3 without a remainder?
   (A)   231
   (B)   233
   (C)   235
   (D)   239

3. Which whole number is divisible by 5 without a remainder?
   (A)   96
   (B)   98
   (C)   100
   (D)   102

4. Which whole number is divisible by 2 without a remainder?
   (A)   109
   (B)   111
   (C)   112
   (D)   113

5. Which whole number is divisible by 3 without a remainder?
   (A)   1,372
   (B)   1,373
   (C)   1,375
   (D)   1,377

6. Which whole number is divisible by 5 without a remainder?
   (A)   15
   (B)   17
   (C)   19
   (D)   21

7. Which whole number is divisible by 9 without a remainder?
   (A)   939
   (B)   941
   (C)   943
   (D)   945

8. 54 is divisible by which of the following numbers?
   (A)   3 only
   (B)   9 only
   (C)   3 and 9
   (D)   2, 3, and 9

9. 270 is divisible by which of the following numbers?
   (A)   3 only
   (B)   5 only
   (C)   3, 5, and 9
   (D)   2, 3, 5, 9, and 10

10. 303 is divisible by which of the following numbers?
   (A)   3 only
   (B)   9 only
   (C)   3 and 9
   (D)   2, 3, and 9

Answer Key – Applied Arithmetic

Math Definitions

1.   Possible answers include -50, -8, 0, 1, 2, 34, etc
2.   Possible answers include 2, 3, 5, 7, 11, 13, 17, 19, etc
3.   No
4.   Yes
5.   Possible answers include 1, 3, 5, 7, or -11, -9, -7, -5, etc
6.   20
7.   Possible answers include 4, 8, 12, 16, 20, 24, etc
8.   6
9.   10
10.   Possible answers include 4, 6, 8, 9, 12, 15, etc
11.   13
12.   31
13.   29
14.   41
15.   10
16.   5
17.   5
18.   11

Intro to Exponents

1.   9
2.   36
3.   81
4.   64
5.   64
6.   16

PEMDAS

1.   18
2.   22
3.   8
4.   17
5.   12
6.   4
7.   1
8.   10
9.   6
10.   7
11.   8
12.   24
13.   C
14.   D
15.   A
16.   B
17.   B
18.   C

Reducing Fractions

Reduce

1. $\frac{1}{2}$

2. $\frac{3}{5}$

3. $\frac{1}{3}$

4. $\frac{1}{1}$ or 1

5. $\frac{58}{111}$

6. $\frac{5}{9}$

7. $\frac{1}{3}$

8. $\frac{63}{47}$

9. $\frac{4}{3}$

10. $\frac{2}{1}$ or 2

11. $\frac{16}{17}$

12. $\frac{1}{5}$

13. $\frac{1}{10}$

14. $\frac{1}{3}$

15. $\frac{1}{2}$

16. $\frac{1}{8}$

17. $\frac{1}{3}$

18. $\frac{4}{5}$

19. $\frac{2}{5}$

20. $\frac{2}{3}$

Improper Fractions and Mixed Numbers

Convert to Mixed Numbers

1. $2\frac{1}{4}$

2. $2\frac{2}{5}$

3. $1\frac{19}{80}$

4. $1\frac{1}{4}$

5. $6\frac{3}{4}$

6. $1\frac{1}{16}$

7. $1\frac{1}{2}$

8. $1\frac{43}{45}$

Convert to Improper Fractions

9. $\frac{9}{7}$

10. $\frac{11}{4}$

11. $\frac{17}{12}$

12. $\frac{35}{8}$

13. $\frac{31}{9}$

14. $\frac{26}{5}$

15. $\frac{14}{3}$

16. $\frac{80}{9}$

Convert to Whole Numbers

17. 2
18. 10
19. 4
20. 1
21. 3

Operations with Fractions

Add, subtract, multiply, or divide

1. $\dfrac{7}{9}$

2. $\dfrac{45}{44}$ or $1\dfrac{1}{44}$

3. $\dfrac{18}{49}$

4. $\dfrac{2}{12}$ or $\dfrac{1}{6}$

5. $\dfrac{57}{40}$ or $1\dfrac{17}{40}$

6. $\dfrac{28}{25}$ or $1\dfrac{3}{25}$

7. $\dfrac{4}{13}$

8. $\dfrac{3}{8}$

9. $\dfrac{36}{33}$ or $\dfrac{12}{11}$ or $1\dfrac{1}{11}$

10. $\dfrac{6}{63}$ or $\dfrac{2}{21}$

Which Fraction is Larger?

11. $\dfrac{3}{8}$

12. $\dfrac{3}{4}$

13. $\dfrac{1}{6}$

14. The fractions are equal

15. $\dfrac{6}{8}$

Which Fraction is the Largest?

16. C
17. B
18. D

Which Fraction is Between the Two Fractions?

19. A
20. B
21. D
22. B

Solve

23. $3\dfrac{4}{7}$

24. $8\dfrac{5}{35}$ or $8\dfrac{1}{7}$

25. $2\dfrac{32}{54}$ or $2\dfrac{16}{27}$

26. $2\dfrac{2}{3}$

27. $4\dfrac{1}{8}$

28. $3\dfrac{3}{10}$

Decimals

1. 2.044
2. 3.3302
3. 5.509
4. 18.84
5. 0.292
6. 10.94
7. 10.202
8. 0.7274
9. 3.52
10. 11.25
11. 4.6875
12. 7.44
13. 19.6875
14. $\frac{55}{100}$ or $\frac{11}{20}$
15. $\frac{9}{100}$
16. $\frac{40}{100}$ or $\frac{2}{5}$
17. $\frac{12}{100}$ or $\frac{3}{25}$
18. $\frac{95}{100}$ or $\frac{19}{20}$
19. 0.43
20. 0.06
21. 0.93
22. 0.01
23. 0.55
24. $3\frac{4}{10}$ or $3\frac{2}{5}$
25. $3\frac{8}{10}$ or $3\frac{4}{5}$
26. $8\frac{6}{10}$ or $8\frac{3}{5}$
27. $6\frac{7}{10}$

Negative Numbers

1. 32
2. 12
3. 80
4. 28
5. -5
6. -47
7. 2
8. 17
9. -28
10. -14
11. -24
12. -300
13. -10
14. 14
15. 35
16. 11

Percents

Convert the Fractions to Percents

1. 14%
2. 65%
3. 50%
4. 90%
5. 80%
6. 75%

Convert the Percents to Decimals

7. 0.90
8. 0.65
9. 0.03
10. 0.12

Convert the Percents to Fractions

11. $\frac{15}{100}$ or $\frac{3}{20}$
12. $\frac{28}{100}$ or $\frac{7}{25}$
13. $\frac{63}{100}$
14. $\frac{44}{100}$ or $\frac{11}{25}$

Units of Measurement

1.   Inches, centimeters
2.   Grams, kilograms, pounds
3.   Ounces, milliliters
4.   Liters, gallons
5.   Pounds, kilograms
6.   Feet, meters
7.   Pounds, kilograms
8.   Inches, centimeters

Perimeter and Area

1.   36 square centimeters
2.   20 inches
3.   48 square feet
4.   25 inches
5.   32 square feet
6.   9 square centimeters
7.   20 centimeters
8.   20 feet
9.   28 square feet
10. 120 square feet
11. 3 square inches
12. 24 square centimeters
13. 30 meters
14. 4 inches
15. 65 square feet
16. 22 square centimeters
17. 4 inches
18. 60 inches
19. 9 inches
20. 32 square feet
21. 9 feet
22. 78 square feet

Mathematical Properties

Identify the Property

1.   Identity
2.   Commutative
3.   Identity
4.   Associative
5.   Distributive
6.   Identity
7.   Associative
8.   Commutative
9.   Distributive
10. Commutative

Select the Best Answer

11. D
12. B
13. D
14. A
15. C
16. C
17. B

Clocks and Telling Time

Determine the Elapsed Time

1.   1 hour
2.   3 hours 25 minutes
3.   2 hours 40 minutes
4.   1 hour 40 minutes
5.   2 hours 15 minutes
6.   2 hours 20 minutes
7.   45 minutes
8.   2 hours 30 minutes

Determine the Ending Time

9.   5:00
10.   10:35
11.   7:55
12.   12:00
13.   6:20 P.M.
14.   5:10 P.M.
15.   6:10 P.M.

Convert Minutes to Hours

16.   2 hours 25 minutes
17.   1 hour 8 minutes
18.   3 hours 50 minutes
19.   2 hours 50 minutes
20.   5 hours 10 minutes

Determine the Time Shown

21.   3:35
22.   11:55
23.   9:40
24.   10:10
25.   9:20
26.   12:20

Number Lines

1. $x = 5, y = 15, z = 30$

2. $x = 23, y = 37, z = 58$

3. $x = \frac{1}{5}, y = \frac{4}{5}, z = \frac{7}{5}$ or $1\frac{2}{5}$

4. $x = \frac{2}{3}, y = \frac{4}{3}$ or $1\frac{1}{3}, z = \frac{8}{3}$ or $2\frac{2}{3}$

5. $\frac{6}{8}$

6. $\frac{5}{5}$

7. $\frac{6}{16}$

Mean, Median, Mode, and Range

1.   18
2.   Range
3.   Mean = 14, Median = 15,
      Mode = 21, Range = 17
4.   Mean = 26, Median = 27,
      Mode = 22, Range = 16
5.   4.2
6.   2.53
7.   7.55

Probability

1.   0.6

2.   B

3. $\frac{3}{5}$

4. $\frac{4}{9}$

5.   C

6.   A

7.   A

8. $\frac{7}{13}$

9.   C

10.   D

11. $\frac{1}{2}$

12.   B

13.   C

14.   A

Rates

1.   28 pens
2.   30 cakes
3.   165 minutes
4.   18 hours
5.   40 miles
6.   500 miles

Ratios

1.   13 : 28
2.   Yes
3.   35
4.   30
5.   21
6.   12
7.   No
8.   7 : 6
9.   15
10. Yes
11. 45

Standard Form

Write the Value of the Underlined Digit

1.   900
2.   40
3.   4
4.   9,000
5.   2,000
6.   300
7.   100,000

Write in Standard Form

8.   903
9.   14,221
10. 301,465
11. 67,012
12. 115

Write in Word Form

13. Twelve thousand fifty two
14. Nine hundred one
15. One hundred one thousand ten
16. Six hundred seventy thousand twenty five
17. Two hundred two thousand one hundred twenty
18. Fourteen thousand two hundred thirty One

Translating English into Math

1.   A
2.   B
3.   A
4.   C
5.   B
6.   C
7.   D
8.   D
9.   B
10. B
11. C
12. D

Rules of Divisibility

1.   B
2.   A
3.   C
4.   C
5.   D
6.   A
7.   D
8.   D
9.   D
10. A

Chapter 3
Algebra and Geometry

Basic Algebra

In algebra, letters or symbols are used to represent numbers in an equation.

There are a few definitions you should be familiar with before beginning this section:
- *variable*: a letter used to represent a number (x, y, etc)
- *coefficient*: a number that appears before a variable ($5x$, $10y$, etc)
- *equation*: an expression that has been set equal to something ($x + 5 = 6$, $3y - 6 = 10$, etc)

Combining Like Terms

Some questions on the ISEE will ask you to simplify an expression or ask you which of the answer choices is equivalent to a given expression. The most important thing to remember is that only "like terms" can be combined. That means that a variable like x can only be combined with another variable x, z can only be combined with z, and so on. These questions are only tricky because it can be difficult to keep track of all the like terms. *You should cross off terms as you go so that you don't get confused!*

Examples $a + a = 2a$ $7z + 10z = 17z$ $a + 2b + 4b + 3a - b = 4a + 5b$

Evaluating Algebraic Expressions

You'll need only a basic understanding of algebra for the Lower Level ISEE. For example, if you know that x is equal to some number, and $x + 4 = 6$, you can probably tell that $x = 2$. Some questions will simply test your ability to plug in a number for a variable and simplify the expression. Here, it is most important that you remember your order of operations and that you show your work.

Examples

If $y = 4$, what is the value of $4y$?
$4(4) = 16$

If $x = 3$, what is the value of $2x + 4$?
$2(3) + 4 = 6 + 4 = 10$

Solving Equations with One Variable

In the simplest equations, you can eyeball what the answer should be.

Example
$x + 2 = 7$
In this example, just ask yourself "*what plus two equals seven?*"

On the Lower Level ISEE, the best way to solve more difficult equations is to work backwards using the given answer choices.

Example:
$4x + 8 = 16$
What is the value of x?
(A)   1
(B)   2
(C)   3
(D)   4

$4(1) + 8 = 12$, so you can eliminate (A).
$4(2) + 8 = 8 + 8 = 16$. **(B) is the correct answer.**

Sometimes, it may not be possible to work backwards. In those questions, you will need to know the basics of rearranging algebraic equations. In an algebraic equation, you need to isolate the variable to solve. You can do this if you know that addition and subtraction are opposites, and that multiplication and division are opposites.

Example

If the area of a rectangle is 20 cm², which equation can be used to determine the width of that rectangle? ($A = lw$, where A = Area, l = length, and w = width.)

(A) $w = \dfrac{20}{l}$

(B) $w = \dfrac{l}{20}$

(C) $w = 20 - l$

(D) $w = 20 + l$

First, plug in the information you know. $A = 20$, so we can rewrite the original equation as $20 = lw$. The question asks us to isolate w, which means we need to move l to the left side of the equation. Because lw means "length times width," and division is the opposite of multiplication, we need to divide both sides by l to move l to the other side. We are left with $\dfrac{20}{l} = w$. **(A) is the correct answer.**

Example

If the area of a triangle is 40 m², which equation can be used to determine the base of that triangle? ($A = \frac{1}{2}bh$, where A = Area, b = base, and h = height.)

(A) $b = 80 - h$

(B) $b = 80 + h$

(C) $b = \dfrac{h}{80}$

(D) $b = \dfrac{80}{h}$

First, plug in 40 for A, which gives you $40 = \frac{1}{2}bh$. The question tells us to isolate b, so we must move $\frac{1}{2}$ and h to the left side of the equation. $\frac{1}{2}bh$ means "$\frac{1}{2}$ times base times height," so once again we will need to use division, since that is the opposite of multiplication. You can divide both sides by $\frac{1}{2}$ to get $2(40) = bh$. Where did the 2 come from? Remember, dividing by $\frac{1}{2}$ is the same as multiplying by $\frac{2}{1}$. Then, divide both sides by h to get $\dfrac{2(40)}{h} = b$. Finally, Simplify $2(40)$ to 80. **The correct answer is (D).**

Example
Use the equations to answer the question.

$a + 2 = 8$
$b - 4 = 6$

What is the value of $2(a + b)$?

(A)   6
(B)   10
(C)   16
(D)   32

This question is very easy, but it contains several trick answers. First, find the values of a and b. $6 + 2 = 8$, so $a = 6$. $10 - 4 = 6$, so $b = 10$. Replace a and b in the final equation. $2(6 + 10) = 2(16) = 32$. **(D) is the correct answer.** Remember that the parentheses indicate multiplication. (A) represents the value of a, (B) represents the value of b, and (C) represents the value of $(a + b)$.

Practice Problems

Simplify

1. $a + 4a$

2. $10y - 6y$

3. $2b + 2b - 3b$

4. $5x + 4y + x - 2y$

5. $6d + 4f + 3f - 2d$

6. $x + y + z + x + y + z$

7. $4x - 3 + 5x + 8$

8. $10 - 5y - 3 + 8y$

9. $12a + 4 - 2a + 7$

10. $18 + 13k - 18 - 13k$

Solve

11. $x + 6 = 10$

12. $z - 3 = 4$

13. $4x = 20$

14. $\frac{36}{a} = 6$

15. $4x + 3 = 19$. What is the value of x?
    (A)   1
    (B)   2
    (C)   3
    (D)   4

16. $5y - 2 = 28$. What is the value of y?
    (A)   3
    (B)   4
    (C)   5
    (D)   6

17. $2z + 5z = 35$. What is the value of z?
    (A)   5
    (B)   6
    (C)   7
    (D)   8

18. $4(2x + 1) = 12$. What is the value of x?
    (A)   1
    (B)   2
    (C)   3
    (D)   4

19. $\frac{36}{a} + 5 = 8$. What is the value of a?
    (A)   6
    (B)   9
    (C)   12
    (D)   15

20. If the area of a rectangle is 12 cm^2, which equation can be used to determine the length of that rectangle?
($A = lw$, where A = Area, l = length, and w = width.)

(A) $l = \dfrac{12}{w}$

(B) $l = \dfrac{w}{12}$

(C) $l = 12 - w$

(D) $l = 12 + w$

21. If the area of a square is 100 m^2, which equation can be used to determine the width of that square?
($A = lw$, where A = Area, l = length, and w = width.)

(A) $w = 100 - l$

(B) $w = \dfrac{l}{100}$

(C) $w = 100 + l$

(D) $w = \dfrac{100}{l}$

22. If the area of a rectangle is 77 in^2, which equation can be used to determine the length of that rectangle?
($A = lw$, where A = Area, l = length, and w = width.)

(A) $l = 77 - w$

(B) $l = 77 + w$

(C) $l = \dfrac{77}{w}$

(D) $l = \dfrac{w}{77}$

23. If the length of a rectangle is 14 cm and the width of that rectangle is $\dfrac{1}{2}$ cm, which equation can be used to determine the area of that rectangle?
($A = lw$, where A = Area, l = length, and w = width.)

(A) $A = 7$

(B) $A = 14$

(C) $A = \dfrac{7}{h}$

(D) $A = \dfrac{l}{14}$

24. If the area of a triangle is 50 in^2, which equation can be used to determine the height of that triangle?
($A = \dfrac{1}{2}bh$, where A = Area, b = base, and h = height.)

(A) $h = 100 - b$

(B) $h = 100 + b$

(C) $h = \dfrac{b}{100}$

(D) $h = \dfrac{100}{b}$

25. If the height of a triangle is 20 in, which equation can be used to determine the base of that triangle?
($A = \dfrac{1}{2}bh$, where A = Area, b = base, and h = height.)

(A) $b = \dfrac{10}{A}$

(B) $b = \dfrac{A}{10}$

(C) $b = A + 10$

(D) $b = A - 10$

26. Use the equations to answer the question.

$$c + 4 = 5$$
$$d - 5 = 2$$

What is the value of $3(c + d)$?

(A)   8
(B)   16
(C)   24
(D)   32

27. Use the equations to answer the question.

$$a + 1 = 6$$
$$b - 3 = 5$$
$$c + 4 = 7$$

What is the sum of $a + b + c$?

(A)   13
(B)   16
(C)   19
(D)   22

28. Use the equations to answer the question.

$$x + 3 = 3$$
$$y - 5 = 5$$

What is the value of $x(y + 2)$?

(A)   0
(B)   6
(C)   12
(D)   18

29. Use the equations to answer the question.

$$l - 1 = 6$$
$$m - 2 = 2$$
$$n + 4 = 8$$

What is the value of $m + l \times n$?

(A)   7
(B)   16
(C)   23
(D)   32

30. Use the equations to answer the question.

$$a + 1 = 3$$
$$b - 3 = 5$$
$$c + 4 = 7$$

What is the value of $3(a + b - c)$?

(A)   18
(B)   21
(C)   27
(D)   30

31. Use the equations to answer the question.

$$j + 4 = 10$$
$$k - 6 = 6$$

What is the value of jk?

(A)   6
(B)   12
(C)   18
(D)   72

32. Use the equations to answer the question.

$$x + 4 = 6$$
$$x - y = 1$$
$$z + 2 = 8$$

What is the value of $2(x + y + z)$?

(A)   9
(B)   18
(C)   27
(D)   36

Shapes

You will need to know the names of shapes up to 10 sides on the Lower Level ISEE.

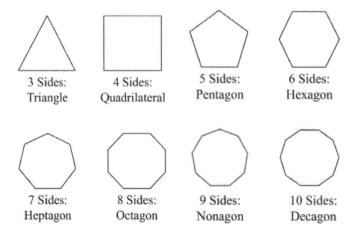

The shapes shown above are all *regular* shapes. That means they have sides that are all equal and interior (inside) angles that are all equal.

Irregular shapes have sides and angles of any length and size. Examples of irregular shapes are given below.

Note that irregular shapes are still named according to the number of sides they have.

Practice Problems

1. A family is building a pool in the shape of a nonagon. How many sides will the pool have?

2. What shape has six sides?

3. How many total sides are there in a hexagon and a heptagon?

4. An octagon is a shape with how many sides?

5. A mosaic is made of hundreds of tiny tiles that each have seven sides. What type of shape are the tiles?

6. A coin has ten sides. What shape is the coin?

7. How many total sides are there in a nonagon and an octagon?

8. Which shape has more sides: a pentagon or a heptagon?

9. What is the length of one side of a regular pentagon with a perimeter of 25 centimeters?

10. What is the length of one side of a regular octagon with a perimeter of 64 inches?

11. The length of one side of a regular heptagon is 7 inches. What is the perimeter of the heptagon?

12. The length of one side of a regular nonagon is 3 meters. What is the perimeter of the nonagon?

13. What is the length of one side of a regular decagon with a perimeter of 120 centimeters?

14. The length of one side of a regular hexagon is 7 inches. What is the hexagon's perimeter?

15. How many total sides are there in a pentagon and a decagon?

16. A regular hexagon has side lengths of 5 inches. If each of the side lengths of the hexagon is doubled, what is the perimeter of the new hexagon?

17. A decagon is a shape with how many sides?

18. Which shape has the greater perimeter: a regular hexagon with side lengths of 7 inches or a regular octagon with side lengths of 5 inches?

19. List the names of shapes in order, starting with a shape that has three sides and going until a shape that has ten sides.

20. What does is mean when a shape is *regular*?

21. How many total sides are there in a pentagon, a hexagon, and an octagon?

Quadrilaterals

A quadrilateral is a four-sided shape. There are six quadrilaterals that you must be familiar with on the Lower Level ISEE.

Squares

A *square* is a quadrilateral with four equal sides and four right angles. A right angle has 90 degrees.

- Perimeter = $4s$ = the sum of all four sides
- Area = $s \times s$
- Squares are always rectangles, parallelograms, and rhombi. In other words, squares are a subset of rectangles, parallelograms, and rhombi

Rectangles

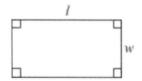

A *rectangle* is a quadrilateral with two pairs of equal sides and four right angles.

- Opposite sides are equal
- Perimeter = $2l + 2w$ = the sum of all four sides
- Area = $l \times w$
- A rectangle is a square if all of its sides are the same length. Rectangles are always parallelograms. In other words, rectangles are a subset of parallelograms.

Parallelograms

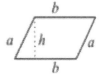

A *parallelogram* is a quadrilateral with two pairs of parallel sides.

- Opposite sides are equal
- Opposite angles are equal
- Perimeter = $2a + 2b$
- Parallelograms are rectangles if they contain four right angles. Parallelograms are squares if they contain four right angles and all four sides are the same length

Rhombi or Diamonds*

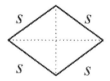

A *rhombus* (plural: *rhombi*), or *diamond*, is a quadrilateral with four equal sides and two pairs of parallel sides.

- Perimeter = $4s$ = the sum of all four sides
- Opposite angles are equal
- A rhombus is always a parallelogram
- A rhombus is a rectangle and a square if it has four right angles

Kites

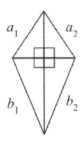

A *kite* is a quadrilateral with two pairs of adjacent sides whose lengths are equal.

- Adjacent sides (the sides next to each other) are the same length
- Diagonals (the lines in the figure above that intersect) cross at right angles

Trapezoids

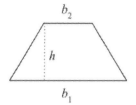

On the ISEE, a *trapezoid* is a quadrilateral with only one pair of parallel sides.

- The sides that are parallel are called *bases*
- The other sides are called *legs*

*The Lower Level ISEE may use the term *diamond*. This is not a formal mathematical term and does not have a precise definition. You can think of a diamond as a square that has been rotated 45 degrees.

Practice Problems

1. What is the name of a quadrilateral with two pairs of adjacent sides of equal length and no right angles?
   (A)   rectangle
   (B)   trapezoid
   (C)   kite
   (D)   pentagon

2. What is the name of the quadrilateral below?

   (A)   parallelogram
   (B)   diamond
   (C)   square
   (D)   trapezoid

3. What is the name of a quadrilateral with sides that measure 4 inches each and four 90-degree angles?
   (A)   parallelogram
   (B)   square
   (C)   rhombus
   (D)   trapezoid

4. What is the name of the quadrilateral below?

   (A)   parallelogram
   (B)   trapezoid
   (C)   rhombus
   (D)   kite

5. How many pairs of parallel sides does a parallelogram have?
   (A)   1
   (B)   2
   (C)   3
   (D)   4

6. A quadrilateral with four equal sides must be:
   (A)   a rectangle or a trapezoid
   (B)   a parallelogram or a trapezoid
   (C)   a square or a rhombus
   (D)   a kite or a square

7. The points with coordinates (1,1)(1,5)(5,5)(5,1) are the vertices of a quadrilateral. If all four points are connected to form a quadrilateral, which term best describes the quadrilateral formed?
   (A)   kite
   (B)   pentagon
   (C)   square
   (D)   trapezoid

8. Which of the following shapes is also always a parallelogram?
   (A)   trapezoid
   (B)   rhombus
   (C)   kite
   (D)   triangle

9. The points with coordinates (1,3)(5,3)(2,5)(6,5) are the vertices of a quadrilateral. If all four points are connected to form a quadrilateral, which term best describes the quadrilateral formed?
   (A)   kite
   (B)   trapezoid
   (C)   square
   (D)   parallelogram

Triangles

Triangles are plane figures with three straight sides and three angles. Triangles always contain a total of 180 degrees.

Perimeter
Like all other shapes, to find the perimeter of a triangle you must add together the lengths of its sides.

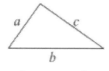

$$a + b + c = \text{perimeter}$$

Area
The equation for finding the area of a triangle is $\frac{bh}{2}$ or $\frac{1}{2}bh$, where b = base and h = height. Height must be perpendicular to the base.

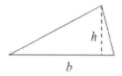

Isosceles Triangles   *Equilateral Triangles*

An isosceles triangle has two sides that are the same length; the angles opposite these sides are also the same measure. A question might tell you that a given triangle is isosceles. Otherwise, you might see markings like those in the figure above which indicate two equal sides and two equal angles.

The sides of an equilateral triangle are all the same length, and the angles are all equal to 60 degrees. A figure may indicate a triangle is equilateral using the dashes shown in the figure above. The question might also tell you a given triangle is equilateral.

Practice Problems

1.   A triangle's base is 10 inches and its height is 12 inches. What is its area?

2.   If one side of an equilateral triangle is 10 inches long, what is the perimeter of the triangle?

3.   What is the perimeter of the triangle shown below?

4.   An equilateral triangle has a perimeter of 24 cm. What is the length of each side?

5.   What is the measure of Angle *B*?

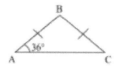

6.   A triangle's base is 5 cm and its height is 6 cm. What is its area?

7.   If the perimeter of an equilateral triangle is 45 inches, what is the length of one side?

Volume

Volume is a measure of the amount of space an object occupies. On the Lower Level ISEE, you will only need to know how to find the volume of cubes and rectangular prisms. A cube is a regular solid with six equal square sides. Dice are cubes. A rectangular prism is a solid object with six faces that are rectangles. A box of cereal is a rectangular prism.

Cube   Rectangular
                  Prism

Both shapes have the same equation for volume: $l \times w \times h$, where l = length, w = width, and h = height. Volume is measured in *cubic* units, otherwise notated as units^3.

Example #1

What is the volume of a prism with a length of 4 feet, a width of 6 feet, and a height of 2 feet?

(A)   8 ft^3
(B)   12 ft^3
(C)   24 ft^3
(D)   48 ft^3

$4 \times 6 \times 2 = 48$. **The correct answer is (D)**.

Example #2

What is the length of one side of a cube whose volume is 27 in^3?

(A)   2 in
(B)   3 in
(C)   4 in
(D)   5 in

The length, width, and height of a cube are equal. $3 \times 3 \times 3 = 27$. **The correct answer is (B)**.

Example #3

Use the diagram of the cube to answer the question.

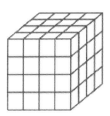

How many small cubes are being used to build the large cube?

(A)   32
(B)   48
(C)   64
(D)   96

The larger cube is composed of 4 smaller cubes on each side. $4 \times 4 \times 4 = 64$. **The correct answer is (C).**

Example #4

The volume of the smaller cube is 8 mm³. The larger cube is three times as wide as the smaller cube.

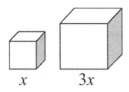

x $3x$

What is the volume of the larger cube?

(A)   6 mm³
(B)   18 mm³
(C)   36 mm³
(D)   216 mm³

The length, width, and height of a cube are all equal. First, figure out the length of each side of the smaller cube. $1 \times 1 \times 1 = 1$, but the volume of the smaller cube is 8, so that doesn't work. $2 \times 2 \times 2 = 8$. That means each side of the smaller cube is 2 mm long. If each side of the larger cube is three times as long as the corresponding side of the smaller cube, that means each side of the larger cube is 6 mm long. $6 \times 6 \times 6 = 216$. **The correct answer is (D).**

Practice Problems

1. What is the volume of a prism with a length of 3 feet, a width of 5 feet, and a height of 4 feet?
    (A)   12 ft³
    (B)   15 ft³
    (C)   60 ft³
    (D)   90 ft³

2. Each side of the smaller cube is 2 cm. Each side of the larger cube is 4 cm.

    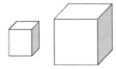

    How many of the smaller cubes could fit into the larger cube?
    (A)   2
    (B)   4
    (C)   6
    (D)   8

3. What is the length of one side of a cube whose volume is 8 cm³?
    (A)   1 cm
    (B)   2 cm
    (C)   3 cm
    (D)   4 cm

4. What is the volume of a prism with a length of 4 feet, a width of 6 feet, and a height of 2 feet?
    (A)   12 ft³
    (B)   24 ft³
    (C)   48 ft³
    (D)   64 ft³

5. The volume of the smaller cube is 1 in³. The larger cube is two times as wide as the smaller cube.

    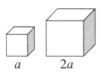

    a $2a$

    What is the volume of the larger cube?
    (A)   2 in³
    (B)   4 in³
    (C)   8 in³
    (D)   16 in³

6. What is the volume of a prism with a length of 2 inches, a width of 9 inches, and a height of 4 inches?
    (A)   18 in³
    (B)   72 in³
    (C)   80 in³
    (D)   144 in³

7. Use the diagram of the cube to answer the question.

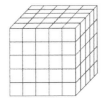

How many small cubes are being used to build the large cube?
(A)   25
(B)   75
(C)   100
(D)   125

8. What is the length of one side of a cube whose volume is 64 m³?
(A)   2 meters
(B)   3 meters
(C)   4 meters
(D)   8 meters

9. What is the length of one side of a cube whose volume is 125 cm³?
(A)   5 centimeters
(B)   6 centimeters
(C)   7 centimeters
(D)   8 centimeters

10. The volume of the larger cube is 64 ft³. The larger cube is four times as wide as the smaller cube.

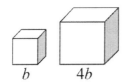

What is the volume of the smaller cube?
(A)   1 ft³
(B)   2 ft³
(C)   4 ft³
(D)   16 ft³

11. Each side of the smaller cube is 1 ft. Each side of the larger cube is 5 ft.

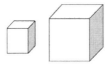

How many of the smaller cubes could fit into the larger cube?
(A)   5
(B)   25
(C)   100
(D)   125

12. The volume of the larger cube is 8 cm³. The larger cube is two times as wide as the smaller cube.

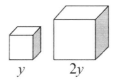

What is the volume of the smaller cube?
(A)   1 cm³
(B)   2 cm³
(C)   16 cm³
(D)   64 cm³

13. Use the diagram of the cubes to answer the question.

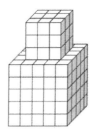

What is the total number of cubes in the diagram?
(A)   27
(B)   125
(C)   152
(D)   200

14. What is the volume of a prism with a length of 6 feet, a width of 6 feet, and a height of 4 feet?
    (A)   36 ft³
    (B)   72 ft³
    (C)   124 ft³
    (D)   144 ft³

15. The volume of the smaller cube is 27 mm³. The larger cube is two times as wide as the smaller cube.

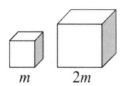

    m   *2m*

    What is the volume of the larger cube?
    (A)   6 mm³
    (B)   18 mm³
    (C)   216 mm³
    (D)   432 mm³

16. What is the length of one side of a cube whose volume is 1,000 in³?
    (A)   1 inches
    (B)   5 inches
    (C)   10 inches
    (D)   100 inches

17. Each side of the smaller cube is 3 ft. Each side of the larger cube is 6 ft.

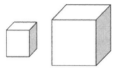

    How many of the smaller cubes could fit into the larger cube?
    (A)   2
    (B)   4
    (C)   6
    (D)   8

Answer Key – Algebra and Geometry

Basic Algebra

1. $5a$
2. $4y$
3. $1b$ or b
4. $6x + 2y$
5. $4d + 7f$
6. $2x + 2y + 2z$
7. $9x + 5$
8. $3y + 7$
9. $10a + 11$
10. 0
11. $x = 4$
12. $z = 7$
13. $x = 5$
14. $a = 6$
15. D
16. D
17. A
18. A
19. C
20. A
21. D
22. C
23. A
24. D
25. B
26. C
27. B
28. A
29. D
30. B
31. D
32. B

Shapes

1. 9
2. Hexagon
3. 13
4. 8
5. Heptagons
6. Decagon
7. 17
8. Heptagon
9. 5 centimeters
10. 8 inches
11. 49 inches
12. 27 meters
13. 12 centimeters
14. 42 inches
15. 15
16. 60 inches
17. 10
18. Hexagon
19. Triangle, Quadrilateral, Pentagon, Hexagon, Heptagon, Octagon, Nonagon, Decagon
20. All the shape's sides are equal and all of the shape's interior angles are equal
21. 19

Quadrilaterals

1. C
2. D
3. B
4. A
5. B
6. C
7. C
8. B
9. D

Triangles

1. 60 square inches
2. 30 inches
3. 39 inches
4. 8 centimeters
5. 108 degrees
6. 15 square centimeters
7. 15 inches

Volume

1. C
2. D
3. B
4. C
5. C
6. B
7. D
8. C
9. A
10. A
11. D
12. A
13. C
14. D
15. C
16. C
17. D

Part IV
Mathematics Question Types

Chapter 4
Mathematics Question Types

Fractions

Fractions questions may test you on basic knowledge of adding, subtracting, multiplying, or dividing fractions, or they may present you with a figure or word problem. You must always remember that a fraction represents "part out of whole." These questions often contain trick answers.

Example #1
What fraction of the figure below is shaded?

(A) $\frac{1}{12}$

(B) $\frac{4}{8}$

(C) $\frac{8}{12}$

(D) $\frac{1}{3}$

First, note that the question asks about the *shaded* part of the figure. There are 4 shaded squares, and 12 squares total. The fraction should be $\frac{4}{12}$, but that's not an option. Try reducing the fraction. 4 and 12 are both divisible by 4, so the fraction can be reduced to $\frac{1}{3}$. **(D) is the correct answer**. (C) is a trick answer – it represents the unshaded portion of the figure. (B) contains a common misconception. It represents shaded squares over unshaded squares.

Example #2
What fraction is between $\frac{1}{2}$ and $\frac{4}{5}$?

(A) $\frac{1}{4}$

(B) $\frac{1}{3}$

(C) $\frac{6}{10}$

(D) $\frac{9}{10}$

If possible, try to change the given fractions so that they have the same denominator. This will make comparing the fractions much easier. $\frac{1}{2} = \frac{5}{10}$, and $\frac{4}{5} = \frac{8}{10}$, so ideally you will see an answer with a denominator of 10. In this question, **the correct answer is (C)**.

Example #3

Jeffrey brought some pieces of candy to school. He gave $\frac{1}{4}$ of the candy to his friend Jack, and $\frac{1}{2}$ of the candy to his teacher. If Jack got 4 pieces of candy from Jeffrey, how many pieces of candy does Jeffrey have now?

(A)   4
(B)   8
(C)   12
(D)   16

This is a very difficult question. To answer it, you need to figure out how many pieces of candy Jeffrey had when he got to school. Jack got 4 pieces of candy, which was $\frac{1}{4}$ of Jeffrey's total candy. 4 pieces is $\frac{1}{4}$ of how many total pieces? You may have to think about this for a while. $\frac{1}{4}$ of 4 is 1, so 4 is definitely not enough. $\frac{1}{4}$ of 12 is 3, so that's still not quite enough. $\frac{1}{4}$ of 16 is 4, so you know that Jeffrey brought 16 pieces of candy to school. That means he must have given 8 pieces to his teacher. $16 - 8 - 4 = 4$, so Jeffrey has 4 pieces of candy left. **(A) is the correct answer**. (B) represents how many pieces of candy Jeffrey gave to his teacher; (C) shows how many pieces he gave away in total, and (D) is the number of pieces he started with. Make sure you choose the answer that addresses what the question asks!

Example #4

Which fraction is the least?

(A) $\frac{3}{5}$

(B) $\frac{5}{9}$

(C) $\frac{6}{13}$

(D) $\frac{8}{15}$

You could compare each fraction individually using the method described in the Math Fundamentals section of this book. However, questions like this most likely will be designed so that you don't have to spend that much time in order to get the right answer. Notice that of the four answer choices, only (C) is less than $\frac{1}{2}$. Therefore, **(C) is the correct answer.**

Example #5

A lake has an area of about 21,400 mi². Which area is closest to that of $\frac{1}{4}$ of the lake's area?

(A)   4,000 mi²
(B)   5,000 mi²
(C)   6,000 mi²
(D)   7,000 mi²

First, round 21,400 down to 20,000, and then multiply by $\frac{1}{4}$. $\frac{20,000}{1} \times \frac{1}{4} = \frac{20,000}{4} = 5,000$. **The correct answer is (B)**. If you'd like to think about this question a different way, you can ask yourself, "what number goes into 20,000 four times?" 5,000 goes into 20,000 four times, so $\frac{1}{4}$ of 20,000 is 5,000.

Practice Problems

1. Florencia brought some pieces of candy to school. She gave $\frac{1}{6}$ of the candy to her friend Isadora, and $\frac{4}{6}$ of the candy to her teacher. If Isadora got 1 piece of candy from Florencia, how many pieces of candy does Florencia have now?

   (A)   1
   (B)   2
   (C)   3
   (D)   4

2. A lake has an area of about 32,600 mi². Which area is closest to that of $\frac{3}{4}$ of the lake's area?
   (A)   10,000 mi²
   (B)   16,000 mi²
   (C)   22,000 mi²
   (D)   24,000 mi²

3. What fraction is between $\frac{1}{8}$ and $\frac{1}{2}$?
   (A) $\frac{1}{9}$

   (B) $\frac{1}{4}$

   (C) $\frac{2}{3}$

   (D) $\frac{3}{4}$

4. Which fraction is the least?
   (A) $\frac{5}{9}$

   (B) $\frac{6}{11}$

   (C) $\frac{4}{8}$

   (D) $\frac{7}{13}$

5. What fraction of the figure below is shaded?

   (A) $\frac{5}{11}$

   (B) $\frac{1}{4}$

   (C) $\frac{5}{16}$

   (D) $\frac{1}{3}$

6. What fraction is between $\frac{1}{2}$ and $\frac{11}{16}$?
   (A) $\frac{1}{3}$

   (B) $\frac{4}{9}$

   (C) $\frac{5}{8}$

   (D) $\frac{3}{4}$

7. Ori brought some pieces of candy to school. He gave $\frac{2}{6}$ of the candy to his friend Hydar, and $\frac{1}{6}$ of the candy to his teacher. If Hydar got 2 pieces of candy from Ori, how many pieces of candy does Ori have now?
   (A)   1
   (B)   2
   (C)   3
   (D)   4

8. A lake has an area of about 17,700 mi^2. Which area is closest to that of $\frac{1}{3}$ of the lake's area?
    (A)   4,000 mi^2
    (B)   5,000 mi^2
    (C)   5,250 mi^2
    (D)   6,000 mi^2

9. Which is the largest fraction?

    (A) $\frac{51}{100}$

    (B) $\frac{1}{2}$

    (C) $\frac{3}{7}$

    (D) $\frac{2}{5}$

10. Lara created the design below.

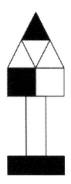

    What fraction of the shapes in her design is shaded?

    (A) $\frac{3}{8}$

    (B) $\frac{5}{3}$

    (C) $\frac{3}{5}$

    (D) $\frac{8}{3}$

11. What fraction is between $\frac{3}{5}$ and $\frac{15}{20}$?

    (A) $\frac{1}{4}$

    (B) $\frac{3}{8}$

    (C) $\frac{1}{2}$

    (D) $\frac{7}{10}$

12. Which is the largest fraction?

    (A) $\frac{11}{20}$

    (B) $\frac{3}{4}$

    (C) $\frac{8}{15}$

    (D) $\frac{5}{10}$

13. A lake has an area of about 58,600 mi^2. Which area is closest to that of $\frac{3}{5}$ of the lake's area?
    (A)   30,000 mi^2
    (B)   36,000 mi^2
    (C)   40,000 mi^2
    (D)   48,000 mi^2

14. Xiaoyan brought some pieces of candy to school. She gave $\frac{1}{8}$ of the candy to her friend Jesse, and $\frac{3}{8}$ of the candy to her teacher. If Jesse got 1 piece of candy from Xiaoyan, how many pieces of candy did her teacher get?
    (A)   1
    (B)   2
    (C)   3
    (D)   4

15. Which fraction is the least?

   (A) $\frac{5}{10}$

   (B) $\frac{4}{7}$

   (C) $\frac{6}{11}$

   (D) $\frac{7}{13}$

16. Which is the largest fraction?

   (A) $\frac{6}{11}$

   (B) $\frac{2}{11}$

   (C) $\frac{5}{11}$

   (D) $\frac{7}{11}$

17. What fraction of the figure below is shaded?

   (A) $\frac{4}{12}$

   (B) $\frac{1}{3}$

   (C) $\frac{1}{4}$

   (D) $\frac{5}{16}$

18. What fraction is between $\frac{3}{7}$ and $\frac{24}{28}$?

   (A) $\frac{1}{3}$

   (B) $\frac{9}{14}$

   (C) $\frac{13}{14}$

   (D) $\frac{9}{10}$

19. A lake has an area of about 12,315 mi^2. Which area is closest to that of $\frac{3}{4}$ of the lake's area?
   (A)   3,000 mi^2
   (B)   6,000 mi^2
   (C)   9,000 mi^2
   (D)   10,000 mi^2

20. Which fraction is the least?

   (A) $\frac{1}{2}$

   (B) $\frac{1}{3}$

   (C) $\frac{1}{4}$

   (D) $\frac{7}{10}$

21. Robin brought some pieces of candy to school. She gave $\frac{1}{4}$ of the candy to her friend Aron, and $\frac{1}{2}$ of the candy to her teacher. If Aron got 2 pieces of candy from Robin, how many pieces of candy does Robin have now?
   (A)   2
   (B)   3
   (C)   4
   (D)   8

22. What fraction is between $\frac{1}{3}$ and $\frac{3}{4}$?
   (A) $\frac{1}{2}$

   (B) $\frac{1}{4}$

   (C) $\frac{1}{5}$

   (D) $\frac{5}{6}$

23. Which is the largest fraction?

   (A) $\frac{2}{3}$

   (B) $\frac{3}{4}$

   (C) $\frac{4}{8}$

   (D) $\frac{6}{10}$

24. Elias brought some pieces of candy to school. He gave $\frac{1}{3}$ of the candy to his friend Filip, and $\frac{1}{2}$ of the candy to his teacher. If the teacher got 12 pieces of candy from Elias, how many pieces of candy did Filip get?

   (A)   4
   (B)   8
   (C)   9
   (D)   12

25. What fraction is between $\frac{1}{4}$ and $\frac{7}{16}$?

   (A) $\frac{1}{8}$

   (B) $\frac{3}{16}$

   (C) $\frac{3}{8}$

   (D) $\frac{3}{4}$

26. Hugo brought some pieces of candy to school. He gave $\frac{1}{3}$ of the candy to his friend Daniel, and $\frac{1}{6}$ of the candy to his teacher. If the teacher got 3 pieces of candy from Hugo, how many pieces of candy did Daniel get?

   (A)   3
   (B)   4
   (C)   5
   (D)   6

Applied Mean, Median, Mode, and Range

The Lower Level ISEE will not ask you to simply find the mean, median, mode, or range of a data set. Instead, you may have to compare measures or apply them to real-life situations.

Example #1

The ingredients in the recipe were evenly mixed and equally divided into 5 bags.

RECIPE

2 cups of chopped chocolate pieces
2 cups of raisins
3 cups of peanuts
6 cups of pretzel sticks

Approximately how many cups of the mixture were placed in each bag?

(A) $1\frac{3}{5}$

(B) $2\frac{3}{5}$

(C) $2\frac{4}{5}$

(D) $3\frac{2}{5}$

This question requires knowledge of fractions and mean. First, add together the ingredients to find the total: $2 + 2 + 3 + 6 = 13$ cups. Then, find the number of cups that will be placed into each of the 5 bags by dividing by 5. $13 \div 5 = \frac{13}{5} = 2\frac{3}{5}$. **The correct answer is (B).**

Example #2

Use the table to answer the question.

JERRY'S SCHOOL SCORES

Event 1	6.7	8.2	7.0	6.7
Event 2	9.0	8.2	6.7	6.6
Event 3	9.4	6.7	6.6	9.1
Event 4	6.7	5.8	8.2	7.0

What is the mode of the data?
(A)   6.6
(B)   6.7
(C)   8.2
(D)   9.1

There is a time saving strategy on this question: there are only 4 possible answer choices, so ignore all numbers except 6.6, 6.7, 8.2, and 9.1! 6.6 appears 2 times, 6.7 appears 5 times, 8.2 appears 3 times, and 9.1 appears 1 time. The mode is 6.7, **so (B) is the correct answer.**

Example #3

Four students recorded the number of minutes they spent playing video games after school for one night and recorded their data in the graph shown.

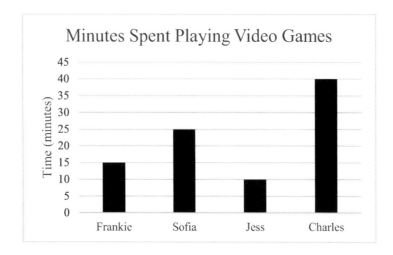

Based on this graph, which conclusion is true about the number of minutes spent playing video games?
(A)   The mean is between 22 and 23
(B)   Sofia played fewer minutes than Frankie
(C)   The range is the same as the number of minutes Sofia played
(D)   Charles played the same number of minutes as Sofia and Jess combined

Remember that you have a limited amount of time to complete each question on the ISEE. As a strategy, you should only do time-consuming tasks if it is absolutely necessary. When it comes to mean, median, mode, and range questions, that means you should always find the mean last. Think about it: finding mode, median, and range only takes a few seconds, while finding the median could take 1 – 2 minutes! Therefore, on this example, look at (B), (C), and (D) first. Sofia played 25 minutes and Frankie played 15 minutes, so that doesn't work. The range is 40 – 10 = 30, and Sofia played 25 minutes, so (C) doesn't work either. Finally, Sofia and Jess played 35 minutes combined, while Charles played 40 minutes. (D) is incorrect. By process of elimination, **(A) must be the correct answer**. You can confirm this by doing the math if you'd like: 15 + 25 + 10 + 40 = 90. 90 ÷ 4 = 22.5.

Practice Problems

1. The ingredients in the recipe were evenly mixed and equally divided into 4 bags.

RECIPE

1 cup of M&Ms
2 cups of cranberries
3 cups of almonds
4 cups of shredded coconut

Approximately how many cups of the mixture were placed in each bag?

(A) $2\frac{1}{2}$

(B) $2\frac{3}{4}$

(C) $3\frac{1}{2}$

(D) $3\frac{3}{4}$

2. A dog had a litter of 5 puppies. Three puppies weighed $7\frac{1}{4}$ ounces each, one puppy weighed $5\frac{3}{4}$ ounces, and one puppy weighed 5 ounces. What is the mean weight of the puppies from the litter?

(A) $6\frac{1}{4}$ ounces

(B) $6\frac{1}{2}$ ounces

(C)   7 ounces

(D) $7\frac{1}{4}$ ounces

3. Use the table to answer the question

JANE'S SCHOOL SCORES

Event 1	4.4	8.2	6.0	5.9
Event 2	9.0	8.6	6.8	9.3
Event 3	9.4	4.7	5.6	6.3
Event 4	6.7	5.4	8.2	7.0

What is the range of the data?

(A)   4.9
(B)   5.0
(C)   5.3
(D)   5.7

4. The ingredients in the recipe were evenly mixed and equally divided into 7 bags.

RECIPE

2 cups of chopped walnuts
2 cups of dried mango
3 cups of peanuts
2 cups of chocolate pieces
8 cups of pretzel sticks

Approximately how many cups of the mixture were placed in each bag?

(A) $2\frac{2}{7}$

(B) $2\frac{3}{7}$

(C) $3\frac{1}{7}$

(D) $3\frac{2}{7}$

5. Use the table to answer the question

KELLY'S SCHOOL SCORES

Event 1	7.8	9.1	7.0	7.0
Event 2	9.0	6.8	7.8	6.6
Event 3	9.4	6.7	6.6	7.8
Event 4	6.5	9.9	7.8	7.0

What is the mode of the data?

(A)   6.6
(B)   7.0
(C)   7.8
(D)   9.4

6. The ingredients in the recipe were evenly mixed and equally divided into 6 bags.

RECIPE

4 cups chopped chocolate pieces
1 cup of raisins
5 cups of peanuts
6 cups of pretzel sticks

Approximately how many cups of the mixture were placed in each bag?

(A) $1\frac{4}{16}$

(B) $1\frac{1}{2}$

(C) $1\frac{3}{4}$

(D) $2\frac{2}{3}$

7. A cat had a litter of 6 kittens. Three kittens weighed $4\frac{1}{2}$ ounces each, two kittens weighed 5 ounces each, and one kitten weighed 11 ounces. What is the mean weight of the kittens from the litter?

(A)   5 ounces

(B) $5\frac{1}{4}$ ounces

(C) $5\frac{3}{4}$ ounces

(D)   6 ounces

8. Use the table to answer the question

LABRON'S SCHOOL SCORES

Event 1	6.7	9.0	7.0	6.7
Event 2	9.0	8.2	4.7	9.0
Event 3	9.4	6.7	6.6	9.1
Event 4	5.7	9.0	8.1	7.0

What is the mode of the data?

(A)   6.6
(B)   7.0
(C)   8.2
(D)   9.0

9. A man bought 4 apples at the store. Two apples weighed $5\frac{3}{4}$ ounces each, one apple weighed 8 ounces, and one apple weighed $8\frac{1}{2}$ ounces. What is the mean weight of the apples?

(A) $6\frac{3}{4}$ ounces

(B)   7 ounces

(C) $7\frac{1}{4}$ ounces

(D)   8 ounces

10. The ingredients in the recipe were evenly mixed and equally divided into 3 bags.

RECIPE

2 cups of pecans
3 cups of dried cherries
1 cup of raisins
1 cup of chopped dark chocolate
4 cups of sunflower seeds

Approximately how many cups of the mixture were placed in each bag?

(A) $2\frac{1}{3}$

(B) $2\frac{2}{3}$

(C) $3\frac{4}{6}$

(D) $3\frac{5}{6}$

11. A cat had a litter of 3 kittens. One kitten weighed $3\frac{1}{2}$ ounces, one kitten weighed 7 ounces, and one kitten weighed $5\frac{1}{4}$ ounces. What is the mean weight of the kittens from the litter?

(A) $5\frac{2}{8}$ ounces

(B) $5\frac{1}{2}$ ounces

(C) $5\frac{6}{8}$ ounces

(D) 6 ounces

12. The ingredients in the recipe were evenly mixed and equally divided into 8 bags.

RECIPE

2 cups of almonds
2 cups of dried banana chips
5 cups of peanuts
3 cups of chocolate chips
1 cup of sunflower seeds

Approximately how many cups of the mixture were placed in each bag?

(A) $1\frac{1}{2}$

(B) $1\frac{5}{8}$

(C) $1\frac{6}{8}$

(D) $1\frac{7}{8}$

13. A student has 5 colored blocks. Two blocks weighed 4.2 ounces each, one block weighed 6.6 ounces, one block weighed 7.5 ounces, and one block weighed 6.5 ounces. What is the mean weight of the blocks?

(A) 5 ounces

(B) $5\frac{8}{100}$ ounces

(C) $5\frac{4}{5}$ ounces

(D) 6 ounces

14. The ingredients in the recipe were evenly mixed and equally divided into 5 bags.

RECIPE

5 cups of chopped walnuts
4 cups of dried mango
3 cups of peanuts
1 cup of chocolate pieces
5 cups of pretzel sticks

Approximately how many cups of the mixture were placed in each bag?

(A) $2\frac{3}{5}$

(B) $3\frac{1}{5}$

(C) $3\frac{6}{10}$

(D) $3\frac{4}{10}$

15. Use the table to answer the question

JAIME'S SCHOOL SCORES

Event 1	6.7	8.2	7.0	6.7
Event 2	4.5	8.2	6.7	9.6
Event 3	9.4	6.7	6.6	9.1
Event 4	6.7	5.8	8.2	7.0

What is the range of the data?

(A) 4.5
(B) 4.9
(C) 5.1
(D) 5.6

16. A dog had a litter of 4 puppies. Two puppies weighed 3.7 ounces each, one puppy weighed 2.5 ounces, and one puppy weighed 2.9 ounces. What is the mean weight of the puppies from the litter?

(A) $3\frac{1}{5}$ ounces

(B) $3\frac{3}{10}$ ounces

(C) $3\frac{1}{2}$ ounces

(D) $3\frac{4}{5}$ ounces

17. Use the table to answer the question

BETH'S SCHOOL SCORES

Event 1	5.5	8.8	7.0	5.5
Event 2	5.1	8.2	6.7	6.6
Event 3	9.4	5.5	8.8	9.1
Event 4	6.7	6.7	5.5	5.1

What is the mode of the data?

(A) 5.1
(B) 5.5
(C) 6.7
(D) 8.8

Questions #18 – 21 refer to the graph below.

The graph shows the total rainfall for six months last year in City A.

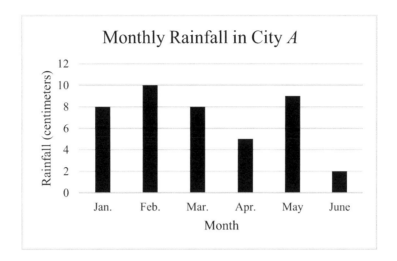

18. Based on this graph, which conclusion is true about the monthly rainfall in City A?
    (A)   The mean is between 7 and 8
    (B)   It rained less in May than it did in February
    (C)   The range is 7
    (D)   It rained the same amount in January as it did in April and June combined

19. According to the graph, what is the mean monthly rainfall?
    (A)   6.5 cm
    (B)   7.0 cm
    (C)   7.5 cm
    (D)   8.0 cm

20. What is the mode of the graph?
    (A)   8 cm
    (B)   9 cm
    (C)   10 cm
    (D)   11 cm

21. Which two measures are equal?
    (A)   The mode and the range
    (B)   The mode and the mean
    (C)   The range and the mean
    (D)   The median and the mean

Questions #22 – 24 refer to the graph below.

Five students recorded the number of minutes they spent practicing piano at home for one night and recorded their data in the graph shown.

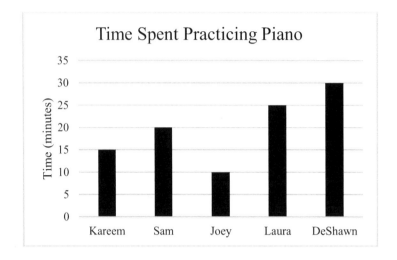

22. Based on this graph, which conclusion is true about the number of minutes spent practicing piano?
    (A)   The mean is between 19 and 21
    (B)   The range and the mode are the same
    (C)   Kareem practiced longer than Laura
    (D)   Sam practiced the same amount of time as Joey and Kareem combined

23. According to the graph, what is the mean amount of time spent practicing piano?
    (A)   18 minutes
    (B)   19 minutes
    (C)   20 minutes
    (D)   21 minutes

24. What is the range of the graph?
    (A)   10
    (B)   20
    (C)   30
    (D)   40

Questions #25 – 28 refer to the graph below.

Six students recorded how far they ran during gym class.

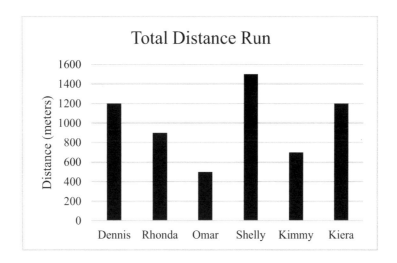

25. Based on this graph, which conclusion is true about the distance students ran in gym class?
    (A)   Shelly ran the same distance as Rhonda and Omar combined
    (B)   The mode is 1,100
    (C)   The range is 1,000
    (D)   No student ran farther than 1,400 meters

26. According to the graph, what is the mean distance the students ran?
    (A)   900 meters
    (B)   1,000 meters
    (C)   1,100 meters
    (D)   1,200 meters

27. What is the mode of the graph?
    (A)   1,000
    (B)   1,050
    (C)   1,200
    (D)   1,500

28. Which two measures are equal?
    (A)   The range and the mode
    (B)   The mode and the median
    (C)   The mean and the mode
    (D)   The mean and the range

Applied Rates and Ratios

Applied rates and ratios questions test simple material at a relatively high level.

Example #1
A teacher put the names of all her students in a hat. The probability that she will pull out a boy's name at random is 4 out of 9. There are 15 girls in the class. How many boys are in the class?
(A) 4
(B) 5
(C) 9
(D) 12

If the probability that the teacher will pull a boy's name is 4 out of 9, then the probability that she will pull a girl's name is 5 out of 9. There are actually 15 girls in the class, which means the multiplier is 3. 4 × 3 = 12, so there are 12 boys in the class. **The correct answer is (D).**

Example #2
Joy and Mark were riding their bikes at the same speed on a bike path. It took Joy 15 minutes to ride 3 miles. How long did it take Mark to ride 9 miles?
(A) 27 minutes
(B) 45 minutes
(C) 70 minutes
(D) 90 minutes

This example is similar to the basic rates questions that were introduced in the Math Fundamentals section. Mark rides three times as far as Joy, so his time will be three times as long as Joy's time. 15 × 3 = 45. **(B) is the correct answer.**

Example #3
Thiago has a box of chocolates with different cream fillings: caramel, vanilla, cinnamon, orange, and cocoa. The probability of choosing a chocolate filled with cinnamon is 6 out of 11. What combination of chocolates is possible?
(A)   6 cinnamon chocolates and 11 others
(B)   24 cinnamon chocolates and 44 others
(C)   18 cinnamon chocolates and 10 others
(D)   30 cinnamon chocolates and 25 others

This is similar to Example #1. If the probability of choosing a cinnamon chocolate is 6 out of 11, then the probability of choosing another type of chocolate is 5 out of 11. That means the possible combination of chocolates could be 6 cinnamon and 5 others, 12 cinnamon and 10 others, 18 cinnamon and 15 others, etc. Notice that the cinnamon chocolates will always be multiples of 6, and the other chocolates will always be multiples of 5. Pay attention to the trick answers in this question. (A) is essentially rewriting the numbers given in the question stem, and (B) simply multiplies both 6 and 11 by 4. Finally, even if the numbers in the answer are the correct multiples, you need to make sure they are also the correct ratio. In (C), the multiples are correct, but the final ratio is wrong. The given ratio is 6 out of 11, but (C) represents 18 out of 28. This reduces to 9 out of 14, *not* 6 out of 11. **The correct answer is (D).** There would be 55 total chocolates, of which 30 are cinnamon. The ratio is 30 out of 55, which reduces to 6 out of 11.

Practice Problems

1. Mahdi has a box of colored marbles: red, yellow, blue, green, and pink. The probability of choosing a red marble is 3 out of 8. What combination of marbles is possible?
   - (A)   3 red marbles and 8 others
   - (B)   12 red marbles and 32 others
   - (C)   15 red marbles and 25 others
   - (D)   16 red marbles and 6 others

2. A teacher put the names of all of her students into a hat. The probability that she will pull out a boy's name is 1 out of 4. There are 15 girls in the class. How many boys are in the class?
   - (A)   1
   - (B)   4
   - (C)   5
   - (D)   11

3. The scale on a map shows that 1.3 inches represents 15 miles. How many inches would it take to represent 45 miles?
   - (A)   3.9
   - (B)   4.0
   - (C)   4.6
   - (D)   5.2

4. Tarik and Filip were walking at the same speed on the beach. It took Tarik 20 minutes to walk 1 mile. How long did it take Filip to walk 5 miles?
   - (A)   4 minutes
   - (B)   60 minutes
   - (C)   80 minutes
   - (D)   100 minutes

5. Diya has a box of chocolates with different cream fillings: caramel, vanilla, cinnamon, orange, and cocoa. The probability of choosing a chocolate filled with caramel is 7 out of 12. What combination of chocolates is possible?
   - (A)   14 caramels and 10 others
   - (B)   7 caramels and 12 others
   - (C)   14 caramels and 12 others
   - (D)   24 caramels and 14 others

6. The scale on a map shows that 0.5 inches represents 12 miles. How many miles do 4.5 inches represent?
   - (A)   24
   - (B)   54
   - (C)   90
   - (D)   108

7. A teacher put the names of all of her students into a hat. The probability that she will pull out a girl's name is 5 out of 8. There are 9 boys in the class. How many girls are in the class?
   - (A)   3
   - (B)   5
   - (C)   13
   - (D)   15

8. Celine has a bag of trail mix made with different ingredients: chocolate, peanuts, raisins, almonds, and dried fruit. The probability of choosing dried fruit is 1 out of 10. What combination of trail mix ingredients is possible?
   - (A)   1 dried fruit and 10 others
   - (B)   4 dried fruit and 36 others
   - (C)   10 dried fruit and 1 other
   - (D)   2 dried fruit and 20 others

9. Larry and Leon were riding their bikes at the same speed on a bike path. It took Larry 18 minutes to ride 4 miles. How long did it take Leon to ride 10 miles?
    (A)   25 minutes
    (B)   36 minutes
    (C)   45 minutes
    (D)   54 minutes

10. The scale on a map shows that 0.7 inches represents 18 miles. How many inches would it take to represent 72 miles?
    (A)   2.1
    (B)   2.8
    (C)   3.5
    (D)   4.2

11. The ratio of girls to boys in a class is 4 to 5. There are 27 students in the class. How many boys are in the class?
    (A)   4
    (B)   5
    (C)   12
    (D)   15

12. Ashley has a box of different colored Legos: green, orange, purple, white, grey, and blue. The probability of choosing a purple Lego is 3 out of 13. What combination of Legos is possible?
    (A)   3 purple out of 10 others
    (B)   6 purple out of 13 others
    (C)   3 purple out of 16 others
    (D)   9 purple out of 3 others

13. Noel and Nathan were sprinting at the same speed on a track. It took Noel 3 minutes to run .5 miles. How long did it take Nathan to run 2.5 miles?
    (A)   1.5 minutes
    (B)   7.5 minutes
    (C)   12 minutes
    (D)   15 minutes

14. The scale on a map shows that 1.8 inches represents 16 miles. How many inches would it take to represent 56 miles?
    (A)   5.4
    (B)   6.3
    (C)   7.0
    (D)   7.2

15. The ratio of boys to girls in a class is 7 to 8. There are 24 girls in the class. How many boys are in the class?
    (A)   7
    (B)   14
    (C)   15
    (D)   21

16. The scale on a map shows that 9.2 inches represents 6 miles. How many inches do 18 miles represent?
    (A)   27.6
    (B)   32.2
    (C)   36.8
    (D)   41.4

Perimeter and Area Questions

The most important thing to do on *perimeter and area questions* is pay attention to what the question is asking. If you are asked to find perimeter, the answer choices will often include the shape's area; if the question asks for area, the answer choices will often include the shape's perimeter. It's very easy to make careless mistakes on these questions.

Example #1

The figure shows a drawing of Mark's bedroom

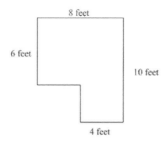

What is the perimeter of Mark's bedroom?

(A)   20 feet
(B)   28 feet
(C)   36 feet
(D)   80 feet

There are two ways of approaching this problem. The harder way is to find the lengths of the missing sides and then add up the 6 different lengths to find the total perimeter. If the total width of the bedroom is 8 feet, and 4 feet are accounted for on the southern end of the bedroom, then the length of the other horizontal section must also be 4 feet (because 8 – 4 = 4). If the width of the bedroom is 10 feet, and 6 feet are accounted for on the western side of the bedroom, then the length of the other vertical section must be 4 feet (because 10 – 6 = 4). Then, add everything together: 8 + 10 + 4 + 4 + 4 + 6 = 36. **The correct answer is (C).**

The other way you can complete these questions is to look at the long edges (here, those edges are 8 and 10 feet). The length across from 8 feet will also be a total of 8 feet, and the width across from 10 feet will also be a total of 10 feet, so you can simply find the sum of 8 + 8 + 10 + 10.

Example #2

The figure shows a drawing of Brad's bedroom.

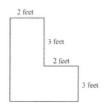

What is the area of Brad's bedroom?

(A)   12 square feet
(B)   18 square feet
(C)   24 square feet
(D)   30 square feet

In this question, you are asked to find area. These questions are a little trickier, because you'll need to split the L-shape into two pieces:

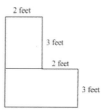

The upper piece is 2 feet by 3 feet, while the lower piece is 3 feet by 4 feet. Where did the 4 come from? You can see that the two horizontal pieces are each 2 feet long. 2 + 2 = 4, so the bottom side of the shape must be 4 feet long. Now, you simply find the area of each shape and add them together. 6 + 12 = 18, so **the correct answer is (B).**

Example #3

Ms. Grabot's dining room table can be lengthened by adding a 5-foot wide, 15-foot long section to the middle of it.

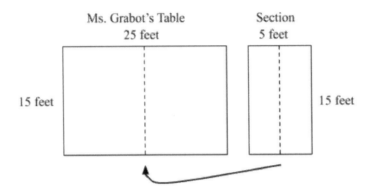

What will happen to the perimeter of Ms. Grabot's table if she adds the 5-foot wide, 15-foot long section to the middle?

(A)   It will increase by 5 feet
(B)   It will increase by 10 feet
(C)   It will increase by 20 feet
(D)   It will increase by 40 feet

Remember, perimeter measures the length of the *outside* of an object. If you place the section in the middle of the table, how many sides of the section will be included when measuring perimeter? Only the top and bottom, because the vertical sides will be *within* the table. The length will increase by 10, so **the correct answer is (B)**. If the section was added to the right side of the table, perimeter would still only increase by 10.

You may be asked a similar question about area. Since area measures the *inside* of a shape, and the area of this section is 75 square feet, the total area of the table will increase by 75 square feet no matter where you place the section: in the middle of the table, on the side of the table, etc.

Practice Problems

1. Mrs. Yarbrough's dining room table can be lengthened by adding a 4-foot wide, 7-foot long section to the middle of it.

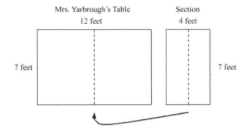

   What will happen to the area of Mrs. Yarbrough's table if she adds the 4-foot wide, 7-foot long section to the middle?
   (A)   It will increase by 4 square feet
   (B)   It will increase by 8 square feet
   (C)   It will increase by 11 square feet
   (D)   It will increase by 28 square feet

2. What is the perimeter of a rectangle that has a length of 1 inch and a width of 10 inches? ($P = 2l + 2w$)
   (A)   11 inches
   (B)   22 inches
   (C)   33 inches
   (D)   44 inches

3. The perimeter of the triangle shown below is 30. The lengths of two sides are shown.

   What is the length of the third side?
   (A)   8
   (B)   10
   (C)   12
   (D)   18

4. Use the triangle to answer the question.

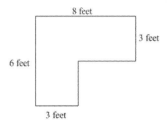

   What is the perimeter of the triangle?
   ($P = s + s + s$)
   (A)   30
   (B)   32
   (C)   33
   (D)   34

5. The figure shows a drawing of Miguel's bedroom

   What is the area of Miguel's bedroom?
   (A)   10 square feet
   (B)   14 square feet
   (C)   33 square feet
   (D)   48 square feet

6. What is the area of a triangle with a base of 16 inches and a height of 4 inches?
   (A)   16 square inches
   (B)   32 square inches
   (C)   64 square inches
   (D)   128 square inches

7. The perimeter of a square is 12s. What is the length of one side?
   (A)   3
   (B)   3s
   (C)   4
   (D)   4s

8. The length of one side of a square is 5 feet. What is the square's area?
    (A) 5 square feet
    (B) 10 square feet
    (C) 20 square feet
    (D) 25 square feet

9. The perimeter of a regular pentagon is 55x. What is the length of one side?
    (A) 11
    (B) 12
    (C) 11x
    (D) 12x

10. What is the area of the triangle shown below?

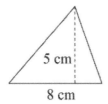

    (A) 20 square centimeters
    (B) 40 square centimeters
    (C) 60 square centimeters
    (D) 80 square centimeters

11. What is the perimeter of a rectangle that has a length of 5 inches and a width of 5 inches? ($P = 2l + 2w$)
    (A) 5 inches
    (B) 10 inches
    (C) 20 inches
    (D) 25 inches

12. What is the area of a triangle with a base of 9 inches and a height of 6 inches?
    (A) 15 square inches
    (B) 27 square inches
    (C) 54 square inches
    (D) 108 square inches

13. The perimeter of a square is 16 meters. What is the square's area?
    (A) 4 square meters
    (B) 8 square meters
    (C) 12 square meters
    (D) 16 square meters

14. The perimeter of the triangle is 40. The lengths of two of the sides are shown.

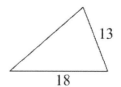

    What is the length of the third side?
    (A) 9
    (B) 10
    (C) 11
    (D) 12

15. Mr. Klein's dining room table can be lengthened by adding a 1-foot wide, 3-foot long section to the middle of it.

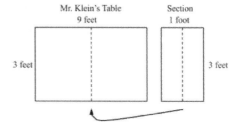

    What will happen to the area of Mr. Klein's table if he adds the 1-foot wide, 3-foot long section to the middle?
    (A) It will increase by 2 square feet
    (B) It will increase by 3 square feet
    (C) It will increase by 4 square feet
    (D) It will increase by 8 square feet

16. A triangle's area is 24 square centimeters. Its height is 6 centimeters. What is the length of the triangle's base?
    - (A)   2 centimeters
    - (B)   4 centimeters
    - (C)   6 centimeters
    - (D)   8 centimeters

17. What is the area of the triangle shown below?

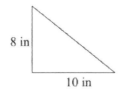

    - (A)   40 square inches
    - (B)   80 square inches
    - (C)   120 square inches
    - (D)   160 square inches

18. The figure shows a drawing of Marty's bedroom

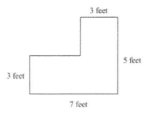

    What is the area of Marty's bedroom?
    - (A)   18 square feet
    - (B)   24 square feet
    - (C)   27 square feet
    - (D)   35 square feet

19. The perimeter of an octagon is $128x$. What is the length of one side?
    - (A)   8
    - (B) $8x$
    - (C)   16
    - (D) $16x$

20. The perimeter of the triangle is 24. The lengths of two of the sides are shown.

    What is the length of the third side?
    - (A)   7
    - (B)   8
    - (C)   9
    - (D)   10

21. A rectangle has a length of 3 inches and a width of 10 inches. What is the rectangle's perimeter?
    - (A)   13 inches
    - (B)   26 inches
    - (C)   30 inches
    - (D)   36 inches

22. Use the triangle to answer the question.

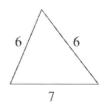

    What is the perimeter of the triangle? $(P = s + s + s)$
    - (A)   12
    - (B)   17
    - (C)   18
    - (D)   19

23. What is the perimeter of a rectangle that has a length of 3 inches and a width of 12 inches? $(P = 2l + 2w)$
    - (A)   12 inches
    - (B)   15 inches
    - (C)   24 inches
    - (D)   30 inches

24. Use the triangle to answer the question.

What is the perimeter of the triangle?
$(P = s + s + s)$
(A)   33
(B)   34
(C)   35
(D)   36

25. The perimeter of a square is $20x$. What is the length of one side?
(A)   5
(B) $5x$
(C)   10
(D) $10x$

26. The perimeter of a heptagon is $49x$. What is the length of one side?
(A)   7
(B) $7x$
(C)   14
(D) $14x$

27. The figure shows a drawing of Manuel's bedroom

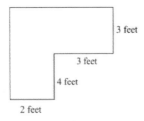

What is the perimeter of Manuel's bedroom?
(A)   24 feet
(B)   25 feet
(C)   26 feet
(D)   27 feet

28. A rectangle is 7 feet by 6 feet. What is the rectangle's perimeter?
(A)   22 feet
(B)   26 feet
(C)   36 feet
(D)   42 feet

29. Use the triangle to answer the question.

What is the perimeter of the triangle?
$(P = s + s + s)$
(A)   50
(B)   51
(C)   52
(D)   53

30. What is the area of the triangle shown below?

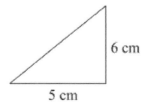

(A)   11 square centimeters
(B)   15 square centimeters
(C)   30 square centimeters
(D)   60 square centimeters

31. A triangle's area is 10 square feet. The base is 5 feet long. What is the triangle's height?
(A)   2 feet
(B)   4 feet
(C)   5 feet
(D)   7 feet

32. Mr. Singh's dining room table can be lengthened by adding a 2-foot wide, 4-foot long section to the side of it.

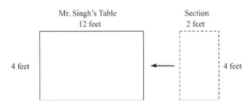

What will happen to the area of Mr. Singh's table if he adds the 2-foot wide, 4-foot long section to the table's side?

(A)   It will increase by 4 square feet
(B)   It will increase by 6 square feet
(C)   It will increase by 8 square feet
(D)   It will increase by 10 square feet

33. The area of the rectangle shown below is 63 square centimeters. What is the length of side x?

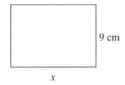

(A)   7 cm
(B)   8 cm
(C)   9 cm
(D)   10 cm

34. The area of the rectangle shown below is 60 square cm. What is the length of side x?

(A)   5 cm
(B)   8 cm
(C)   18 cm
(D)   20 cm

35. What is the perimeter of a rectangle that has a length of 6 inches and a width of 9 inches? ($P = 2l + 2w$)

(A)   15 inches
(B)   30 inches
(C)   60 inches
(D)   63 inches

36. The perimeter of a square is 32 inches. What is the square's area?

(A)   8 square inches
(B)   16 square inches
(C)   32 square inches
(D)   64 square inches

37. Ms. Argerich's dining room table can be lengthened by adding a 5-foot wide, 15-foot long section to the side of it.

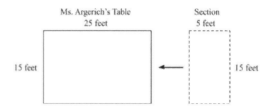

What will happen to the perimeter of Ms. Argerich's table if she adds the 5-foot wide, 15-foot long section to the side?

(A)   It will increase by 10 feet
(B)   It will increase by 20 feet
(C)   It will increase by 25 feet
(D)   It will increase by 40 feet

38. The perimeter of a decagon is 50. What is the length of one side?

(A)   5
(B)   10
(C) $5y$
(D) $10y$

39. The figure shows a drawing of Kimmy's bedroom

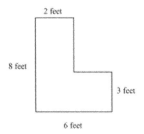

What is the perimeter of Kimmy's bedroom?
(A)   19 feet
(B)   23 feet
(C)   26 feet
(D)   28 feet

40. The perimeter of a square is 20 centimeters. What is the square's area?
(A)   5 square centimeters
(B)   10 square centimeters
(C)   25 square centimeters
(D)   100 square centimeters

Estimating

Estimating questions are quite easy. The most important thing is that you pay attention to what the question asks you to round to. Is it the ones, tens, or hundreds place? In general, you round up for numbers ending in 5 or more, and you round down for numbers ending in 4 or less. As you will see below, there are some exceptions to that rule on this test.

Example #1

Jamie earns $15.24 per hour at her part-time job. Last week, she worked 4.78 hours. Which expression should she use to get the closest estimate of her pay?

(A) 15×4

(B) 20×4

(C) 15×5

(D) 20×5

Notice that this question doesn't tell you which place to round to. You need to look at all the answer choices to determine which one is the closest estimate of Jamie's pay. If you were rounding to the tens place, 15.24 would increase to 20. Two answer choices include 20. However, in this question it is more accurate to round down to 15. Therefore, the answer is either (A) or (C). 4.78 rounds up to 5, so **the correct answer is (C).**

Example #2

A student did the problem shown on his calculator.

$$\frac{41 \times 612}{32}$$

What is a reasonable estimation for his answer?

(A)   between 500 and 600

(B)   between 600 and 900

(C)   between 900 and 1,100

(D)   between 1,100 and 1,300

It will waste too much time to do all the work in this question. Instead, round the numbers and then find an approximate answer. You can change the expression to $\frac{40 \times 600}{30}$ and solve. $40 \times 600 = 24,000$. $24,000 \div 30 = 800$. **The correct answer is (B).**

Example #3

Rasheeda buys five items costing $2.49, $10.99, $4.99, $0.50, and $7.99. What is the estimated total cost of Rasheeda's items?

(A)   between $20 and $25

(B)   between $25 and $30

(C)   between $30 and $35

(D)   between $35 and $40

This question asks you to estimate the total cost, so don't waste time by adding up each individual item precisely. $2.50 + $11 + $5 + $0.50 + $8 = $27. **The correct answer is (B).**

Practice Problems

1. Enzo bought five packages of gum that cost $1.71 each. Which expression should he use to get the closest estimate of how much he paid?
   (A) 5×1.0
   (B) 5×1.5
   (C) 5×2.0
   (D) 5×2.5

2. A student buys four items costing $1.49, $12.99, $3.99, and $0.50. What is the estimated total cost of the student's items?
   (A) between $15 and $18
   (B) between $18 and $21
   (C) between $21 and $24
   (D) between $24 and $27

3. What is a reasonable estimate for $\frac{41 \times 325}{53}$?

   (A) $\frac{40 \times 300}{60}$

   (B) $\frac{40 \times 400}{50}$

   (C) $\frac{40 \times 300}{50}$

   (D) $\frac{50 \times 300}{50}$

4. Noah earns $15.78 per hour at his part-time job. Last week, he worked 12.40 hours. Which expression should he use to get the closest estimate of his pay?
   (A) 15×12
   (B) 16×13
   (C) 15×13
   (D) 16×12

5. A student did the problem shown on his calculator.

   $$\frac{35 \times 425}{43}$$

   What is a reasonable estimation for his answer?
   (A) between 100 and 300
   (B) between 300 and 500
   (C) between 500 and 700
   (D) between 700 and 900

6. What is 89,675 rounded to the nearest hundred?
   (A) 89,000
   (B) 89,600
   (C) 89,700
   (D) 90,000

7. Jeffrey buys five items costing $0.49, $15.99, $7.99, $1.50, and $9.99. What is the estimated total cost of Jeffrey's items?
   (A) between $20 and $25
   (B) between $25 and $30
   (C) between $30 and $35
   (D) between $35 and $40

8. What is a reasonable estimate for $\frac{61 \times 190}{22}$?

   (A) $\frac{60 \times 200}{20}$

   (B) $\frac{60 \times 200}{30}$

   (C) $\frac{70 \times 200}{20}$

   (D) $\frac{70 \times 100}{30}$

9. A warehouse stores 478 boxes, each of which contains 92 calculators. Which expression gives the best approximation of the number of calculators in the warehouse?
   (A) 400×90
   (B) 400×100
   (C) 500×90
   (D) 500×100

10. A student did the problem shown on his calculator.

$$\frac{190 \times 40}{19}$$

What is a reasonable estimation for his answer?
   (A)   between 350 and 450
   (B)   between 450 and 550
   (C)   between 550 and 650
   (D)   between 650 and 750

11. A boy buys five items costing $3.49, $9.49, $2.49, $1.50, and $11.99. What is the estimated total cost of the boy's items?
   (A)   between $20 and $25
   (B)   between $25 and $30
   (C)   between $30 and $35
   (D)   between $35 and $40

12. Agustin's school was collecting cans for recycling. They had 42 bags with 38 cans inside each bag. Which expression shows about how many cans they collected?
   (A) 30×30
   (B) 40×30
   (C) 40×40
   (D) 50×40

13. What is a reasonable estimate for $\frac{11 \times 88}{34}$?
   (A) $\frac{0 \times 90}{30}$
   (B) $\frac{10 \times 90}{30}$
   (C) $\frac{10 \times 100}{30}$
   (D) $\frac{20 \times 100}{30}$

14. What is 52 rounded to the nearest ten?
   (A)   50
   (B)   55
   (C)   60
   (D)   100

15. An airplane has 67 compartments that can hold 6 pieces of luggage each. Which expression shows about how many total pieces of luggage the airplane can hold?
   (A) 60×10
   (B) 70×10
   (C) 60×5
   (D) 70×5

16. What is 49 rounded to the nearest hundred?
   (A)   0
   (B)   40
   (C)   50
   (D)   100

17. What is 528 rounded to the nearest 10?
   (A)   500
   (B)   520
   (C)   530
   (D)   550

18. A student did the problem shown on his calculator.

$$\frac{34 \times 152}{19}$$

What is a reasonable estimation for his answer?
(A)   between 200 and 300
(B)   between 300 and 400
(C)   between 400 and 500
(D)   between 500 and 600

19. Josiah buys five items costing $7.49, $6.99, $3.99, $8.50, and $6.99. What is the estimated total cost of Josiah's items?
(A)   between $20 and $25
(B)   between $25 and $30
(C)   between $30 and $35
(D)   between $35 and $40

20. A delivery company gave each of their 108 trucks 62 boxes each. Which expression shows approximately how many total boxes the trucks held?
(A) 110×60
(B) 100×60
(C) 110×70
(D) 100×70

21. What is a reasonable estimate for $\frac{54 \times 555}{59}$?

(A) $\frac{50 \times 500}{60}$

(B) $\frac{40 \times 500}{50}$

(C) $\frac{60 \times 500}{50}$

(D) $\frac{50 \times 600}{60}$

22. What is 6,821 rounded to the nearest ten?
(A)   6,800
(B)   6,820
(C)   6,830
(D)   6,900

23. A girl buys six items costing $15.49, $5.99, $6.99, $1.50, $11.99, and $4.50. What is the estimated total cost of the girl's items?
(A)   between $35 and $40
(B)   between $40 and $45
(C)   between $45 and $50
(D)   between $50 and $55

24. A student did the problem shown on his calculator.

$$\frac{52 \times 418}{93}$$

What is a reasonable estimation for his answer?
(A)   between 50 and 150
(B)   between 150 and 250
(C)   between 250 and 350
(D)   between 350 and 450

25. What is 700 rounded to the nearest 10?
(A)   700
(B)   710
(C)   800
(D)   1,000

26. Claire buys five items costing $7.99, $9.49, $5.99, $4.50, and $13.99. What is the estimated total cost of Claire's items?
(A)   between $25 and $30
(B)   between $30 and $35
(C)   between $35 and $40
(D)   between $40 and $45

Patterns

You never know what type of shape or figure you'll be presented with on a *patterns* question, so you must train yourself to be able to identify patterns in a variety of situations.

Example #1

A pattern is shown below.

How many squares will there be in the 5th figure?

(A)   16
(B)   25
(C)   30
(D)   36

You can see that there are 4 figures presented in the pattern. Since you are asked to find the 5th figure, you simply need to identify what the next shape will look like. In this pattern, the length and width of the larger squares increase by one in each successive figure. Therefore, the next square will be 5 × 5. The equation for area is length × width, so the area of the 5th figure is 5 × 5 = 25. **The correct answer is (B).** The 6th figure would have 36 squares, so (D) is a trick answer.

Example #2

A pattern is shown below.

What will the 8th shape in the pattern be?

(A)   ○

(B)   ●

(C)   ♡

(D)   ♥

The pattern in this figure is difficult to identify. It goes "circle, heart, circle, heart," so you know the 8th shape will be a heart. You can eliminate (A) and (B). It looks like the color pattern is "2 black, 2 white, 2 black, 2 white," but the pattern has started in the middle, which is why there is only one black shape at the beginning. The 8th shape will be black, so **the correct answer is (D).**

Example #3

Use the pattern to help answer the question.

$1 + 3 = 2^2$
$1 + 3 + 5 = 3^2$
$1 + 3 + 5 + 7 = 4^2$

What is the solution to $1 + 3 + 5 + 7 + 9 + 11$?

(A) 5^2
(B) 6^2
(C) 7^2
(D) 11^2

It's unlikely you've ever seen a pattern like this in school, but if you look closely you'll be able to spot the trick: the base of the exponent is equal to the number of digits that are added together. For example, $1 + 3$ is two total digits, and the answer is 2^2. $1 + 3 + 5$ is three total digits, and the answer is 2^2.

$1 + 3 + 5 + 7 + 9 + 11$ is 6 digits, so **the answer is (B).**

135

Practice Problems

1. Dana used a rule to make a number pattern. Her rule is to multiply by 2. Which number pattern follows Dana's rule?
   (A)   4, 6, 8, 10, 12
   (B)   2, 4, 8, 16, 32
   (C)   5, 7, 9, 11, 13
   (D)   2, 4, 8, 15, 20

2. Use the pattern to help answer the question.

   $1 + 3 = 2^2$
   $1 + 3 + 5 = 3^2$
   $1 + 3 + 5 + 7 = 4^2$

   What is the solution to
   $1 + 3 + 5 + 7 + 9 + 11 + 13$?

   (A) 5^2
   (B) 6^2
   (C) 7^2
   (D) 13^2

3. A pattern is shown below.

   What will the next figure in this pattern be?

   (A)

   (B)

   (C)

   (D)

4. A pattern is shown below.

   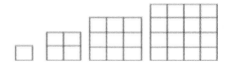

   How many squares will there be in the 8th figure?
   (A)   25
   (B)   36
   (C)   49
   (D)   64

5. Use the number sequence to answer the question.

   2, 4, 8, 16, 32

   What is the next number in the sequence?
   (A)   48
   (B)   54
   (C)   64
   (D)   128

6. Use the figure below to answer the question.

   If one more row was added to the figure, how many small triangles would the fourth row have, assuming the same pattern continues?
   (A)   4
   (B)   5
   (C)   6
   (D)   7

136

7. What number is missing in the pattern?

    12, 16, _____, 24, 28

    (A)   17
    (B)   20
    (C)   29
    (D)   32

8. A subtraction rule was used to make the pattern of numbers in the table.

31	29	27	25	23	?	?

    If the pattern continues, what would the next two numbers be?
    (A)   19, 21
    (B)   22, 21
    (C)   21, 19
    (D)   24, 25

9. Use the number sequence to answer the question.

    144, 72, 36, 18

    What is the next number in the sequence?
    (A)   0
    (B)   9
    (C)   12
    (D)   18

10. A pattern is shown below.

    1, 2, 4, 7, 11, 16, 22

    What will the next number in the pattern be?
    (A)   29
    (B)   30
    (C)   31
    (D)   32

11. A pattern is shown below.

    What will the next shape in the pattern be?

    (A)

    (B)   ●

    (C)   ♡

    (D)   ♥

12. What are the missing numbers in the pattern below?

    21, 24, ____, ____, 33, _____

    (A)   25, 26, 34
    (B)   26, 28, 34
    (C)   27, 29, 35
    (D)   27, 30, 36

13. A pattern is shown below.

    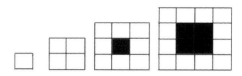

    How many cubes will be shaded in the 6th figure?
    (A)   6
    (B)   7
    (C)   9
    (D)   16

14. Sally is selling candy bars for her school.

Day	Bars Sold
Monday	3
Tuesday	6
Wednesday	9
Thursday	?

If the pattern continues, how many candy bars will Sally sell on Thursday?

(A)　　3
(B)　　10
(C)　　11
(D)　　12

15. Use the number sequence to answer the question.

1, 4, 9, 16, 25

What is the seventh number in the sequence?

(A)　　35
(B)　　36
(C)　　49
(D)　　64

Coordinate Grids

Coordinate geometry is the study of algebraic equations on graphs. It involves plotting points, curves, and lines on an *x*- and *y*-axes. On the Lower Level ISEE, you will only be asked to plot points. The figure below shows an example of a coordinate grid:

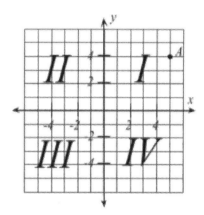

Coordinate grids are divided into four quadrants. The grids are composed of an *x*-axis, which runs horizontally, and a *y*-axis, which runs vertically. The axes intersect at the origin. The coordinates of the origin are (0,0).

To find the coordinates of a point on the coordinate plane, start at the origin (the place where the *x*- and *y*-axes intersect) and count how far you must move on the *x*-axis. If you move to the right, the coordinate is positive. If you move to the left, the coordinate is negative. Then, count how far up and down you must move on the *y*-axis. If you move up, the coordinate is positive. If you move down, the coordinate is negative.

Some students find it helpful to think about coordinates like this: to get to a friend's apartment, first you have to walk to his or her building, then you have to take the elevator up to the apartment. If you walk to the right on the *x*-axis, the coordinate is positive; if you walk to the left on the *x*-axis, the coordinate is negative. Then, if you take the elevator up to your friend's apartment, the second coordinate is positive; if you take the elevator down to the basement, the second coordinate is negative.

Point *A* is labeled in the grid above. Beginning at the origin, move right 5 spaces, then move up 4 spaces. The coordinates of Point *A* are (5, 4).

Example #1

Which point is located at (5,4) on the coordinate grid below?

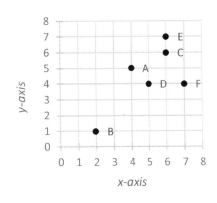

(A)   *A*
(B)   *B*
(C)   *C*
(D)   *D*

The given point is (5,4). Some students find it helpful to think about coordinates like this: to get to a friend's apartment, first you have to walk to his or her building, then you have to take the elevator up to the apartment. In this question, the 5 represents walking to your friend's apartment, so you start at (0,0) and move 5 spaces to the right. The 4 represents taking the elevator up to your friend's apartment. Once you've moved 5 spaces right, you then move 4 spaces up. You land on Point *D*, so **(D) is the correct answer.**

Example #2

Sergei draws a path on the coordinate grid. He begins at point (3,3) and moves 2 spaces right and 3 spaces up.

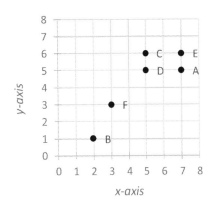

What is the point where Sergei lands?
(A)   *A*
(B)   *B*
(C)   *C*
(D)   *D*

First, move 3 spaces right and 3 spaces up to land on Point *F*: this is your starting point. From there, move 2 spaces right and 3 spaces up to land on Point *C*. **(C) is the correct answer.**

Example #3

A coordinate graph is shown.

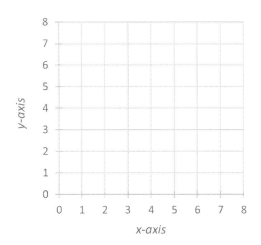

A student plotted the following points on the coordinate grid.

Point *A* (3,3); Point *B* (3,6); Point *C* (7,5); Point *D* (7,2)

A polygon is formed with vertices *A, B, C,* and *D* and sides $\overline{AB}$, $\overline{BC}$, $\overline{CD}$, and $\overline{DA}$. Which type of polygon is formed?
(A)   square
(B)   pentagon
(C)   parallelogram
(D)   trapezoid

On questions like these, you should plot the points onto the coordinate grid provided so that you can visualize the shape. Once you've connected the points, you will need to remember the properties of different types of shapes in order to identify what shape it is. Here, notice that sides $\overline{AB}$ and $\overline{CD}$ are parallel and that sides $\overline{BC}$ and $\overline{DA}$ are parallel. There are no right angles in the figure. This shape is a parallelogram, so **the correct answer is (C).**

Example #4

Use the coordinate grid to answer the question.

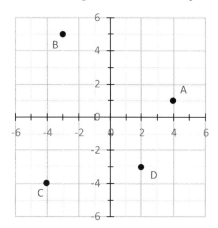

Which of the points on the graph is closest to (4,-2)?
(A)   *A*
(B)   *B*
(C)   *C*
(D)   *D*

First, identify the point (4,-2) on the graph. It is in between Point *A* and Point *D*, but it falls closer to Point *D*. Therefore, **(D) is the correct answer.**

Practice Problems

1. Aisha draws a path on the coordinate grid. She begins at point (3,1) and moves 2 spaces right and 3 spaces up.

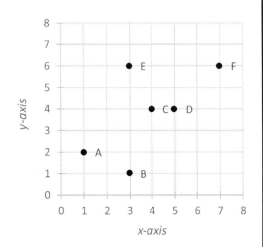

   What is the point where Aisha lands?
   (A)   C
   (B)   D
   (C)   E
   (D)   F

2. What are the coordinates of Point C below?

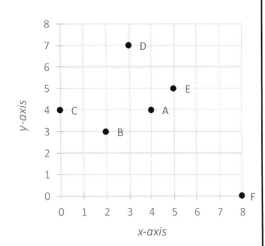

   (A)   (2,3)
   (B)   (3,2)
   (C)   (0,4)
   (D)   (4,0)

3. Which point is located at (0,4) on the coordinate grid below?

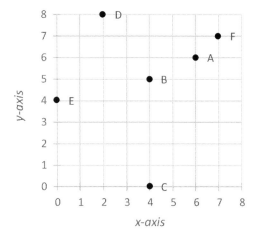

   (A)   B
   (B)   C
   (C)   D
   (D)   E

4. Ivan draws a path on the coordinate grid. He begins at point (0,1) and moves 4 spaces right and 2 spaces up.

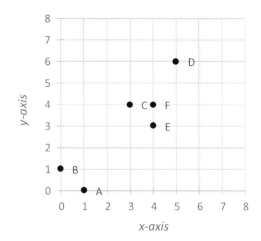

   What is the point where Ivan lands?
   (A)   C
   (B)   D
   (C)   E
   (D)   F

5. Konstantinos draws a path on the coordinate grid. He begins at point (3,0) and moves 2 spaces right and 5 spaces up.

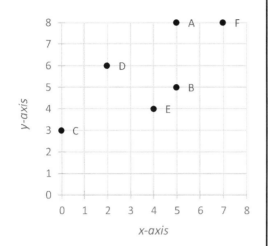

What is the point where Konstantinos lands?
(A)   *A*
(B)   *B*
(C)   *C*
(D)   *D*

6. What are the coordinates of Point *B* below?

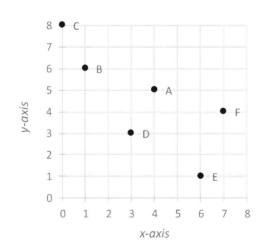

(A)   (1,6)
(B)   (3,3)
(C)   (6,1)
(D)   (0,8)

7. Lina draws a path on the coordinate grid. She begins at point (2,4) and moves 1 space right and 1 space up.

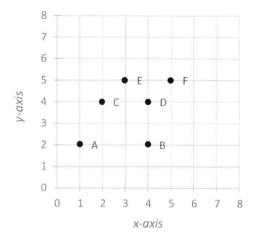

What is the point where Lina lands?
(A)   *B*
(B)   *C*
(C)   *D*
(D)   *E*

8. Which point is located at (3,4) on the coordinate grid below?

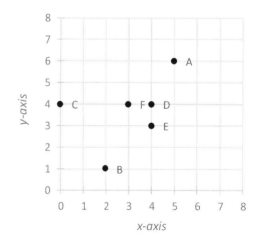

(A)   *C*
(B)   *D*
(C)   *E*
(D)   *F*

9. Ari draws a path on the coordinate grid. He begins at point (1,2) and moves 6 spaces right and 3 spaces up.

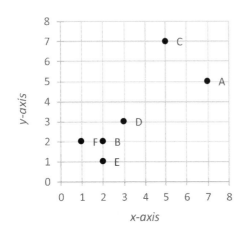

What is the point where Ari lands?
(A)   A
(B)   B
(C)   C
(D)   D

10. Martina draws a path on the coordinate grid. She begins at point (3,1) and moves 2 spaces right and 3 spaces up.

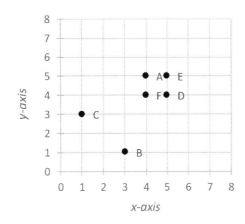

What is the point where Martina lands?
(A)   A
(B)   B
(C)   C
(D)   D

11. Which point is located at (2,5) on the coordinate grid below?

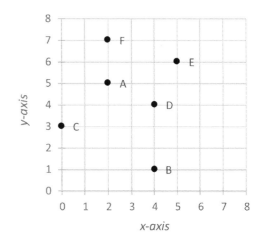

(A)   A
(B)   B
(C)   C
(D)   D

12. Use the coordinate grid to answer the question.

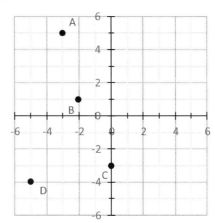

Which of the points on the graph is closest to (-4,-3)?
(A)   A
(B)   B
(C)   C
(D)   D

13. A coordinate graph is shown.

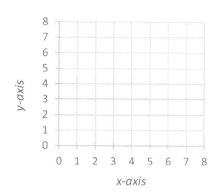

A student plotted the following points on the coordinate grid.

Point W (1,1); Point X (4,1); Point Y (4,4); Point Z (1,4)

A polygon is formed with vertices W, X, Y, and Z and sides $\overline{WX}$, $\overline{XY}$, $\overline{YZ}$, and $\overline{ZW}$. Which type of polygon is formed?
(A)   square
(B)   pentagon
(C)   triangle
(D)   circle

14. A coordinate graph is shown.

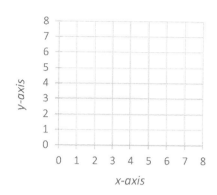

A student plotted the following points on the coordinate grid.

Point Q (2,2); Point R (7,2); Point S (6,5); Point T (3,5)

A polygon is formed with vertices Q, R, S, and T and sides $\overline{QR}$, $\overline{RS}$, $\overline{ST}$, and $\overline{TQ}$. Which type of polygon is formed?
(A)   parallelogram
(B)   rectangle
(C)   rhombus
(D)   trapezoid

15. Use the coordinate grid to answer the question.

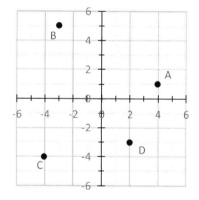

Which of the points on the graph is closest to (-3,3)?
(A) A
(B) B
(C) C
(D) D

16. Use the coordinate grid to answer the question.

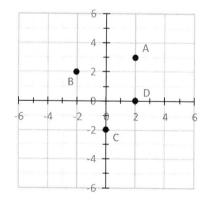

Which of the points on the graph is closest to (1,2)?
(A) A
(B) B
(C) C
(D) D

145

17. A coordinate graph is shown.

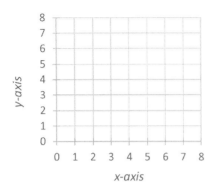

A student plotted the following points on the coordinate grid.

Point *M* (4,7); Point *N* (3,5); Point *O* (4,3); Point *P* (5,5)

A polygon is formed with vertices *M, N, O,* and *P* and sides $\overline{MN}$, $\overline{NO}$, $\overline{OP}$, and $\overline{PM}$. Which type of polygon is formed?
(A)   triangle
(B)   rhombus
(C)   rectangle
(D)   square

18. A coordinate graph is shown.

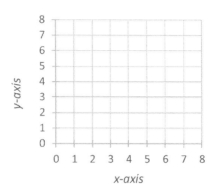

A student plotted the following points on the coordinate grid.

Point *L* (0,5); Point *M* (6,5); Point *N* (6,8); Point *O* (0,8)

A polygon is formed with vertices *L, M, N,* and *O* and sides $\overline{LM}$, $\overline{MN}$, $\overline{NO}$, and $\overline{OL}$. Which type of polygon is formed?
(A)   rectangle
(B)   square
(C)   triangle
(D)   kite

19. Use the coordinate grid to answer the question.

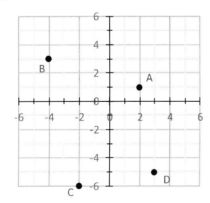

Which of the points on the graph is closest to (2,-4)?
(A)   *A*
(B)   *B*
(C)   *C*
(D)   *D*

20. Use the coordinate grid to answer the question.

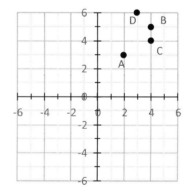

Which of the points on the graph is closest to (6,4)?
(A)   *A*
(B)   *B*
(C)   *C*
(D)   *D*

Graphs

Graphs require that you understand large amounts of information. When you see a graph question, the first thing you should do is look at the x- and y-axes. The x-axis is horizontal; it will be labeled on the bottom part of the graph. The y-axis is vertical; it will be labeled on the left or right side of the graph. There may also be a *key* which provides some additional information. Once you have a general idea of what is going on in the graph, look at the related question so you know where you should focus your attention.

Example #1
Questions #1 – 4 refer to the graph below.

A teacher created a graph to compare the favorite pets of the students in her class.

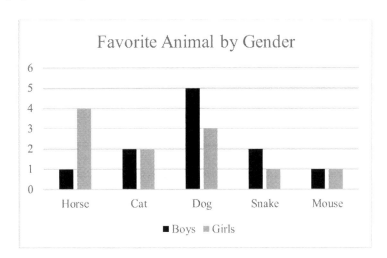

1. Which animal did more girls prefer than boys?
    (A)   Horse
    (B)   Cat
    (C)   Dog
    (D)   Snake

2. How many boys liked either cats or dogs?
    (A)   3
    (B)   4
    (C)   7
    (D)   8

3. Which animal was preferred by the greatest total number of students?
    (A)   Cat
    (B)   Dog
    (C)   Snake
    (D)   Mouse

4. How many more boys than girls preferred snakes?
    (A)   1
    (B)   2
    (C)   3
    (D)   4

On the graph, the *x*-axis shows which animal students preferred, while the *y*-axis indicates how many students preferred each animal. There is also a key at the bottom of the graph that tells you the boys' responses are labeled in black, while the girls' responses are labeled in grey.

Now that you understand what's going on in the graph, answering the questions will be easy. For question #1, you can see that the only animal on the graph which has a taller bar for girls than boys is horses, so **the correct answer is (A).** Question #2 requires that you do a little addition. 2 boys liked cats and 5 boys liked dogs, so 7 boys liked either cats or dogs. **The correct answer is (C).** 8 total students preferred dogs, so **the correct answer for question #3 is (B).** Finally, you can see that 2 boys and 1 girl preferred snakes, so **the correct answer for question #4 is (A).**

Example #2
Questions #1 – 3 refer to the graph below.

A survey of 40 students' favorite colors is displayed on the circle graph shown.

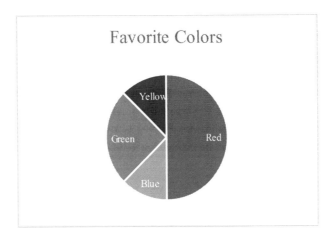

1. About what fraction of the students chose green as their favorite color?

    (A) $\frac{1}{8}$

    (B) $\frac{1}{4}$

    (C) $\frac{1}{3}$

    (D) $\frac{1}{2}$

2. What is the best estimate for how many students chose yellow as their favorite color?

    (A)   5
    (B)   15
    (C)   20
    (D)   25

3. Which two colors did an equal number of students select as their favorites?

    (A)   yellow and red
    (B)   red and green
    (C)   green and yellow
    (D)   yellow and blue

Pie charts are just another way of graphically displaying data. The bigger the slice of pie, the more data points fit into that category. In this example, red is the biggest slice, so that means the most students chose red as their favorite color. You can also see that red takes up half of the circle, which means half of the students chose red as their favorite color. There are 40 students, so 20 students chose red.

It's a little harder to determine what fraction the green slice represents. On your test, you can use your pencil to split the graph into equally sized pieces:

Now, it should be obvious that green represents $\frac{2}{8}$ or $\frac{1}{4}$. **The correct answer for question #1 is (B).** Yellow represents $\frac{1}{8}$ of the pie. There are 40 students, and $\frac{1}{8}$ of 40 would be 5 students. **The correct answer for question #2 is (A).** You should be able to see that the yellow and blue slices are the same size. **The correct answer for question #3 is (D).**

Practice Problems

Questions #1 – 4 refer to the graph below.

A teacher created a graph to compare the number of pets that the boys and girls in his class have.

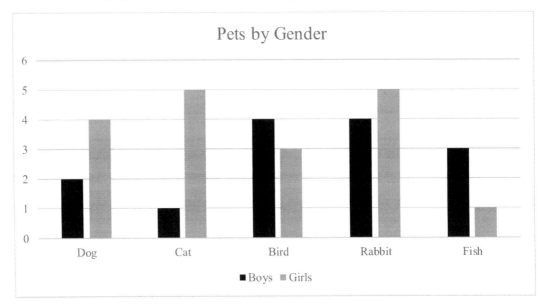

1. Which pet had the greatest difference between the number of boys and the number of girls who owned that pet?
    (A)   Dog
    (B)   Cat
    (C)   Bird
    (D)   Fish

2. How many boys owned either a bird or a fish?
    (A)   3
    (B)   4
    (C)   7
    (D)   8

3. Which type of animal had the greatest total number of boys and girls who owned that pet?
    (A)   Cat
    (B)   Rabbit
    (C)   Fish
    (D)   Dog

4. How many more boys than girls owned a fish?
    (A)   1
    (B)   2
    (C)   3
    (D)   4

Questions #5 – 10 refer to the graph below.

Students in a class voted for their favorite movie.

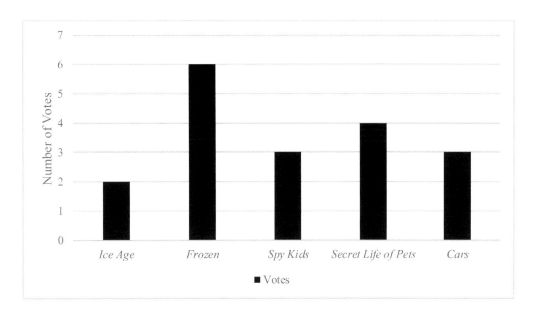

5. How many people voted for *Spy Kids*?
    (A) 1
    (B) 2
    (C) 3
    (D) 4

6. Which movie received the most votes?
    (A) *Ice Age*
    (B) *Spy Kids*
    (C) *Cars*
    (D) *Frozen*

7. Which two *Spy Kids* movies received the same number of votes?
    (A) *Ice Age* and *Spy Kids*
    (B) *Spy Kids* and *Cars*
    (C) *Frozen* and *Secret Life of Pets*
    (D) *Ice Age* and *Frozen*

8. Which movie received 4 votes?
    (A) *Frozen*
    (B) *Spy Kids*
    (C) *Secret Life of Pets*
    (D) *Cars*

9. How many more votes did *Spy Kids* receive than Ice Age?
    (A) 1
    (B) 2
    (C) 3
    (D) 4

10. What is the combined number of people who voted for *Cars* and *Spy Kids*?
    (A) 3
    (B) 4
    (C) 5
    (D) 6

Questions #11 – 14 refer to the graph below.

The graph represents the number of boys and girls in all the classes in each grade at an elementary school.

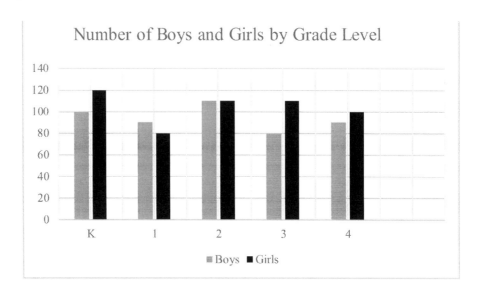

11. Based on the data in this graph, which question can be answered?
    (A)   Which grade has the most classrooms?
    (B)   How many boys and girls are in 5th grade?
    (C)   Which grade has the greatest number of students?
    (D)   How many boys and girls will be in kindergarten next year?

12. How many more boys are there in Kindergarten than there are in 3rd grade?
    (A)   1
    (B)   2
    (C)   10
    (D)   20

13. Which grade has fewer girls than boys?
    (A)   Kindergarten
    (B)   1st
    (C)   2nd
    (D)   3rd

14. Which grade has the same number of boys and girls?
    (A)   1st
    (B)   2nd
    (C)   3rd
    (D)   4th

15. Determine which graph best represents the information in the table.

Name	Faye	Pierre	Hannah	Anik	Kelly
States Lived In	2	3	7	2	7

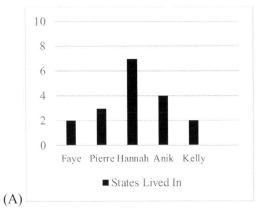

(A)

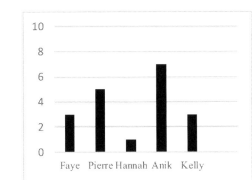

(B)

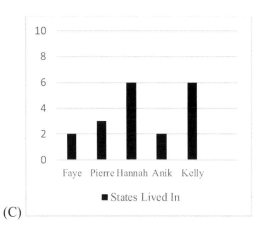

(C)

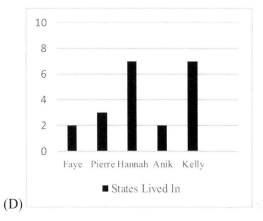

(D)

Questions #16 – 18 refer to the circle graph below.

A survey of 40 students' favorite pets is displayed on the circle graph shown.

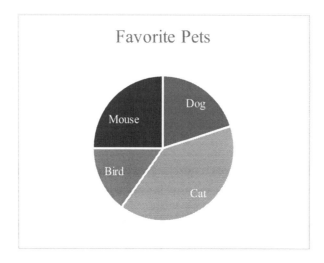

16. About what fraction of the students chose mice as their favorite pets?

(A) $\frac{1}{8}$

(B) $\frac{1}{4}$

(C) $\frac{1}{3}$

(D) $\frac{1}{2}$

17. Which animal did the most students choose as their favorite?
(A)   Mouse
(B)   Dog
(C)   Cat
(D)   Bird

18. What is the closest approximation of how many students chose mice as their favorite pet?
(A)   10
(B)   20
(C)   30
(D)   50

Questions #19 – 21 refer to the circle graph below.

A survey of 100 students' favorite colors is displayed on the circle graph shown.

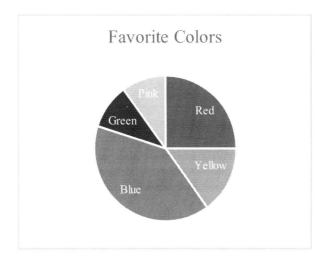

19. About what fraction of the students chose red as their favorite color?

(A) $\frac{1}{8}$

(B) $\frac{1}{4}$

(C) $\frac{1}{3}$

(D) $\frac{1}{2}$

20. Which color did the most students choose as their favorite?
(A) Red
(B) Blue
(C) Yellow
(D) Pink

21. What is the closest approximation of how many students chose red as their favorite color?
(A) 10
(B) 25
(C) 40
(D) 75

Function Machines

Function machines show the relationship between input and output.

Example #1

Determine what rule the function machine is using.

In	Out
20	10
26	16
38	28
52	42

(A)   Add 6

(B)   Subtract 6

(C)   Add 10

(D)   Subtract 10

When working on function tables, you must determine the relationship between what goes in and what comes out. In the table above, when 20 goes in, 10 comes out. When 26 goes in, 16 comes out. Notice that the second number is 10 less than the first number in both instances. That means that you must subtract 10 to find the relationship between the two columns. **The correct answer is (D).**

These questions may contain trick answers. If you look only at the left column, you might think the relationship is add 6, because 26 is 6 greater than 20. Don't make this common mistake! Remember, you must find the relationship between the left and the right columns.

Example #2

Use the table to determine the rule.

Input ▲	Output ■
4	9
7	15
10	21
12	25

What is the rule for the function?

(A) $▲ + 5 = ■$

(B) $▲ \times 2 + 1 = ■$

(C) $▲ \times 3 - 3 = ■$

(D) $▲ + 3 = ■$

This question is a little trickier. Plug in a number from the Input side of the table into each equation, and see which equation pops out the correct number on the Output side. These questions will always contain trick answers, so you need to test at least two of the numbers on the Input side before selecting an answer. (A) works when the input is 4, because $4 + 5 = 9$. However, when you try it with 7, you'll see that $7 + 5 \neq 15$, so (A) is incorrect. **(B) is the correct answer**.

Example #3

The function machine only accepts even numbers as input. It performs the same operation on each input number to create an output number.

Input ▲	Output ■
4	13
10	31
12	37
22	67

Which input number creates an output of 43?

(A)   14
(B)   16
(C)   18
(D)   20

This is the hardest type of function machine question that you may see on the Lower Level ISEE. Here, you'll have to figure out the rule before you can answer the question. Notice that each input number is an even number and is smaller than its output number. That means that multiplication and / or addition will be involved. $4 + 9 = 13$, so does that mean the rule is "plus 9?" $10 + 9 = 19$, not 31, so that doesn't work. That means you'll need to do multiplication, as well. $4 \times 3 = 12$, and $12 + 1 = 13$, so the rule may be "(input number $\times$ 3) + 1 = output number. Let's try that with 10. $(10 \times 3) + 1 = 31$, so it seems this rule is correct! Now, use the answer choices to figure out which one will result in an output value of 43. $(14 \times 3) + 1 = 43$, so **(A) is the correct answer.**

Practice Problems

1. Determine what rule the function machine is using.

In	Out
20	15
26	21
38	33
52	47

(A)   Add 6
(B)   Subtract 6
(C)   Add 5
(D)   Subtract 5

2. Use the table to determine the rule.

Input ▲	Output ■
0	2
15	17
17	19
22	24

What is the rule for the function?
(A) $▲ + 13 = ■$
(B) $▲ - 4 = ■$
(C) $▲ + 2 = ■$
(D) $▲ × 0 + 2 = ■$

3. A function machine is shown.

In	Out
19	15
27	23
32	28
33	29

What number would result in an output of 55?
(A)   51
(B)   57
(C)   59
(D)   61

4. Use the table to determine the rule.

Input ▲	Output ■
8	0
16	2
20	3
44	9

What is the rule for the function?
(A) $▲ - 8 = ■$
(B) $▲ + 8 = ■$
(C) $(▲ × 2) - 16 = ■$
(D) $▲ ÷ 4 - 2 = ■$

5. Determine what rule the function machine is using.

In	Out
11	22
23	34
35	46
43	54

(A)   Add 12
(B)   Subtract 12
(C)   Add 11
(D)   Subtract 11

6. Use the table to determine the rule.

Input ▲	Output ■
0	0
1	3
9	27
12	36

What is the rule for the function?
(A) $▲ × 3 = ■$
(B) $▲ + 0 = ■$
(C) $▲ + 1 = ■$
(D) $▲ ÷ 3 = ■$

7. A function machine is shown.

In	Out
10	3
18	7
22	9
30	13

What number would result in an output of 21?

(A)   40
(B)   42
(C)   44
(D)   46

8. Use the table to determine the rule.

Input ▲	Output ■
1	1
4	16
6	36
8	64

What is the rule for the function?

(A) $▲ \times 1 = ■$
(B) $▲ + 3 = ■$
(C) $▲ + 5 = ■$
(D) $▲ \times ▲ = ■$

9. Determine what rule the function machine is using.

In	Out
20	16
22	18
23	19
42	38
44	40

(A)   Subtract 4
(B)   Add 6
(C)   Subtract 6
(D)   Add 4

10. Use the table to determine the rule.

Input ▲	Output ■
10	15
16	24
22	33
26	39

What is the rule for the function?

(A) $▲ \div 2 + ▲ = ■$
(B) $▲ + 5 = ■$
(C) $▲ + 6 \div ▲ = ■$
(D) $▲ \div 2 = ■$

11. A function machine is shown.

Input ▲	Output ■
12	4
15	7
20	12
25	17

What number would result in an output of 100?

(A)   93
(B)   98
(C)   105
(D)   108

12. Determine what rule the function machine is using.

In	Out
4	12
7	21
15	45
20	60

(A)   Plus 3
(B)   Plus 8
(C)   Times 3
(D)   Divided by 3

13. Use the table to determine the rule.

Input ▲	Output ■
6	10
10	18
13	24
15	28

What is the rule for the function?
(A) $▲ + 4 = ■$
(B) $▲ - 2 + ▲ = ■$
(C) $(▲ - 2) × 2 = ■$
(D) $▲ × 2 + ▲ = ■$

14. Determine what rule the function machine is using.

In	Out
4	0
9	0
11	0
24	0
32	0

(A)   Minus 4
(B)   Plus 5
(C)   Times 0
(D)   Times 1

15. A function machine is shown.

In	Out
4	11
9	21
12	27
15	33

What number would result in an output of 63?
(A)   17
(B)   28
(C)   30
(D)   33

16. Determine what rule the function machine is using.

In	Out
6	2
15	5
24	8
30	10
33	11

(A)   Plus 6
(B)   Minus 4
(C)   Times 3
(D)   Divided by 3

17. A function machine is shown.

Input ▲	Output ■
3	5
5	9
9	17
13	25

What number would result in an output of 11?
(A)   6
(B)   7
(C)   8
(D)   9

18. Determine what rule the function machine is using.

In	Out
4	13
5	14
9	18
11	20
14	23

(A)   Plus 9
(B)   Plus 1
(C)   Times 3
(D)   Divided by 2

Math Stories

Math stories ask you to translate English into math or vice versa.

Example #1

Which story best fits the equation $3 \times 9 = 27$?

(A)   I have 27 cookies. After eating 3 cookies, how many cookies do I have left?

(B)   I want to share 27 cookies with 9 friends. How many cookies do they each get?

(C)   I have 3 boxes of cookies, with 9 cookies in each box. How many cookies do I have altogether?

(D)   I have 3 boxes of cookies, and my friend has 9 boxes of cookies. How many boxes of cookies do we have altogether?

On these questions, the four answer choices will usually include an option for addition, subtraction, multiplication, and division. Here, (A) represents subtraction. If you were to rewrite this answer choice, it would be $27 - 3 = 24$. (B) represents division; it would be rewritten as $27 \div 9 = 3$. (C) represents multiplication and would be rewritten as $3 \times 9 = 27$. (D) represents addition, and would be rewritten as $3 + 9 = 12$. **(C) is the correct answer.**

Example #2

A student has 42 candy bars and gives a certain number of candy bars away. The student has 20 candy bars remaining. Which equation would tell how many candy bars (c) the student gave away?

(A) $42 + 20 = c$

(B) $42 \div 20 = c$

(C) $42 - 20 = c$

(D) $42 \times 20 = c$

This is the opposite of Example #1; here, you are translating words into math, rather than the other way around. If you have 42 candy bars and you give away 20, you will have 22 remaining. Now, look at the answer choices. $42 + 20 = 62$, so that doesn't work. $42 \div 20$ definitely does not equal 22, so don't even bother trying to do the division. 42×20 would be far larger than 22, so that leaves (C). $42 - 20 = 22$, so this matches the work you have already done. **(C) is the correct answer.**

Practice Problems

1. Which story best fits the equation $4 \times 6 = 24$?

   (A) I have 24 cookies. After eating 6 cookies, how many cookies do I have left?

   (B) I want to share 24 cookies with 6 friends. How many cookies do we each get?

   (C) I have 4 boxes of cookies, with 6 cookies in each box. How many cookies do I have altogether?

   (D) I have 6 boxes of cookies, and my friend has 4 boxes of cookies. How many boxes of cookies do we have altogether?

2. A student has 25 candy bars and gives a certain number of candy bars away. The student has 15 candy bars remaining. Which equation would tell how many candy bars (c) the student gave away?

   (A) $25 + 15 = c$

   (B) $c = 25 \div 15$

   (C) $25 - 15 = c$

   (D) $15 \times c = 25$

3. Which story best fits the equation $100 \div 10 = 10$?

   (A) I have 100 pencils and I give 10 pencils to my friend. How many pencils do I have remaining?

   (B) I have 10 boxes of pencils, and each box has 10 pencils in it. How many pencils do I have?

   (C) I have 100 pencils, and my friend gives me 10 more pencils. How many pencils do I have now?

   (D) I want to share 100 pencils evenly with 10 friends. How many pencils do they each get?

4. Which story best fits the equation $2 \times 15 = 30$?

   (A) A homework assignment is 2 pages, and there are 15 questions on each page. How many questions are there altogether?

   (B) One teacher gives a student 2 homework questions, and another teacher gives the same student 15 homework questions. How many questions does the student have to do?

   (C) A student completes 15 homework questions out of 30 total questions. How many questions remain?

   (D) A student has 30 homework questions. The student's friend helps him complete 2 questions. How many questions remain?

5. Which story best fits the equation $24 \div 4 = 6$?

   (A) I have 24 stuffed animals, and I put the stuffed animals into groups of 4 and place them in boxes. How many boxes do I have?

   (B) I have 24 boxes of stuffed animals, and each box has 4 animals in it. How many total stuffed animals do I have?

   (C) I have 24 stuffed animals, and I give away 4. How many stuffed animals do I have remaining?

   (D) I want to share 24 stuffed animals equally with 6 friends. How many stuffed animals do they each get?

6. Which story best fits the equation
   $5 \times 5 = 25$?

   (A)   I have 5 coffee cups, and my
          friend gives me 5 more. How
          many total coffee cups do I have
          now?
   (B)   Each of my 5 friends has 5
          coffee cups. How many total
          coffee cups do my friends have?
   (C)   I have 25 coffee cups, and I
          want to give an equal number of
          coffee cups to each of my 5
          friends. How many coffee cups
          does each friend get?
   (D)   I have 25 coffee cups, and I give
          away 5 of them. How many
          coffee cups do I have left?

7. Which story best fits the equation
   $9 + 6 = 15$?

   (A)   One student gives a teacher 9
          pieces of candy, and another
          student gives the same teacher 6
          pieces of candy. How many
          pieces of candy does the teacher
          have?
   (B)   A student gives her friend 9
          boxes of candy. Each box has 6
          pieces of candy in it. How many
          pieces of candy did the student
          give to her friend?
   (C)   A student has 15 pieces of
          candy and gives away 6 pieces.
          How many pieces are left?
   (D)   A student has 15 pieces of
          candy and puts the candy into
          boxes. If she puts 6 pieces of
          candy into each box, how many
          boxes are there?

8. A box contains 40 toys that are
   packaged into groups of 5. If n
   represents the number of packages in the
   box, which equation would tell how
   many packages are in the box?
   (A) $5 + n = 40$
   (B) $n = 40 \div 5$
   (C) $n - 5 = 40$
   (D) $40 \times n = 5$

9. A zoo has 14 lions and 6 tigers. Which
   equation represents the total number (n)
   of lions and tigers?
   (A) $6 + 14 = n$
   (B) $n = 14 \div 6$
   (C) $n - 14 = 6$
   (D) $6 \times n = 14$

10. Which story best fits the equation
    $8 - 6 = 2$?

    (A)   The tiger enclosure at a zoo has
           8 tigers. The zoo gives 6 tigers
           to another zoo. How many
           tigers remain?
    (B)   A zoo has 8 tiger enclosures,
           and each enclosure has 2 tigers
           in it. How many total tigers does
           the zoo have?
    (C)   A zoo has 8 tigers and wants to
           put an equal number of tigers
           into 2 enclosures. How many
           tigers are placed in each
           enclosure?
    (D)   A zoo has 2 tigers, and another
           zoo gives this zoo 6 more tigers.
           How many total tigers does the
           zoo have now?

11. Which story best fits the equation
$15 + 9 = 24$?

(A)   A school has 15 classrooms, and I have 9 friends in each classroom. How many friends do I have?

(B)   I have 15 friends. Over the summer, 9 of them transfer to different schools. How many friends do I have now?

(C)   I have 15 friends, and I want to give each of them 9 pieces of candy. How many pieces of candy do I give away?

(D)   I have 15 friends. On the first day of 4th grade, I make 9 new friends. How many friends do I have now?

12. Which story best fits the equation
$20 - 3 = 17$?

(A)   Each of my 3 friends has 20 bananas. How many total bananas do my friends have?

(B)   I have 20 bananas, and my friend gives me 3 more. How many total bananas do I have?

(C)   I have 20 bananas, and I divide them equally into 3 boxes. How many bananas are in each box?

(D)   I have 20 bananas, and I give 3 to a friend. How many bananas do I have remaining?

13. A zoo has a certain number of lions. The zoo plans to give a certain number of lions to another zoo. How would the zoo figure out how many lions (l) it has after it gives a certain number away?

(A) l = the number of lions it has × the number of lions it gives away

(B) l = the number of lions it has + the number of lions it gives away

(C) l = the number of lions it has ÷ the number of lions it gives away

(D) l = the number of lions it has – the number of lions it gives away

14. A student is organizing his stuffed animal collection. He knows how many stuffed animals he has, and he knows how many boxes he has that he wants to place the stuffed animals into. He wants to place the same number of stuffed animals into each box. How would he figure out how many stuffed animals (s) go in each box, based on the number of boxes that he has?

(A) s = the number of stuffed animals × the number of boxes

(B) s = the number of stuffed animals + the number of boxes

(C) s = the number of stuffed animals ÷ the number of boxes

(D) s = the number of stuffed animals – the number of boxes

15. A boy has 12 friends. On the first day of 4th grade, he makes 8 new friends. How would he figure out how many friends (f) he has now?

(A) f = the original number of friends × the number of new friends

(B) f = the original number of friends + the number of new friends

(C) f = the original number of friends ÷ the number of new friends

(D) f = the original number of friends – the number of new friends

16. A student is ordering candy bars for all her friends. She knows how many friends she wants to buy candy bars for, and she knows how many candy bars come in a box. How would she figure out how many boxes (b) to order?

   (A) b = the number of friends $\times$ the number of candy bars per box

   (B) b = the number of friends $+$ the number of candy bars per box

   (C) b = the number of friends $\div$ the number of candy bars per box

   (D) b = the number of friends $-$ the number of candy bars per box

17. A student has several pieces of candy. Her friend gives her some more candy. How would the student figure out how many pieces of candy (c) she has now?

   (A) c = the original number of pieces of candy $\times$ the number of pieces of candy her friend gives her

   (B) c = the original number of pieces of candy $+$ the number of pieces of candy her friend gives her

   (C) c = the original number of pieces of candy $\div$ the number of pieces of candy her friend gives her

   (D) c = the original number of pieces of candy $-$ the number of pieces of candy her friend gives her

18. A student is ordering toys for all the students in her school. She knows how many students are in the school, and she knows how many toys come in a box. How would she figure out how many boxes (b) to order?

   (A) b = the number of students $\times$ the number of toys per box

   (B) b = the number of students $+$ the number of toys per box

   (C) b = the number of students $\div$ the number of toys per box

   (D) b = the number of students $-$ the number of toys per box

Number Theory

Number theory questions look difficult, but when you know the trick to answering them, they're a piece of cake!

Example #1

If x can be divided by both 3 and 7 without leaving a remainder, then x can also be divided by which number without leaving a remainder?

(A)   8
(B)   10
(C)   14
(D)   21

On divisibility and remainder questions, working backwards it almost always your best option. The question tells us that x is divisible by both 3 and 7. Can you think of a number for x? 3×7 is 21, which means 21 must be divisible by both 3 and 7. Let's say that $x = 21$, since that's the smallest integer that is divisible by both 3 and 7. Now, look at the answer choices given. The correct answer must be divisible by 21. **(D) is the correct answer**.

Example #2

Kaitlyn wrote down a whole number greater than 9 and less than 13. When Ben tried to guess the number, Kaitlyn told him it was greater than 11 and less than 15. What is Kaitlyn's number?

(A)   10
(B)   11
(C)   12
(D)   13

This question type is not difficult at all, but many students answer it incorrectly because they've never seen a question like this. On these questions, you should write out the numbers by hand and then cross off numbers according to what the question says. We know the number is greater than 9 and less than 13.

~~9~~ 10 11 12 ~~13~~

So far, the number could be 10, 11, or 12. You can cross off (D).

The number is also greater than 11 and less than 15.

~~9~~ 10 11 **12** ~~13~~
      ~~11~~ **12** ~~13~~ 14 ~~15~~

Neither 11 nor 15 fit into the range given in the second part of the question. 13 was already crossed off in the first part of the question. 14 was not included in the range of the first question. The only number that fits into both categories is 12, so **the correct answer is (C).**

Example #3

Use the set of numbers shown to answer the question.

{-2, 0, 2, 5, 15}

Which describes the set of numbers?
(A)   whole numbers
(B)   consecutive even integers
(C)   distinct numbers
(D)   prime numbers

This is a definition question. If you aren't familiar with the definitions of each of these answer choices, review the Math Definitions section in the Fundamentals chapter. Whole numbers refer to positive integers and zero, but there is a negative number in this set, so (A) is incorrect. There are two odd numbers in the set, so (B) also doesn't work. 0 and 15 are not prime, so you can eliminate (D). Distinct means different, and all of these numbers are different from one another, so **(C) is the correct answer.**

Example #4

The total combined weight of a sphere, a pyramid, and a cube is 12 grams. If the pyramid weighs the same as 2 spheres and the cube weighs the same as 3 spheres, how many grams does the sphere weigh?
(A)   2 grams
(B)   3 grams
(C)   5 grams
(D)   6 grams

One way the answer can be found is by recognizing the information given:
1 sphere + 1 pyramid + 1 cube = 12 grams. Therefore, 1 sphere + (2 spheres) + (3 spheres) = 12 grams. 6 spheres = 12 grams. $12 \div 6 = 2$. Each sphere weighs 2 grams. **The correct answer is (A).**

You can also work backwards on these questions. Start with (B). If the sphere weighs 3 grams, then the pyramid weighs 6 grams and the cube weighs 9 grams. $3 + 6 + 9 = 18$. This is too high, so you know the answer must be smaller. (A) is the only option.

Practice Problems

1. Kimiko wrote down a whole number greater than 2 and less than 6. When Said tried to guess the number, Kimiko told him it was greater than 4 and less than 8. What is Kimiko's number?
   (A) 2
   (B) 3
   (C) 4
   (D) 5

2. Use the set of numbers shown to answer the question.

   {2, 3, 5, 7, 11, 13}

   Which describes the set of numbers?

   (A) consecutive odd numbers
   (B) composite numbers
   (C) irrational numbers
   (D) prime numbers

3. The total combined weight of a sphere, a pyramid, and a cube is 16 grams. If the cube weighs as much as 5 pyramids and the sphere weighs as much as 10 pyramids, how much does the cube weigh?
   (A) 1 gram
   (B) 5 grams
   (C) 10 grams
   (D) 16 grams

4. If y can be divided by both 4 and 6 without leaving a remainder, then y can also be divided by which number without leaving a remainder?
   (A) 10
   (B) 12
   (C) 16
   (D) 20

5. Petros wrote down a whole number greater than 15 and less than 19. When Helen tried to guess the number, Petros told her it was greater than 17 and less than 21. What is Petros's number?
   (A) 18
   (B) 19
   (C) 20
   (D) 21

6. If z can be divided by both 2 and 9 without leaving a remainder, then z can also be divided by which number without leaving a remainder?
   (A) 11
   (B) 16
   (C) 18
   (D) 20

7. The total combined weight of a sphere, a pyramid, and a cube is 24 grams. If the sphere weighs as much as 3 cubes and the pyramid weighs as much as 4 cubes, how much does the sphere weigh?
   (A) 3 grams
   (B) 6 grams
   (C) 9 grams
   (D) 12 grams

8. Use the set of numbers shown to answer the question.

   {-2, 0, 4, 6, 6, 45}

   Which describes the set of numbers?

   (A) even numbers
   (B) odd numbers
   (C) integers
   (D) distinct numbers

9. Santino wrote down a whole number greater than 12 and less than 16. When James tried to guess the number, Santino told him it was greater than 14 and less than 18. What is Santino's number?
   (A)   15
   (B)   16
   (C)   17
   (D)   18

10. If a can be divided by both 11 and 4 without leaving a remainder, then a can also be divided by which number without leaving a remainder?
   (A)   15
   (B)   22
   (C)   33
   (D)   45

11. The total combined weight of a sphere, a pyramid, and a cube is 34 grams. If the pyramid weighs as much as 4 spheres and the cube weighs as much as 12 spheres, how much does 1 sphere weigh?
   (A)   2 grams
   (B)   4 grams
   (C)   6 grams
   (D)   8 grams

12. Wilson wrote down a whole number greater than 8 and less than 13. When Alysha tried to guess the number, Wilson told her it was greater than 6 and less than 11, and that the number is not 10. What is Wilson's number?
   (A)   7
   (B)   8
   (C)   9
   (D)   11

13. Use the set of numbers shown to answer the question.

$$\{0, 2, 4, 6, 7, 10\}$$

Which describes the set of numbers?

   (A)   even numbers
   (B)   whole numbers
   (C)   composite numbers
   (D)   prime numbers

14. If k can be divided by both 5 and 6 without leaving a remainder, then k can also be divided by which number without leaving a remainder?
   (A)   9
   (B)   12
   (C)   15
   (D)   35

15. The total combined weight of a sphere, a pyramid, and a cube is 40 grams. If the sphere weighs as much as 2 pyramids and the cube weighs as much as 5 pyramids, how much does the sphere weigh?
   (A)   5 grams
   (B)   10 grams
   (C)   20 grams
   (D)   25 grams

16. Valeria wrote down a whole number greater than 14 and less than 19. When Moe tried to guess the number, Valeria told him it was greater than 15 and less than 18, and that the number is not 16. What is Valeria's number?
   (A)   14
   (B)   15
   (C)   16
   (D)   17

17. Use the set of numbers shown to answer the question.

$$\{-8, -4, -3, -2, -1\}$$

Which describes the set of numbers?

(A)   positive numbers
(B)   negative numbers
(C)   even numbers
(D)   odd numbers

18. The total combined weight of a sphere, a pyramid, and a cube is 36 grams. If the pyramid weighs as much as 2 cubes and the sphere weighs as much as 6 cubes, how much does the sphere weigh?

(A)   4 grams
(B)   8 grams
(C)   24 grams
(D)   28 grams

Measurement

There isn't much strategy involved in *measurement* questions. If you have studied the units of measurement in Section III, these questions will be very easy!

Example #1
What units are most appropriate for measuring the length of a football field?
(A)   millimeters
(B)   meters
(C)   centimeters
(D)   kilograms

You're probably more familiar with some of these units than others. For example, even if you don't know exactly how long a centimeter is, you may know that 1 centimeter is pretty short; therefore, you definitely should *not* select (C) as your answer. If there are any other units of measurement that you recognize, and you also know they are not appropriate for measuring the length of a football field, then cross them off! **The correct answer is (B).** 1 meter is equal to approximately 3 feet. Millimeters are much too small to measure the length of a football field. Kilograms measure weight, not length.

Example #2
Amit was painting his room. How much paint did he most likely use?
(A)   2 milliliters
(B)   2 gallons
(C)   2 pounds
(D)   2 ounces

In this question, we need a measure of volume. Pounds measure weight, so cross off (C). Milliliters and ounces measure very small amounts of either liquid or weight. Maybe you've seen a bucket of paint in your house or in a hardware store – do you remember how it was labeled? *Gallons* are the best unit of measurement, so **the correct answer is (B).**

Practice Problems

1. Mohammed recorded a measurement of his notebook as 400 grams. Which notebook measurement did Mohammed record?
    (A)   length
    (B)   area
    (C)   weight
    (D)   volume

2. What is the best estimate for how many gallons of water are needed to fill the average sink?
    (A)   1
    (B)   10
    (C)   100
    (D)   1,000

3. What units are most appropriate for measuring the weight of a person?
    (A)   kilograms
    (B)   grams
    (C)   feet
    (D)   meters

4. Ibrahim knows that a raisin weighs about one gram. Which object weighs about one kilogram?
    (A)   an elephant
    (B)   a person
    (C)   a car
    (D)   a hardcover book

5. Yu Yang is pouring milk for her cereal. How much milk did she likely pour?
    (A)   1 gallon
    (B)   1 liter
    (C)   1 ounce
    (D)   1 cup

6. What is the best estimate for how many liters of water a bathtub holds?
    (A)   30
    (B)   300
    (C)   3,000
    (D)   30,000

7. Jesse recorded a measurement of his computer screen as 100 square inches. Which measurement did Jesse record?
    (A)   area
    (B)   length
    (C)   perimeter
    (D)   width

8. What units are most appropriate for measuring the volume of a swimming pool?
    (A)   ounces
    (B)   milliliters
    (C)   gallons
    (D)   feet

9. What is the best estimate for how much a car weighs?
    (A)   50 kilograms
    (B)   4,000 pounds
    (C)   200 ounces
    (D)   1,000 gallons

10. Santiago knows that the width of the average pinkie finger is about one centimeter. Which object is about one meter long?
    (A)   a computer screen
    (B)   a TV remote control
    (C)   a notebook
    (D)   the width of a doorway

11. Amir was watering a house plant. How much water did he most likely use?
    (A)   1 ounce
    (B)   10 ounces
    (C)   100 ounces
    (D)   1,000 ounces

12. Keira recorded a measurement of her door frame as 85 inches. Which measurement did Keira record?
    (A)   area
    (B)   length
    (C)   weight
    (D)   volume

13. What is the best estimate for the length of a tree leaf?
    (A)   5 centimeters
    (B)   5 feet
    (C)   5 meters
    (D)   5 millimeters

14. What units are most appropriate for measuring the height of a tree?
    (A)   centimeters
    (B)   inches
    (C)   meters
    (D)   gallons

15. About how much shampoo does a shampoo bottle hold?
    (A)   1 ounce
    (B)   16 ounces
    (C)   160 ounces
    (D)   1,600 ounces

16. Ahmed knows that a stick of gum weighs about one gram. Which object weighs about one kilogram?
    (A)   a small cantaloupe
    (B)   a large dog
    (C)   a flat screen TV
    (D)   a cell phone

17. Shane recorded a measurement of his fingernail as 7 millimeters. Which measurement did Shane record?
    (A)   area
    (B)   length
    (C)   weight
    (D)   volume

Shapes

There are a variety of *shapes* questions that you can expect will be tested on the Lower Level ISEE.

Net Shapes
These questions test spatial reasoning abilities. That means the questions test how well you can imagine what a 3-D shape looks like in your head.

Example #1
Jerome has a box shaped like a cube. He cuts some of the edges to make the box flat. Which drawing shows the flattened box?

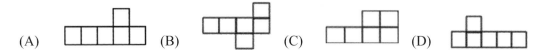

One way to practice these questions is to draw the shapes on paper, cut them out, and then see if it's possible to fold them into cubes. You should also remember that each figure must have one portion that is 4 boxes long. If there are 3 boxes or 5 boxes in a row, it is impossible to create a cube. Finally, you can memorize the following nets:

These four nets will all form cubes. Therefore, **the correct answer to the question above is (B).**

Example #2
A solid shape is shown below.

Which shows the faces of the shape?

(A)

(B)

(C)

(D)

On a question like this, it may be helpful to think about a real-life object. The shape above looks similar to a can of soup, so you should think about how many faces that can has. There is a circular bottom and top, as well as the side of can. If you unfolded the side of the can and laid it flat, it would form a rectangle, so **(B) is the correct answer**

Incomplete Shapes
These questions will provide a partial shape and ask you which answer choice completes the shape.

Example #3
Use the diagram to answer the question.

Which piece would complete the diagram to make a square?

(A)   (B)   (C)   (D)

On the real test, the best way to complete these questions is to draw in the missing boxes on the given shape, and then match your drawing with one of the answer choices. This is a 4 × 4 square, so you'll have to draw two boxes in the top row, one box in the second row, and two boxes in the third row. **The correct answer is (B).**

Dividing Shapes into Smaller Regions

Example #4
Use the figure shown to answer the question.

How many triangular regions can be made in the figure by only drawing line segments from vertex *A* to the other vertices?
(A)   3
(B)   4
(C)   5
(D)   6

The best way to do these questions is to pick up your pencil and draw in the lines yourself! A vertex is where two line segments meet. You can think of a vertex as a "corner" of a shape. Use your pencil to draw straight lines from vertex *A* to each of the other vertices.

Now you can see that 5 triangles can be created in this figure. **The correct answer is (C).** As a rule, you will always be able to draw 2 fewer triangles than the number of sides in the shape. So, if the shape has 8 sides, you can draw 6 triangles, etc.

Practice Problems

1. Malik has a box shaped like a cube. He cuts some of the edges to make the box flat. Which drawing shows the flattened box?

(A)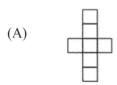

(B)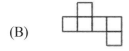

(C)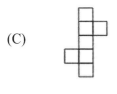

(D)

2. Use the figure shown to answer the question.

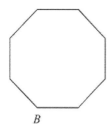

How many triangular regions can be made in the figure by only drawing line segments from vertex B to the other vertices?

(A)   4
(B)   5
(C)   6
(D)   7

3. A solid shape is shown below.

Which shows the faces of the shape?

(A)

(B)

(C)

(D)

4. A solid shape is shown below.

Which shows the faces of the shape?

(A)

(B)

(C)

(D)

5. Aina has a box shaped like a cube. She cuts some of the edges to make the box flat. Which drawing shows the flattened box?

(A)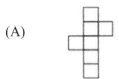

(B)

(C)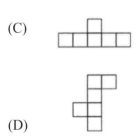

(D)

6. Use the figure shown to answer the question.

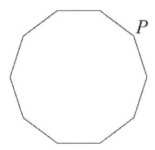

How many triangular regions can be made in the figure by only drawing line segments from vertex P to the other vertices?

(A)   5
(B)   6
(C)   7
(D)   8

7. A solid shape is shown below.

Which shows the faces of the shape?

(A)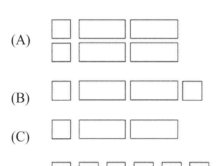

(B)

(C)

(D)

8. Davis has a box shaped like a cube. He cuts some of the edges to make the box flat. Which drawing shows the flattened box?

(A)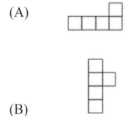

(B)

(C)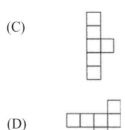

(D)

9. Use the diagram to answer the question.

Which piece would complete the diagram to make a square?

(A)   (B)   (C)   (D)

---

10. Use the diagram to answer the question.

Which piece would complete the diagram to make a square?

(A)   (B)   (C)   (D)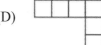

11. Use the diagram to answer the question.

Which piece would complete the diagram to make a circle?

(A)   (B)   (C)   (D)

12. Use the diagram to answer the question.

Which piece would complete the diagram to make a square?

(A)   (B)   (C)   (D)

Reflections and Lines of Symmetry

Reflections and Lines of Symmetry questions ask what a shape would look like if it were reflected over a line. Some questions on the Lower Level ISEE may ask you to reflect an object over two different lines.

Example #1
Use the figure to answer the question.

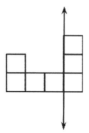

Which shows the figure after being flipped over the vertical line?

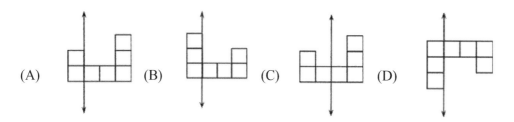

In the original figure, there are four boxes to the left of the vertical line and three boxes to the right of the vertical line. Therefore, when the figure is reflected over the vertical line, there will be three boxes to the left of the vertical line and four boxes to the right of the vertical line. You can eliminate (A). Choice (C) has simply moved the vertical line one space to the left, but the figure has not been reflected over the line. The figure in choice (D) has been flipped over the vertical line, but it has *also* been flipped upside down. Therefore, **the correct answer is (B).**

___

If something is *symmetrical*, that means that is has halves that are mirror images of each other. Let's look at a few examples:

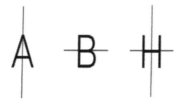

Each letter's line of symmetry has been drawn in. Notice how if you fold the letter over the line of symmetry, it will create a mirror image. *A* and *B* both have one line of symmetry, while *H* has two lines of symmetry.

Example #2

In which pair of letters do both letters have an equal number of lines of symmetry?

(A)   A C

(B)   O Z

(C)   L M

(D)   G T

To answer this question, you must know that symmetry means a figure can be folded in half so that the two halves match. *A* and *C* both have one line of symmetry, so **the correct answer is (A)**. *O* has an infinite number of lines of symmetry, while *Z* has zero lines of symmetry. *L* has zero lines of symmetry, while *M* has one line of symmetry. *G* has zero lines of symmetry, while *T* has one line of symmetry.

Example #3

The figure shown may be folded along one or more of the dotted lines.

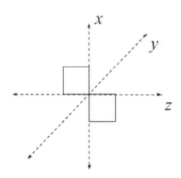

Which line or pair of lines, when folded, will allow the squares to exactly match the original figure?
(A)   line *x* only
(B)   line *z* only
(C)   both line *x* and line *y*
(D)   both line *x* and line *z*

If folded only over line *x* or line *z*, the squares will not land on top of one another. If folded over line *x* and then over line *z*, the squares would land on top of one another. **The correct answer is (D).** Folding the squares over line *y* would also allow the squares to match, but this is not an answer choice.

Practice Problems

1. Use the figure to answer the question.

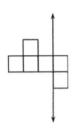

Which shows the figure after being flipped over the vertical line?

(A)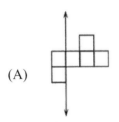

(B)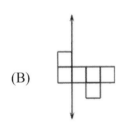

(C)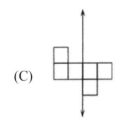

(D)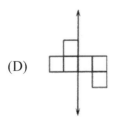

2. The figure shown may be folded along one or more of the dotted lines.

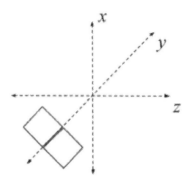

Which line or pair of lines, when folded, will allow the squares to exactly match the original figure?
(A)   line *x* only
(B)   line *y* only
(C)   both line *x* and line *y*
(D)   both line *y* and line *z*

3. In which pair of letters do both letters have an equal number of lines of symmetry?

(A)   N A

(B)   O K

(C)   Z H

(D)   E C

4. Use the figure to answer the question.

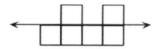

Which shows the figure after being flipped over the horizontal line?

(A)
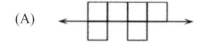

(B)
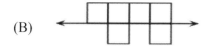

(C)
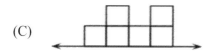

(D)
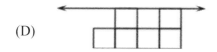

5. The figure shown may be folded along one or more of the dotted lines.

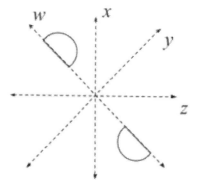

Which line or pair of lines, when folded, will allow the semicircles to exactly match the original figure?
(A)   line w only
(B)   line y only
(C)   both line w and line z
(D)   both line w and line y

6. In which pair of letters do both letters have an equal number of lines of symmetry?

(A)   R   A

(B)   O   C

(C)   T   M

(D)   E   F

7. Use the figure to answer the question.

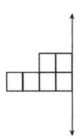

Which shows the figure after being flipped over the vertical line?

(A)

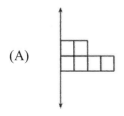

(B)

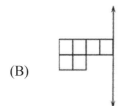

(C)

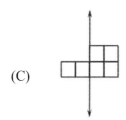

(D)

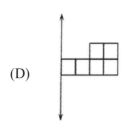

8. The figure shown may be folded along one or more of the dotted lines.

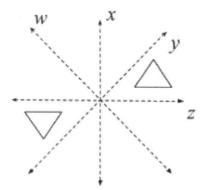

Which line or pair of lines, when folded, will allow the triangles to exactly match the original figure?
(A)   line x only
(B)   line y only
(C)   both line x and line y
(D)   both line x and line z

9. In which pair of letters do both letters have an equal number of lines of symmetry?

(A)   O H

(B)   G C

(C)   W X

(D)   T A

10. Use the figure to answer the question.

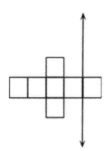

Which shows the figure after being flipped over the vertical line?

(A)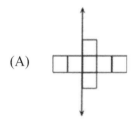

(B)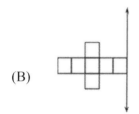

(C)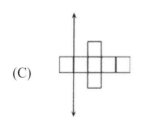

(D)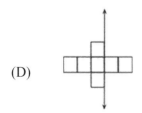

11. The figure shown may be folded along one or more of the dotted lines.

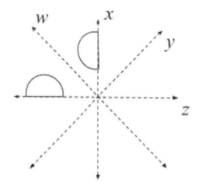

Which line or pair of lines, when folded, will allow the semicircles to exactly match the original figure?

(A)   line w only
(B)   line z only
(C)   both line x and line w
(D)   both line x and line z

12. In which pair of letters do both letters have an equal number of lines of symmetry?

(A)   E   R

(B)   Q   C

(C)   V   O

(D)   H   I

13. Use the figure to answer the question.

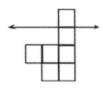

Which shows the figure after being flipped over the horizontal line?

(A)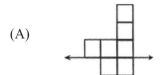

(B)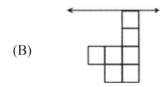

(C)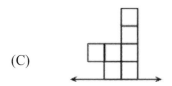

(D)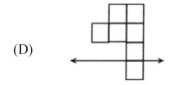

14. In which pair of letters do both letters have an equal number of lines of symmetry?

(A)   O D

(B)   C H

(C)   Y U

(D)   L W

Decimals

Decimals questions on the Lower Level ISEE will often involve shaded figures. Remember that the easiest way to find a decimal value is to create a fraction with a denominator of 100, and then move the decimal of the top number of the fraction two places to the left.

Example #1

Convert $\frac{1}{4}$ to a decimal.

(A)   0.10
(B)   0.25
(C)   0.40
(D)   0.50

You need to find a way to make the denominator of this fraction equal 100. To do this, multiply by 25. Then, since you multiplied by 25 on the bottom, you need to do the same thing on top. This results in $\frac{25}{100}$. The number on top is 25.00. Moving the decimal two places to the left results in 0.25. **The correct answer is (B).**

Example #2

Which fraction is less than 0.4?

(A) $\frac{3}{4}$

(B) $\frac{4}{10}$

(C) $\frac{6}{10}$

(D) $\frac{3}{8}$

First, convert the decimal to a fraction. Move the decimal two places to the right, put the resulting number in the numerator of a fraction, add 100 to the denominator, and reduce: $0.4 = \frac{40}{100} = \frac{2}{5}$. Now, focus on the fractions in the answer choices that are easiest to compare to $\frac{2}{5}$. $\frac{4}{10} = \frac{2}{5}$, and $\frac{6}{10} = \frac{3}{5}$, so you can eliminate both (B) and (C). Finally, compare $\frac{2}{5}$ with the remaining two answer choices using the method described in Part III: Operations with Fractions. **The correct answer is (D).**

Example #3

What decimal represents the shaded region of the figure below?

(A)   0.15
(B)   0.25
(C)   0.50
(D)   1.00

First, create a fraction. There are 16 boxes total, and 8 of the boxes are shaded, so the fraction is $\frac{8}{16}$. There is no way to make 16 multiply to 100, so you can try reducing the fraction first. The fraction is equal to $\frac{1}{2}$. Now, you can multiply the top and bottom of the fraction by 50 to get $\frac{50}{100}$. The number on top of the fraction is 50.00. Move the decimal 2 places to the left to get 0.50. **The correct answer is (C).**

Practice Problems

1. What decimal represents the shaded region of the figure below?

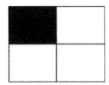

    (A)   0.10
    (B)   0.25
    (C)   0.50
    (D)   0.75

2. Convert $\frac{1}{5}$ to a decimal.

    (A)   0.20
    (B)   0.40
    (C)   0.50
    (D)   0.70

3. Which fraction is equivalent to 0.75?

    (A) $\frac{1}{3}$

    (B) $\frac{6}{8}$

    (C) $\frac{7}{5}$

    (D) $\frac{75}{10}$

4. Which decimal represents the number of unshaded shapes in the figure below?

    (A)   0.50
    (B)   0.70
    (C)   0.75
    (D)   1.00

5. Convert $\frac{3}{25}$ to a decimal.

    (A)   0.12
    (B)   0.30
    (C)   0.24
    (D)   0.60

6. Which fraction is greater than 0.7?

    (A) $\frac{3}{5}$

    (B) $\frac{4}{7}$

    (C) $\frac{3}{4}$

    (D) $\frac{5}{8}$

7. Which decimal represents the number of shaded circles in the figure below?

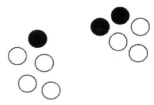

    (A)   0.10
    (B)   0.20
    (C)   0.30
    (D)   0.40

8. Convert $\frac{7}{20}$ to a decimal.

    (A)   0.07
    (B)   0.14
    (C)   0.35
    (D)   0.70

9. Which decimal represents the number of unshaded shapes below?

(A)　　0.20
(B)　　0.25
(C)　　0.40
(D)　　0.60

10. Which fraction is less than 0.3?

(A)　　$\frac{1}{3}$

(B)　　$\frac{1}{4}$

(C)　　$\frac{2}{5}$

(D)　　$\frac{3}{8}$

11. Carol's marble collection is shown.

Which decimal represents the number of black marbles in Carol's collection?

(A)　　0.10
(B)　　0.20
(C)　　0.40
(D)　　0.50

12. Convert $\frac{99}{100}$ to a decimal.

(A)　　0.99
(B)　　9.9
(C)　　99.00
(D)　　0.099

13. Which fraction is equivalent to 0.55?

(A)　　$\frac{5}{55}$

(B)　　$\frac{7}{5}$

(C)　　$\frac{11}{20}$

(D)　　$\frac{55}{10}$

14. Which decimal represents the shaded region of the figure below?

(A)　　0.40
(B)　　0.50
(C)　　0.60
(D)　　0.70

15. Which fraction is greater than 0.2?

(A)　　$\frac{1}{10}$

(B)　　$\frac{3}{11}$

(C)　　$\frac{3}{20}$

(D)　　$\frac{2}{10}$

16. Which fraction is equivalent to 0.30?

(A)　　$\frac{3}{10}$

(B)　　$\frac{3}{100}$

(C)　　$\frac{100}{30}$

(D)　　$\frac{3}{5}$

17. Which decimal represents the number of shaded shapes in the figure below?

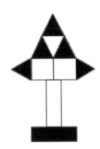

    (A)   0.60
    (B)   0.70
    (C)   0.80
    (D)   0.90

18. Which fraction is greater than 0.35?

    (A) $\frac{1}{4}$

    (B) $\frac{3}{10}$

    (C) $\frac{7}{20}$

    (D) $\frac{9}{25}$

19. Marina's marble collection is shown.

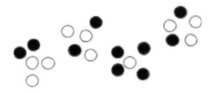

Which decimal represents the number of white marbles in Marina's collection?

    (A)   0.25
    (B)   0.50
    (C)   0.75
    (D)   1.00

20. Convert $\frac{1}{4}$ to a decimal.

    (A)   0.10
    (B)   0.25
    (C)   0.40
    (D)   0.75

21. Which fraction is equivalent to 0.45?

    (A) $\frac{2}{5}$

    (B) $\frac{45}{1{,}000}$

    (C) $\frac{4}{5}$

    (D) $\frac{9}{20}$

22. What decimal represents the unshaded region of the figure below?

    (A)   0.25
    (B)   0.50
    (C)   0.75
    (D)   1.00

Venn Diagrams

A *Venn diagram* is a way of classifying groups of objects with the same properties. Typically, a Venn diagram has two or three circles that intersect each other. There is also a space outside the circles where objects are placed if they do not fit any of the properties. The figures below show how to interpret Venn diagrams.

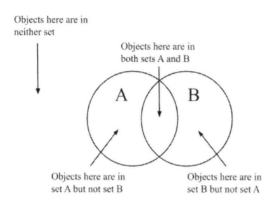

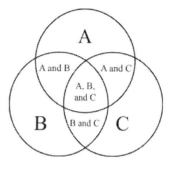

Example #1
Use the Venn diagram to answer the question.

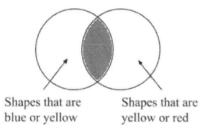

What shape could be found in the shaded part of the Venn diagram?
(A)   a blue square
(B)   a yellow triangle
(C)   a red rectangle
(D)   a blue triangle

There are three types of shapes listed in this Venn diagram: blue shapes, yellow shapes, and red shapes. The two large circles share one type of shape in common: yellow shapes. Therefore, the white space in the left circle will contain blue shapes, the white space in the right circle will contain red shapes, and the shaded area will contain yellow shapes. **The correct answer is (B).**

Example #2

The Venn diagram below shows the number of students enrolled in music, drama, or both.

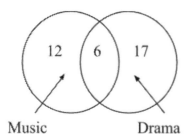

How many total students are enrolled in drama?

(A)   12
(B)   17
(C)   23
(D)   35

Don't make the mistake of choosing (B). This is a trick answer that does not take into consideration the 6 students who are taking both drama and music. Therefore, the total number of students taking drama is $17 + 6 = 23$. **The correct answer is (C).**

Example #3

Use the data set and the Venn diagram below to answer the question.

{6, 68, 74, 92, 101, 104, 115, 299, 360, 361}

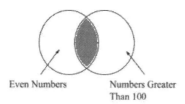

How many numbers belong in the shaded section of the diagram?

(A)   2
(B)   4
(C)   6
(D)   8

The best way to approach this question is to write the numbers in the spaces on the Venn diagram where they belong.

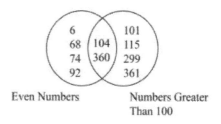

Only 104 and 360 are both even and greater than 100. Therefore, **the correct answer is (A).** (B) represents the number of even numbers less than 100, (C) represents the total number of even numbers, and (D) represents even numbers less than 100 and odd numbers greater than 100. Be careful not to select a trick answer!

Practice Problems

1. Use the Venn diagram to answer the question.

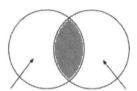

Shapes that are red or orange   Shapes that are orange or green

What shape could be found in the shaded part of the Venn diagram?
(A)   a red parallelogram
(B)   a green circle
(C)   a red square
(D)   an orange circle

2. The Venn diagram shows students who take music classes, English classes, or math classes.

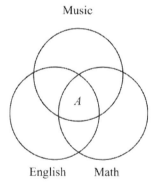

What classes do students take who are in part *A* of the Venn diagram?
(A)   music and English
(B)   music and math
(C)   English and math
(D)   music, English, and math

3. Use the data set and the Venn diagram below to answer the question.

$$\{2, 3, 8, 17, 23, 29\}$$

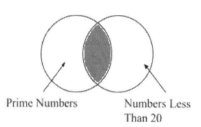

Prime Numbers   Numbers Less Than 20

How many numbers belong in the shaded section of the diagram?
(A)   2
(B)   3
(C)   4
(D)   5

4. The Venn diagram below shows the attributes of flowers in a flower shop.

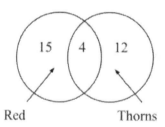

Red   Thorns

How many flowers only had thorns?
(A)   4
(B)   12
(C)   16
(D)   31

5. Use the Venn diagram to answer the question.

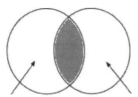

Shapes that are pink or purple

Shapes that are pink or blue

What shape could be found in the shaded part of the Venn diagram?
(A)   a pink kite
(B)   a purple square
(C)   a blue rhombus
(D)   a purple rectangle

6. The Venn diagram below shows the pets that students in a class owned.

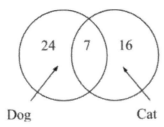

Dog   Cat

How many students owned cats?
(A)   7
(B)   16
(C)   23
(D)   47

7. Use the data set and the Venn diagram below to answer the question.

$$\{4, 6, 9, 11, 12, 15, 17, 18\}$$

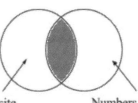

Composite Numbers

Numbers Greater than 10

How many numbers belong in the shaded section of the diagram?
(A)   1
(B)   2
(C)   3
(D)   4

8. The Venn diagram shows students who have cats, dogs, or hamsters as pets.

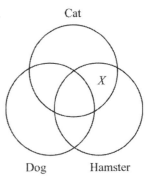

What pets do students own who are in part X of the Venn diagram?
(A)   cats and hamsters
(B)   cats and dogs
(C)   dogs and hamsters
(D)   cats, dogs, and hamsters

9. Use the Venn diagram to answer the question.

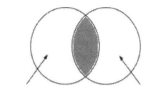

Shapes that are   Shapes that are
black or white   black or blue

What shape could be found in the shaded part of the Venn diagram?
(A)   a white trapezoid
(B)   a blue square
(C)   a black quadrilateral
(D)   a blue circle

10. The Venn diagram shows students who ate hot dogs, hamburgers, or pizza for lunch.

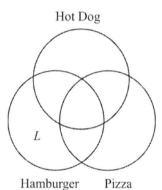

Hot Dog

L

Hamburger   Pizza

What foods did students eat who are in part L of the Venn diagram?
(A)   hot dogs
(B)   hamburgers
(C)   hot dogs and hamburgers
(D)   pizza

11. The Venn diagram below shows the sports that people watched on TV this weekend.

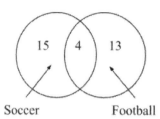

Soccer   Football

How many people watched both soccer and football?
(A)   4
(B)   17
(C)   19
(D)   31

12. Use the data set and the Venn diagram below to answer the question.

{0, 2, 4, 7, 9, 12, 13, 14}

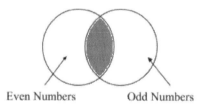

Even Numbers   Odd Numbers

How many numbers belong in the shaded section of the diagram?
(A)   0
(B)   1
(C)   2
(D)   3

Number Lines

Number lines were introduced in the Math Fundamentals section. Here, we will learn about some of the specific number line questions that may be tested on the Lower Level ISEE.

Example #1
Use the number line to answer the question.

What three numbers are the vertical arrows pointing to on the number line?
(A)   2.6,   2.8,   5.6
(B)   2.8,   3.4,   5.8
(C)   3.0,   4.0,   6.0
(D)   3.2,   4.6,   6.2

Treat this as you would treat any number line question. You need to determine the increase that each tick mark represents. To do so, do $5.5 - 2.5 = 3.0$. Then, divide by the number of equal spaces. $3.0 \div 6 = 0.5$. Therefore, each tick mark represents an increase of 0.5. $2.5 + 0.5 = 3.0$. The tick mark to the right of 2.5 is equal to 3.0. Based on the answer choices, you already know **the correct answer must be (C)**.

Example #2
The length of *AB* is *x* and the length of *AC* is *y*.

A   B   C

What is the length of *BC*?
(A) $y - x$
(B) $y + x$
(C) $x - y$
(D) xy

You'll need to use logic on this question. It will help if you make up your own values for the lengths of *AC* and *AB*.

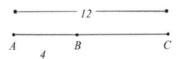

If $AC = 12$ and $AB = 4$, to find *BC* you would do $12 - 4$. *Y* corresponds to the 12, and *x* corresponds to the 4, so this is the same as doing $y - x$. **The correct answer is (A).**

Example #3

Use the number line shown to answer the question.

B is the average of A and another number. What is the other number?

(A)   18
(B)   26
(C)   32
(D)   36

Once again, you'll need to determine the value of each of the tick marks. $20 - 4 = 16$. $16 \div 4 = 4$. Each tick mark represents an increase of 4, so you can fill in the number line like this:

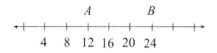

Now, you can reword the question to say, "24 is the average of 12 and some other number. What is the other number?" Use the answer choices to your advantage. $\frac{12 + 32}{2} = 22$. This is too small. $\frac{12 + 36}{2} = 24$.
The correct answer is (D).

Practice Problems

1. Use the number line below to answer the question.

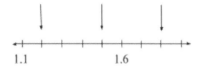

Which three numbers are the vertical arrows pointing to on the number line?
(A)   1.2,   1.5,   1.8
(B)   1.2,   1.4,   1.7
(C)   1.3,   1.4,   1.7
(D)   1.3,   1.4,   1.8

2. The length of *QS* is *a* and the length of *RS* is *b*.

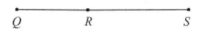

What is the length of *QR*?
(A) $a - b$
(B) $a + b$
(C) $b - a$
(D) ab

3. Use the number line below to answer the question.

D is the average of *C* and another number. What is the other number?
(A)   0
(B)   2
(C)   4
(D)   8

4. Use the number line below to answer the question.

Which three numbers are the vertical arrows pointing to on the number line?
(A)   2.3,   2.6,   2.8
(B)   2.3,   2.6,   3.3
(C)   2.2,   2.8,   3.2
(D)   2.2,   2.8,   3.3

5. The length of *DE* is *x* and the length of *EF* is *y*.

What is the length of *DF*?
(A) $x - y$
(B) $x + y$
(C) $y - x$
(D) xy

6. Use the number line below to answer the question.

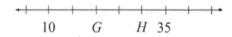

H is the average of *G* and another number. What is the other number?
(A)   20
(B)   30
(C)   40
(D)   50

7. Use the number line below to answer the question.

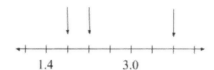

    Which three numbers are the vertical arrows pointing to on the number line?
    (A)   1.8, 2.2, 3.8
    (B)   1.5, 1.6, 3.3
    (C)   1.6, 1.8, 3.4
    (D)   1.7, 2.0, 3.6

8. The length of *LN* is *c* and the length of *LM* is *d*.

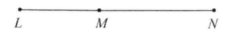

    What is the length of *MN*?
    (A) $c - d$
    (B) $c + d$
    (C) $d - c$
    (D) cd

9. Use the number line below to answer the question.

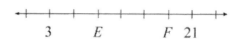

    F is the average of *E* and another number. What is the other number?
    (A)   9
    (B)   18
    (C)   27
    (D)   36

10. Use the number line below to answer the question.

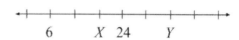

    X is the average of *Y* and another number. What is the other number?
    (A)   0
    (B)   12
    (C)   18
    (D)   36

Scales

Scales questions can be tricky. They usually show a balanced scale and ask you how much objects on the scale must weigh in relation to one another.

Example #1

The figure shows Carlos and Samuel's containers.

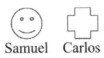

Samuel   Carlos

If each scale is balanced, which diagram shows that Carlos's container weighs 1 pound more than Samuel's container? Let ⬜ = 1 pound.

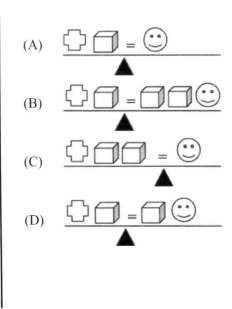

Let's go through these answer choices one by one. Note that the cubes each weigh one pound. For the scale in (A) to be balanced, one pound had to be added to Carlos's side. This means that Carlos's container weighs one pound *less* than Samuel's container. To make this easier to visualize, you can assign a weight to the containers. For example, let's say Samuel's container weighs 5 pounds. That means there are 5 pounds on the right side of the scale. On the left side, you know that the cube weighs 1 pound. That means Carlos's container must weigh 4 pounds, since $4 + 1 = 5$, and this would balance the scale.

In answer choice (B), cross out one cube on both sides of the scale. You can do this because each cube weighs one pound, so they cancel each other out. This leaves you with one cube on the right side of the scale. Based on the work you did for (A), you know that Samuel's container weighs one pound less than Carlos's container. In other words, Carlos's container weighs one pound *more* than Samuel's container. **(B) is the correct answer**.

In (C), Carlos's container weighs two pounds less than Samuel's container. In (D), both containers weigh the same amount.

Practice Problems

1. The figure shows Alex and Jack's containers.

    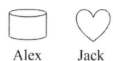

    Alex   Jack

    If each scale is balanced, which diagram shows that Alex's container weighs 2 pounds more than Jack's container? Let 🔲 = 1 pound.

    (A)

    (B)

    (C)

    (D)

2. The figure shows Zahid and Feng's containers.

    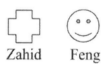

    Zahid   Feng

    If each scale is balanced, which diagram shows that Zahid's container weighs 2 pounds more than Feng's container? Let 🔲 = 2 pounds.

    (A)

    (B)

    (C)

    (D)

3. The figure shows Selma and Omar's containers.

    Selma   Omar

    If each scale is balanced, which diagram shows that Selma's container weighs the same as Omar's container? Let 🔲 = 1 pound.

    (A)

    (B)

    (C)

    (D)

201

4. The figure shows Logan and Nareh's containers.

Logan   Nareh

If each scale is balanced, which diagram shows that Logan's container weighs 4 pounds less than Nareh's container? Let [cube] = 2 pounds.

(A)

(B)

(C)

(D)

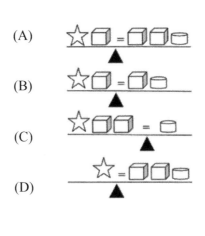

5. The figure shows Nicola and Gustav's containers.

Nicola   Gustav

If each scale is balanced, which diagram shows that Gustav's container weighs 1 pound more than Nicola's container? Let [cube] = 1 pound.

(A)

(B)

(C)

(D)

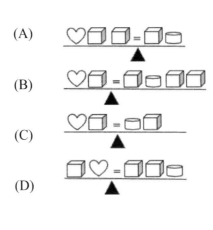

6. The figure shows Ivan and Aloysha's containers.

Ivan   Aloysha

If each scale is balanced, which diagram shows that the combined weight of Ivan and Aloysha's containers is 6 pounds? Let [cube] = 3 pounds.

(A)

(B)

(C)

(D)

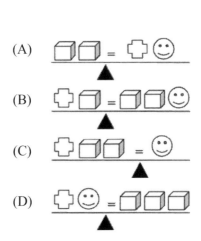

7. The figure shows Martine and
    Nathalie's containers.

    Martine   Nathalie

    If each scale is balanced, which diagram
    shows that Martine's container weighs 2
    pounds more than Nathalie's container?
    Let 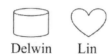 = 1 pound.

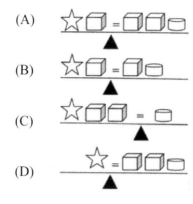

(A)

(B)

(C)

(D)

8. The figure shows Delwin and Lin's
    containers.

    Delwin   Lin

    If each scale is balanced, which diagram
    shows that Delwin's container weighs 4
    pounds less than Lin's container? Let
    = 2 pounds.

(A)

(B)

(C)

(D)

Tables

Tables questions usually test your ability to identify trends with decimals or rates.

Example #1

Mehmet recorded how much time he spent doing dishes for 10 consecutive days.

DISHWASHING TIMES FOR NOVEMBER 3-12	
Nov 3	7.55 minutes
Nov 4	7.78 minutes
Nov 5	7.91 minutes
Nov 6	8.01 minutes
Nov 7	8.19 minutes
Nov 8	8.47 minutes
Nov 9	8.41 minutes
Nov 10	8.65 minutes
Nov 11	9.00 minutes
Nov 12	9.05 minutes

The amount of time Mehmet spent washing dishes each day increased for several days, then decreased. On which day did the amount of time Mehmet spent washing dishes decrease?

(A)   Nov 7
(B)   Nov 8
(C)   Nov 9
(D)   Nov 10

There is a lot of information in this table. To save yourself time, you can focus on only four pieces of information: November 7th, 8th, 9th, and 10th. If the amount of time Mehmet spent washing dishes on one of these days *decreased*, then the amount of time he spent washing dishes the day before should be *higher* than the amount of time he spent washing dishes on one of the given dates.

So, look at November 6th: 8.01 is less than 8.19, so this answer is incorrect. On November 7th, Mehmet spent 8.19 minutes washing dishes, which is less than 8.47 minutes. On November 8th, he spent 8.47 minutes, which is *greater* than the 8.41 minutes he spent washing dishes on November 9th. Therefore, **(C) is the correct answer**. You don't even need to bother looking at (D)!

Example #2

The table shows the number of copies made per minute with the school's new copy machine.

NEW COPY MACHINE	
Number of Copies	Minutes
60	5
120	6
180	7

Jenny needs to make 360 copies. How long will it take Jenny to make 360 copies?

(A)   9 minutes
(B)   10 minutes
(C)   11 minutes
(D)   12 minutes

It takes 5 minutes to make the first 60 copies and 1 minute to make 60 copies after that. Jenny needs to make 180 + 60 + 60 + 60 = 360 copies. This will take 7 + 1 + 1 + 1 = 10 minutes. **The correct answer is (B).**

Example #3

The table shows items that a man bought at the grocery store. He bought at least one of each item on the list.

GROCERY LIST

Item	Price for One	Total Cost for Item
pasta	$1.50	$3.00
carton of eggs	$2.50	$2.50
ice cream	$5.75	$5.75
gallon of milk	$3.25	?

If he spent a total of $17.75, how many gallons of milk did he buy?
(A)   1
(B)   2
(C)   3
(D)   4

First, add up how much the man has already spent: $3.00 + $2.50 + $5.75 = $11.25. Then, subtract this amount from the total amount he spent: $17.75 − $11.25 = $6.50. Finally, divide this number by the cost of 1 gallon of milk: $6.50 ÷ $3.25 = 2. **The correct answer is (B).**

Practice Problems

1. Alban recorded how long it took him to run a mile for 9 consecutive days.

MILE TIMES FOR JUNE 20-28	
June 20	9.25 minutes
June 21	9.17 minutes
June 22	9.05 minutes
June 23	8.55 minutes
June 24	8.37 minutes
June 25	7.59 minutes
June 26	7.51 minutes
June 27	7.55 minutes
June 28	7.45 minutes

Alban's times decreased each day for several days and then increased. On which day did his time increase?
(A)   June 23
(B)   June 25
(C)   June 27
(D)   June 28

2. The table shows the number of copies made per minute with the school's new copy machine.

NEW COPY MACHINE	
Number of Copies	Minutes
60	5
120	6
180	7
240	8

Aria needs to make 420 copies. How long will it take Aria to make 420 copies?
(A)   9 minutes
(B)   10 minutes
(C)   11 minutes
(D)   12 minutes

3. The table shows items that a man bought at the grocery store. He bought at least one of each item on the list.

GROCERY LIST

Item	Price for One	Total Cost for Item
yogurt	$1.00	$2.00
cheese	$3.25	$6.50
olive oil	$4.75	?
turkey	$6.50	$6.50

If he spent a total of $19.75, how much money did he spend just on olive oil?
(A) $4.75
(B) $9.50
(C) $14.25
(D) $19.00

4. The table shows how far Mateo walks in a certain amount of time.

Distance Walked (miles)	Minutes
0.50	10
1.00	20
1.50	30
2.00	40

At his current rate, how far will Mateo walk in 100 minutes?
(A)   2.50 miles
(B)   4.00 miles
(C)   5.00 miles
(D)   6.50 miles

5. A coach recorded a swimmer's swim times for 10 consecutive days.

SWIM TIMES FOR APRIL 10-19	
April 10	32.4 seconds
April 11	31.8 seconds
April 12	31.6 seconds
April 13	31.4 seconds
April 14	31.2 seconds
April 15	31.6 seconds
April 16	30.8 seconds
April 17	30.6 seconds
April 18	30.4 seconds
April 19	29.8 seconds

The swimmer's times decreased each day for several days and then increased. On which day did the time increase?
(A)   April 13
(B)   April 14
(C)   April 15
(D)   April 16

6. The table shows items that a woman bought at the grocery store. She bought at least one of each item on the list.

GROCERY LIST

Item	Price for One	Total Cost for Item
cream	$3.25	$3.25
eggs	$2.50	$7.50
tomato	$0.25	?
bread	$4.75	$4.75

If she spent a total of $20.00, how many tomatoes did she buy?
(A)   5
(B)   7
(C)   11
(D)   18

7. The table shows the distance Liam swims in a certain amount of time.

Distance (meters)	Seconds
30	20
50	40
70	60
90	80

At his current rate, how many seconds will it take for Liam to swim 120 meters?
(A)   100
(B)   110
(C)   120
(D)   130

8. Yosef recorded how long it took him to complete his homework each day for 10 consecutive days.

HOMEWORK TIME FOR JANUARY 12-21	
Jan 12	46.20 minutes
Jan 13	45.90 minutes
Jan 14	43.10 minutes
Jan 15	43.05 minutes
Jan 16	43.50 minutes
Jan 17	43.60 minutes
Jan 18	43.65 minutes
Jan 19	44.10 minutes
Jan 20	44.25 minutes
Jan 21	44.90 minutes

Yosef's homework completion time decreased for several days before beginning to increase again. On which day did his time begin to increase?
(A)   Jan 15
(B)   Jan 16
(C)   Jan 17
(D)   Jan 18

9. The table shows how far Ximena ran in a certain amount of time.

Distance (miles)	Minutes
4	28
6	42
8	56
10	70

At her current rate, how far will Ximena run in 91 minutes?
(A)   11 miles
(B)   12 miles
(C)   13 miles
(D)   14 miles

10. Aya recorded how much time she spent watching TV each day for 10 consecutive days.

TV TIME FOR DECEMBER 15-24	
Dec 15	36.40 minutes
Dec 16	33.15 minutes
Dec 17	30.50 minutes
Dec 18	36.75 minutes
Dec 19	37.15 minutes
Dec 20	36.65 minutes
Dec 21	31.45 minutes
Dec 22	32.50 minutes
Dec 23	33.00 minutes
Dec 24	29.25 minutes

On which day did Aya watch 0.50 fewer minutes of TV than she did the day before?
(A)   Dec 16
(B)   Dec 19
(C)   Dec 20
(D)   Dec 22

11. The table shows items that a man bought at the grocery store. He bought at least one of each item on the list.

GROCERY LIST

Item	Price for One	Total Cost for Item
spaghetti	$2.25	$5.50
corn	$1.00	$4.00
popsicle	$0.75	?
soda	$2.50	$5.00

If he spent a total of $16.75, how much money did he spend on popsicles?
(A) $0.75
(B) $1.50
(C) $1.75
(D) $2.25

12. The table shows how many pieces of music David plays on the piano in a certain amount of time.

Number of Pieces	Minutes
4	12
5	15
6	18
7	21

At his current rate, how many pieces can David play in 36 minutes?
(A)   8
(B)   9
(C)   11
(D)   12

13. The table shows how many pushups Zeinab can do in a certain amount of time.

Number of Pushups	Minutes
30	2
45	3
60	4
75	5

At her current rate, how many pushups can Zeinab do in 8 minutes?
(A)   100
(B)   120
(C)   140
(D)   160

14. Oskar recorded his 200-meter dash times for 10 consecutive days.

200-METER DASH TIMES FOR OCTOBER 18-27	
Oct 18	49.24 seconds
Oct 19	49.15 seconds
Oct 20	49.01 seconds
Oct 21	48.91 seconds
Oct 22	48.95 seconds
Oct 23	48.68 seconds
Oct 24	48.55 seconds
Oct 25	48.15 seconds
Oct 26	47.47 seconds
Oct 27	47.40 seconds

Oskar's time decreased for several days and then increased. For how many days did Oskar's time decrease before it increased?
(A)   4
(B)   5
(C)   6
(D)   7

15. The table shows items that a woman bought at the grocery store. She bought at least one of each item on the list.

GROCERY LIST

Item	Price for One	Total Cost for Item
lettuce	$1.50	$3.00
apple	$2.50	$5.00
avocado	$1.50	$4.50
bread	$3.25	$3.25

What is the total number of items the woman purchased?
(A)   6
(B)   7
(C)   8
(D)   9

16. The table shows how many jumping jacks Jing can do in a certain amount of time.

Number of Jumping Jacks	Minutes
30	3
50	5
70	7
90	9

At her current rate, how many minutes will it take Jing to do 120 jumping jacks?
(A)   12
(B)   13
(C)   14
(D)   15

Time Zones

Time zones questions require knowledge of reading clocks and interpreting time zone changes between different locations.

Example #1
Use the Time Zone map to answer the question.

An airplane leaves San Francisco at 12:00 P.M. and arrives 4 hours later in Chicago. What time is it in Chicago?
(A)   10:00 A.M.
(B)   12:00 P.M.
(C)   4:00 P.M.
(D)   6:00 P.M.

The clocks at the bottom of the figure show you the relationship between each city's time zone. When it is 2:00 P.M. in the Pacific time zone, where San Francisco located, it is 4:00 P.M. in the Central time zone, where Chicago is located. That means Chicago is 2 hours ahead of San Francisco. If the flight departs at 12:00 P.M. and lasts for 4 hours, that means it lands at 4:00 P.M. San Francisco time. Then, you must add 2 hours to get the local Chicago time. **(D) is the correct answer.**

Practice Problems

1. Use the Time Zone map to answer the question.

STANDARD TIME ZONES

Pacific   Mountain   Central   Eastern

An airplane leaves Seattle at 2:00 P.M. and arrives 5 hours later in Boston. What time is it in Boston?

(A)   7:00 P.M.
(B)   9:00 P.M.
(C)   10:00 P.M.
(D)   11:00 P.M.

---

2. The clocks below show the time difference between Seattle and Boston.

Seattle   Boston

If a plane leaves Seattle at 1:00 P.M. and arrives 5 hours later in Boston, what time will it be in Boston when the plane lands?

(A)   6:00 P.M.
(B)   7:00 P.M.
(C)   8:00 P.M.
(D)   9:00 P.M.

3. The clocks below show the time difference between Hawaii and San Francisco.

Hawaii   San Francisco

If a plane leaves Hawaii at 8:00 A.M. and arrives 6 hours later in San Francisco, what time will it be in San Francisco when the plane lands?

(A)   4:00 P.M.
(B)   5:00 P.M.
(C)   6:00 P.M.
(D)   7:00 P.M.

4.   Use the Time Zone map to answer the question.

STANDARD TIME ZONES

An airplane leaves New York at 3:00 P.M. and arrives 4 hours later in Denver. What time is it in Denver?

(A)   4:00 P.M.

(B)   5:00 P.M.

(C)   9:00 P.M.

(D)   10:00 P.M.

---

5.   The clocks below show the time difference between New York and London.

If a plane leaves New York at 6:00 A.M. and arrives 6 hours later in London, what time will it be in London when the plane lands?

(A)   12:00 P.M.

(B)   4:00 P.M.

(C)   5:00 P.M.

(D)   7:00 P.M.

6.   The clocks below show the time difference between Seattle and Boston.

If a plane leaves Boston at 8:00 P.M. and arrives 5 hours later in Seattle, what time will it be in Seattle when the plane lands?

(A)   9:00 P.M.

(B)   10:00 P.M.

(C)   11:00 P.M.

(D)   12:00 A.M.

7.   Use the Time Zone map to answer the question.

STANDARD TIME ZONES

An airplane leaves Denver at 6:00 A.M. and arrives 3 hours later in Atlanta. What time is it in Atlanta?

(A)   9:00 A.M.

(B)   10:00 A.M.

(C)   11:00 A.M.

(D)   12:00 P.M.

---

8.   The clocks below show the time difference between Hawaii and San Francisco.

If a plane leaves San Francisco at 5:00 P.M. and arrives 6 hours later in Hawaii, what time will it be in Hawaii when the plane lands?

(A)   6:00 P.M.

(B)   7:00 P.M.

(C)   8:00 P.M.

(D)   9:00 P.M.

9.   The clocks below show the time difference between New York and London.

If a plane leaves London at 2:00 P.M. and arrives 6 hours later in New York, what time will it be in New York when the plane lands?

(A)   3:00 P.M.

(B)   4:00 P.M.

(C)   8:00 P.M.

(D)   1:00 A.M.

Charts

The Lower Level ISEE has some *charts* questions that are unique to this test.

Example #1

An ice cream man counted the number of ice cream cones he sold each day for 5 days. He sold 24 more cones on Thursday and Friday combined than he did on Monday.

ICE CREAM CONES SOLD PER DAY

Monday	🍦 🍦 🍦
Tuesday	🍦
Wednesday	🍦 🍦 🍦 🍦 🍦 🍦
Thursday	🍦 🍦 🍦
Friday	🍦 🍦 🍦 🍦

Based on the data, how many ice cream cones are represented by the 🍦 ?
(A)   4
(B)   5
(C)   6
(D)   7

The best way to answer these questions is by working backwards. If (A) is correct, the ice cream man sold 28 cones on Thursday and Friday combined (because 3 + 4 = 7, and 7 × 4 = 28) and 12 cones on Monday. 28 − 12 = 16, but the question says he sold 24 more cones on Thursday and Friday combined, so this answer is incorrect. Let's jump to (C). If (C) is correct, the ice cream man sold 42 cones on Thursday and Friday combined (because 3 + 4 = 7, and 7 × 6 = 42) and 18 cones on Monday. 42 − 18 = 24, so **(C) is the correct answer**.

If you don't want to work backwards, you should first find how many cones the ice cream man sold on Thursday and Friday combined. Based on the chart, there are 7 cones. On Monday, he sold 3 cones. 7 − 3 = 4, so there is a difference of 4 cones. Then, ask yourself "4 times what equals 24?" 4 × 6 = 24, so you know (C) is the correct answer.

Practice Problems

1. Dan recorded the number of toy dinosaurs he had in five different toy boxes. He counted 4 more toy dinosaurs in boxes 3, 4, and 5 combined than he did in box 2.

DINOSAURS PER TOY BOX

Based on the data, how many toy dinosaurs are represented by the ?

(A)   1
(B)   2
(C)   3
(D)   4

---

2. Rasmus recorded the number of hummingbirds at the bird feeder each day for five days. He spotted 3 more hummingbirds on Friday than he did on Monday and Thursday combined.

HUMMINGBIRDS SPOTTED EACH DAY

Based on the data, how many hummingbirds are represented by the ?

(A)   1
(B)   3
(C)   5
(D)   7

3. Emil recorded the number of ladybugs on a plant each day for five days. He spotted 16 more ladybugs on Thursday than he did on Wednesday.

LADYBUGS SPOTTED EACH DAY

Monday	🐞 🐞 🐞
Tuesday	🐞 🐞 🐞 🐞 🐞
Wednesday	🐞 🐞
Thursday	🐞 🐞 🐞 🐞 🐞 🐞
Friday	🐞 🐞 🐞

Based on the data, how many ladybugs are represented by the 🐞 ?

(A)   2
(B)   4
(C)   6
(D)   8

---

4. Lucy recorded the number of beakers in each of the 5 science labs at her high school. There were 15 more beakers in Room 5 than there were in Rooms 3 and 4 combined.

BEAKERS PER CLASSROOM

Room 1	🧪 🧪
Room 2	🧪 🧪 🧪 🧪
Room 3	🧪
Room 4	🧪
Room 5	🧪 🧪 🧪 🧪 🧪

Based on the data, how many beakers are represented by the ?

(A)   1
(B)   3
(C)   5
(D)   7

5. Teresa surveyed the students in 5 classrooms. She asked how many students per room took piano lessons. There were 9 more piano students in Rooms 2 and 4 combined than there were in Rooms 1 and 3 combined.

PIANISTS PER CLASSROOM

Based on the data, how many piano students are represented by the [piano] ?

(A)   1
(B)   3
(C)   5
(D)   7

6. Pippa recorded the number of lions she saw on a 5 day safari. She spotted 20 more lions on Tuesday than she did on Wednesday and Thursday combined.

LIONS SPOTTED EACH DAY

Based on the data, how many lions are represented by the [lion] ?

(A)   2
(B)   5
(C)   10
(D)   20

Observations

Observations questions test your knowledge of quantitative and qualitative data. Quantitative data can be counted, measured, or expressed using numbers, while qualitative data is categorized based on traits and characteristics.

Example #1

Malika's class spent time at the zoo collecting data about animals and their habitats. The students had to list, in categories or groups, what they observed.

> **MALIKA'S OBSERVATION LIST**
>
> 1. kinds of animals at the zoo: pandas, bears, crocodiles, deer, elephants
> 2. ?
> 3. food that the animals at the zoo eat: hay, meat, insects, nuts, berries

What information completes Malika's observation list?

(A)   dimensions of the animal cages at the zoo

(B)   colors of the animals at the zoo

(C)   number of animals at the zoo

(D)   ages of the animals at the zoo

So far, Malika has only collected *qualitative* data: data that is based on traits and characteristics. Therefore, the missing data must also be qualitative. Answer choices (A), (C), and (D) can all be measured or expressed with numbers. **The correct answer is (B)**.

Practice Problems

1.   Desiree collected data about gym members and their workouts. She listed the data she observed.

> **DESIREE'S OBSERVATION LIST**
>
> 1. number of exercises completed at the gym: 1-3, 4-6, 7+
> 2. heart rate of the gym members: 20-60 beats per minute (bpm), 60-100 bpm, 100+ bpm
> 3. ?

What information completes Desiree's observation list?

(A)   lengths of workouts at the gym

(B)   colors of outfits worn by gym members

(C)   names of the exercises completed at the gym

(D)   kinds of beverages preferred at the gym

2. A student recorded his observations about the other students in his class.

    ┌───┐
    │   OBSERVATION LIST   │
    │   │
    │   1. favorite subjects: history, math, science, English   │
    │   2. least favorite teacher: history teacher, math teacher, English teacher │
    │   3. ?   │
    └───┘

    What information completes the student's observation list?

    (A)   number of students in the class
    (B)   colors of the students' t-shirts
    (C)   ages of the students
    (D)   heights of the students

3. A teenager recorded his observations about the cars driving past his house.

    ┌───┐
    │   OBSERVATION LIST   │
    │   │
    │   1. number of cars that drove past   │
    │   2. speed of the cars driving past: 0-20 mph, 20-50 mph, 50+ mph │
    │   3. ?   │
    └───┘

    What information completes the teenager's observation list?

    (A)   colors of the cars that drove past
    (B)   makes and models of the cars that drove past
    (C)   number of Toyotas that drove past
    (D)   direction that the cars were driving

4. Joffrey's class spent time at the zoo collecting data about animals and their habitats. The students had to list, in categories or groups, what they observed.

    ┌───┐
    │   OBSERVATION LIST   │
    │   │
    │   1. ?   │
    │   2. number of animals at the zoo   │
    │   3. dimensions of the zoo cages   │
    └───┘

    What information completes Joffrey's observation list?

    (A)   types of animals at the zoo
    (B)   ages of the animals at the zoo
    (C)   colors of the animals at the zoo
    (D)   types of food eaten by the animals at the zoo

5. Rolph recorded his observations about the weather for a week.

    ┌──┐
    │   OBSERVATION LIST   │
    │   │
    │   1. daily temperatures: 0-40 degrees, 40-80 degrees, 80+ degrees │
    │   2. sunset times   │
    │   3. ?   │
    └──┘

    What information completes Rolph's observation list?

    (A)   types of precipitation
    (B)   wind direction
    (C)   total hours of sunlight per day
    (D)   types of clouds

6. A bodybuilder recorded information about the members at her gym.

    ┌──┐
    │   OBSERVATION LIST   │
    │   │
    │   1. kinds of beverages preferred: water, protein shake, milk, soda │
    │   2. ?   │
    │   3. types of exercises completed: chest and back, biceps, legs, abs │
    └──┘

    What information completes the bodybuilder's observation list?

    (A)   weights of the gym members
    (B)   number of exercises completed
    (C)   minutes spent working out
    (D)   color of clothing worn

7. Cassie recorded her observations about her classmates' internet habits.

    ┌──┐
    │   OBSERVATION LIST   │
    │   │
    │   1. average number of minutes spent online each day   │
    │   2. number of sites visited each day   │
    │   3. ?   │
    └──┘

    What information completes Cassie's observation list?

    (A)   purpose of going online
    (B)   who each student interacted with on social media
    (C)   types of sites visited each day
    (D)   number of posts on social media sites each day

Answer Key - Mathematics Question Types

Fractions	Applied Mean, Median, Mode, and Range	Applied Rates and Ratios	Perimeter and Area
1. A	1. A	1. C	1. D
2. D	2. B	2. C	2. B
3. B	3. B	3. A	3. C
4. C	4. B	4. D	4. D
5. C	5. C	5. A	5. C
6. C	6. D	6. D	6. B
7. C	7. C	7. D	7. B
8. D	8. D	8. B	8. D
9. A	9. B	9. C	9. C
10. A	10. C	10. B	10. A
11. D	11. A	11. D	11. C
12. B	12. B	12. A	12. B
13. B	13. C	13. D	13. D
14. C	14. C	14. B	14. A
15. A	15. C	15. D	15. B
16. D	16. A	16. A	16. D
17. C	17. B		17. A
18. B	18. B		18. C
19. C	19. B		19. D
20. C	20. A		20. C
21. A	21. A		21. B
22. A	22. A		22. D
23. B	23. C		23. D
24. B	24. B		24. A
25. C	25. C		25. B
26. D	26. B		26. B
	27. C		27. A
	28. D		28. B
			29. B
			30. B
			31. B
			32. C
			33. A
			34. A
			35. B
			36. D
			37. A
			38. A
			39. D
			40. C

Estimating

1. B
2. B
3. C
4. D
5. B
6. C
7. D
8. A
9. C
10. A
11. B
12. C
13. B
14. A
15. D
16. A
17. C
18. A
19. C
20. A
21. D
22. B
23. C
24. B
25. A
26. D

Patterns

1. B
2. C
3. C
4. D
5. C
6. D
7. B
8. C
9. B
10. A
11. A
12. D
13. D
14. D
15. C

Coordinate Grids

1. B
2. C
3. D
4. C
5. B
6. A
7. D
8. D
9. A
10. D
11. A
12. D
13. A
14. D
15. B
16. A
17. B
18. A
19. D
20. C

Graphs

1. B
2. C
3. B
4. B
5. C
6. D
7. B
8. C
9. A
10. D
11. C
12. D
13. B
14. B
15. D
16. B
17. C
18. A
19. B
20. B
21. B

Function Machines

1. D
2. C
3. C
4. D
5. C
6. A
7. D
8. D
9. A
10. A
11. D
12. C
13. B
14. C
15. C
16. D
17. A
18. A

Math Stories

1. C
2. C
3. D
4. A
5. A
6. B
7. A
8. B
9. A
10. A
11. D
12. D
13. D
14. C
15. B
16. C
17. B
18. C

Number Theory

1. D
2. D
3. B
4. B
5. A
6. C
7. C
8. C
9. A
10. B
11. A
12. C
13. B
14. C
15. B
16. D
17. B
18. C

Measurement

1. C
2. B
3. A
4. D
5. D
6. B
7. A
8. C
9. B
10. D
11. B
12. B
13. A
14. C
15. B
16. A
17. B

Shapes

1. B
2. C
3. B
4. A
5. D
6. D
7. A
8. D
9. A
10. B
11. D
12. B

Reflections

1. A
2. B
3. D
4. B
5. D
6. C
7. A
8. D
9. D
10. C
11. A
12. D
13. D
14. C

Decimals

1. B
2. A
3. B
4. A
5. A
6. C
7. C
8. C
9. D
10. B
11. D
12. A
13. C
14. C
15. B
16. A
17. A
18. D
19. B
20. B
21. D
22. C

Venn Diagrams

1. D
2. D
3. B
4. B
5. A
6. C
7. C
8. A
9. C
10. B
11. A
12. A

Number Lines

1. A
2. A
3. D
4. C
5. B
6. C
7. A
8. A
9. C
10. A

Scales

1. C
2. B
3. B
4. C
5. D
6. A
7. C
8. C

Tables

1. C
2. C
3. A
4. C
5. C
6. D
7. B
8. B
9. C
10. C
11. D
12. D
13. B
14. A
15. C
16. A

Times Zones

1. C
2. D
3. A
4. B
5. C
6. B
7. C
8. D
9. A

Charts

1. B
2. B
3. B
4. C
5. B
6. D

Observations

1. A
2. B
3. C
4. B
5. C
6. D
7. D

Part V
*Lower Level ISEE
Mathematics Practice Tests*

Chapter 5
Quantitative Reasoning
Practice Test #1

Section 2
Quantitative Reasoning

35 Questions   **Time: 34 minutes**

Each question is followed by four suggested answers. Read each question and then decide which one of the four suggested answers is best.

Find the row of spaces on your answer document that has the same answer as the question. In this row, mark the space having the same letter as the answer you have chosen. The answer document can be found after Mathematics Achievement Practice Test #1. You may write in your test booklet.

EXAMPLE 1:   Sample Answer
                                                    Ⓐ Ⓑ ● Ⓓ

What is the value of the expression $4 + (2 \times 8) \div (1 + 3)$?

(A)   0
(B)   4
(C)   8
(D)   16

The correct answer is 8, so circle C is darkened.

STOP. Do not go on
until told to do so. **STOP**

QR Practice Test #1

1. What portion of the figure below is shaded?

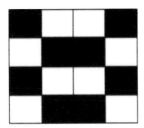

   (A) $\frac{6}{16}$

   (B) $\frac{4}{8}$

   (C) $\frac{3}{8}$

   (D) $\frac{8}{8}$

2. Which story best fits the equation $4 \times 9 = 36$?

   (A) I have 4 pieces of candy, and my friend gives me 9 more pieces of candy. How many pieces of candy do I have now?

   (B) I have 36 pieces of candy, and I want to divide the candy equally among 4 friends. How many pieces of candy does each friend get?

   (C) I have 9 friends, and I want to give each friend 4 pieces of candy. How many pieces of candy do I give away?

   (D) I have 9 pieces of candy, and I give away 4 pieces. How many pieces of candy do I have now?

3. Noam wrote down a whole number greater than 23 and less than 27. When Weiwei tried to guess the number, Noam told her it was greater than 24 and less than 28, and that the number is not 26. What is Noam's number?

   (A) 24

   (B) 25

   (C) 26

   (D) 27

4. The perimeter of the triangle is 36 centimeters. The lengths of two of the sides are shown.

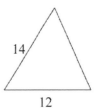

   What is the length of the third side?

   (A) 10 centimeters

   (B) 11 centimeters

   (C) 12 centimeters

   (D) 13 centimeters

5. Use the equations to answer the question.

$$2x + 1 = 7$$
$$5 + y = 10$$

   What is the sum of $x + y$?

   (A) 2

   (B) 3

   (C) 5

   (D) 8

Go on to the next page. ➡

QR Practice Test #1

6. Use the diagram to answer the question.

Which piece would complete the diagram to make a square?

(A)

(B)

(C)

(D)

7. Peter and Jessie were hiking at the same speed on a trail. It took Peter 32 minutes to hike 2 miles. How long did it take Jessie to hike 11 miles?
   (A)   16 minutes
   (B)   176 minutes
   (C)   192 minutes
   (D)   208 minutes

8. Which is the largest fraction?

   (A) $\frac{1}{8}$

   (B) $\frac{1}{10}$

   (C) $\frac{1}{7}$

   (D) $\frac{1}{9}$

9. If q can be divided by both 5 and 8 without leaving a remainder, then q can also be divided by which number without leaving a remainder?
   (A)   13
   (B)   20
   (C)   32
   (D)   70

10. Use the data set and the Venn diagram below to answer the question.

$$\{3, 5, 6, 12, 14, 21, 30, 33\}$$

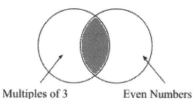

How many numbers belong in the shaded section of the diagram?
   (A)   3
   (B)   4
   (C)   5
   (D)   6

Go on to the next page. ➡

QR Practice Test #1

11. A science teacher asked his class to do an experiment. Each student placed three reactants in three separate beakers filled with different solutions. Over time, the reactants combined with the solution, leading to a decrease in the mass of reactant in each beaker. The class collected the data shown below.

SCIENCE EXPERIMENT

	Reactant 1	Reactant 2	Reactant 3
Start	50.00 mg	50.00 mg	50.00 mg
10 min	47.00 mg	49.50 mg	49.00 mg
20 min	44.00 mg	49.00 mg	47.00 mg
30 min	41.00 mg	48.50 mg	44.00 mg
40 min	38.00 mg	48.00 mg	40.00 mg
50 min	35.00 mg	47.50 mg	35.00 mg

According to the pattern from these data, what would be the predicted milligrams of Reactant 1 remaining after 80 minutes?

(A)   15
(B)   20
(C)   26
(D)   46

12. Use the table to determine the rule.

Input ▲	Output ■
5	8
9	20
10	23
15	38

What is the rule for the function?

(A)   ▲ × 3 − 7 = ■
(B)   ▲ + 3 = ■
(C)   ▲ + 4 = ■
(D)   ▲ × 3 + 7 = ■

13. The perimeter of a square is $40y$. What is the length of one side?

(A)   4
(B) $4y$
(C)   10
(D) $10y$

14. What is the value of x in the math equation $4x + 9 = 41$?

(A)   7
(B)   8
(C)   9
(D)   10

15. Use the pattern to help answer the question.

$$1 + 3 = 2^2$$
$$1 + 3 + 5 = 3^2$$
$$1 + 3 + 5 + 7 = 4^2$$

If the pattern continues, what will be the solution to the 10th row of the pattern?

(A) 10^2
(B) 11^2
(C) 12^2
(D) 13^2

Go on to the next page. ➡

QR Practice Test #1

16. A survey of 80 students' favorite ice cream flavors is displayed on the circle graph shown.

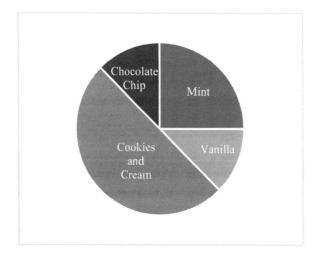

About what fraction of the students chose Vanilla as their favorite flavor?

(A) $\frac{1}{8}$

(B) $\frac{1}{4}$

(C) $\frac{1}{2}$

(D) $\frac{3}{4}$

---

17. A cat had a litter of 4 kittens. Two of the kittens weighed $4\frac{1}{2}$ ounces each, 1 kitten weighed 2 ounces, and 1 kitten weighed 5 ounces. What is the mean weight of the kittens from the litter?

(A) $3\frac{1}{2}$ ounces

(B)   4 ounces

(C) $4\frac{1}{2}$ ounces

(D)   5 ounces

18. Use the number line below to answer the question.

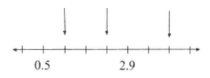

Which three numbers are the vertical arrows pointing to on the number line?
(A)   0.6, 0.8, 4.1
(B)   0.6, 0.8, 3.1
(C)   1.1, 2.2, 4.0
(D)   1.1, 2.3, 4.1

Go on to the next page. ➡

QR Practice Test #1

19. Use the figure below to answer the question.

   If three more rows were added to the figure, how many small triangles would the sixth row have, assuming the same pattern continues?
   (A)   6
   (B)   7
   (C)   9
   (D)   11

20. The length of *HJ* is *x* and the length of *IJ* is *y*.

   What is the length of *HI*?
   (A) $x - y$
   (B) $x + y$
   (C) $y - x$
   (D) xy

21. Stevenson was buying pencils. He bought 14 packs, and each pack had 33 pencils in it. Which expression shows about how many pencils he bought?
   (A) 10×40
   (B) 15×30
   (C) 10×30
   (D) 15×40

22. What is the length of one side of a cube whose volume is 216 in³?
   (A)   2 inches
   (B)   6 inches
   (C)   8 inches
   (D)   36 inches

23. Jar 1 and Jar 2 each hold 1 cup of liquid when filled to the top. The jars shown are not completely filled to the top.

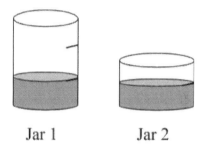

   Jar 1   Jar 2

   If the liquids in the two jars are combined, approximately how much liquid will there be altogether?
   (A)   0.5 cups
   (B)   0.8 cups
   (C)   1.0 cup
   (D)   1.5 cups

24. What is the area of the triangle shown below?

   9 cm

   10 cm

   (A)   19 square centimeters
   (B)   38 square centimeters
   (C)   45 square centimeters
   (D)   90 square centimeters

Go on to the next page. ➡

25. The figure shown may be folded along one or more of the dotted lines.

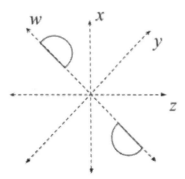

Which line or pair of lines, when folded, will allow the semicircles to exactly match the original figure?

(A)   line *w* only
(B)   line *y* only
(C)   both line *w* and line *z*
(D)   both line *w* and line *y*

26. The ingredients in the recipe were evenly mixed and equally divided into 3 bags.

RECIPE

1 cup of almonds
2 cups of dried banana chips
4 cups of peanuts
6 cups of chocolate chips
1 cup of sunflower seeds

Approximately how many cups of the mixture were placed in each bag?

(A) $3\frac{1}{3}$

(B) $3\frac{2}{3}$

(C)   4

(D) $4\frac{2}{3}$

27. A teacher put the names of all of her students into a hat. The probability that she will pull out a girl's name is 7 out of 9. There are 14 boys in the class. How many girls are in the class?

(A)   7
(B)   14
(C)   49
(D)   55

28. The total combined weight of a sphere, a pyramid, and a cube is 36 grams. If the pyramid weighs the same as 7 spheres and the cube weighs the same as 10 spheres, how many grams does the pyramid weigh?

(A)   2 grams
(B)   14 grams
(C)   20 grams
(D)   24 grams

29. Use the figure shown to answer the question.

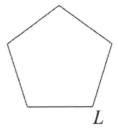

How many triangular regions can be made in the figure by only drawing line segments from vertex *L* to the other vertices?

(A)   3
(B)   4
(C)   5
(D)   6

Go on to the next page. ➡

QR Practice Test #1

30. Four students recorded the number of minutes spent watching TV at home for one night and recorded their data in the graph shown.

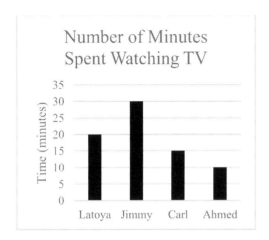

Number of Minutes Spent Watching TV

Based on the graph, which conclusion is true about the number of minutes spent watching TV?
(A)　Jimmy watched fewer minutes than Latoya
(B)　The mean is between 18 and 19
(C)　The range is greater than the number of minutes Latoya watched
(D)　Latoya watched the same number of minutes as Carl and Ahmed combined

31. Which equation can be read as "2 more than 5 times a number equals 8 less than 4 divided by that number" Let n represent the unknown number.

(A)　$(5 \times n) + 2 = \frac{4}{n} - 8$

(B)　$(5 \times n) + 2 = \frac{n}{4} - 8$

(C)　$(5 \times n) + 2 = \frac{4}{n} + 8$

(D)　$(5 \times n) - 2 = \frac{4}{n} - 8$

32. Samantha has a box of chocolates with different cream fillings: caramel, vanilla, cinnamon, orange, and cocoa. The probability of choosing a chocolate filled with vanilla is 9 out of 20. What combination of chocolates is possible?
(A)　9 vanilla and 11 others
(B)　9 vanilla and 20 others
(C)　11 vanilla and 20 others
(D)　18 vanilla and 60 others

33. A student did the problem shown on his calculator.

$$\frac{578 \times 111}{52}$$

What is a reasonable estimation for his answer?
(A)　between 1,000 and 1,250
(B)　between 1,250 and 1,450
(C)　between 1,450 and 1,650
(D)　between 1,650 and 1,850

34. What is the value of n in the expression

$$\frac{15(10 + 60)}{5} = n?$$

(A)　200
(B)　210
(C)　220
(D)　230

35. Use the number line below to answer the question.

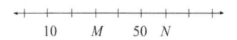

M is the average of N and another number. What is the other number?
(A)　0
(B)　30
(C)　60
(D)　90

Go on to the next page. ➡

Chapter 6
Mathematics Achievement
Practice Test #1

Section 4
Mathematics Achievement

25 Questions   **Time: 25 minutes**

Each question is followed by four suggested answers. Read each question and then decide which one of the four suggested answers is best.

Find the row of spaces on your answer document that has the same answer as the question. In this row, mark the space having the same letter as the answer you have chosen. The answer document can be found after Mathematics Achievement Practice Test #1. You may write in your test booklet.

EXAMPLE 1:   Sample Answer
                                                    Ⓐ Ⓑ ● Ⓓ

    What is the value of the expression $4 + (2 \times 8) \div (1 + 3)$?

    (A) 0
    (B) 4
    (C) 8
    (D) 16

    The correct answer is 8, so circle C is darkened.

STOP. Do not go on
until told to do so. **STOP**

MA Practice Test #1

1. Use the triangle to answer the question.

    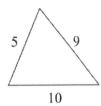

    What is the perimeter of the triangle?
    ($P = s + s + s$)
    (A)   21
    (B)   22
    (C)   23
    (D)   24

2. A total of 33 students were asked which one of three snacks – potato chips, pretzels, or yogurt – they preferred. If 14 students said they preferred potato chips, and 6 students said they preferred pretzels, how many students said they preferred yogurt?
    (A)   12
    (B)   13
    (C)   19
    (D)   27

3. What is the name of a quadrilateral with 2 adjacent sides that are each 2 cm in length, and another two adjacent sides that are each 4 cm in length?
    (A)   square
    (B)   rectangle
    (C)   kite
    (D)   pentagon

4. What is the standard form for three hundred six thousand fifty two?
    (A)   306,052
    (B)   306,520
    (C)   360,052
    (D)   360,520

5. A coordinate graph is shown.

    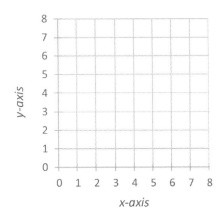

    A student plotted the following points on the coordinate grid.

    Point E (6,6); Point F (4,4); Point G (6,0); Point H (8,4)

    A polygon is formed with vertices E, F, G, and H and sides $\overline{EF}$, $\overline{FG}$, $\overline{GH}$, and $\overline{HE}$. Which type of polygon is formed?
    (A)   trapezoid
    (B)   rhombus
    (C)   kite
    (D)   square

6. Which expression is equal to 30?
    (A) $(6 \times 6) + 2 - 8$
    (B) $6 \times (6 + 2) - 8$
    (C) $6 \times 6 + (8 - 2)$
    (D) $6 \times (6 + 2 - 8)$

7. Which fraction is equivalent to 0.2?

    (A) $\dfrac{2}{100}$

    (B) $\dfrac{1}{5}$

    (C) $\dfrac{1}{4}$

    (D) $\dfrac{2}{20}$

Go on to the next page. ➡

MA Practice Test #1

8. For a science experiment, a class put 15 fruit flies into each of three test tubes. They added a different food source to each test tube. Each day, the class counted how many fruit flies were in each test tube. The class recorded the results in the table below.

SCIENCE EXPERIMENT

	Tube 1	Tube 2	Tube 3
Start	15	15	15
Day 1	17	20	21
Day 2	19	25	27
Day 3	21	30	33
Day 4	23	35	39
Day 5	25	40	45

On Day 5, how many more fruit flies were there in Tube 3 than in Tube 2?
(A)   5
(B)   10
(C)   15
(D)   20

9. What is the value of the expression 3,000 − 482?
(A)   2,418
(B)   2,518
(C)   2,618
(D)   3,482

10. If $4 \times (\blacktriangle + 6) = 40$, what number does $\blacktriangle$ stand for?
(A)   1
(B)   2
(C)   3
(D)   4

11. A lake has an area of about 38,150 mi². Which area is closest to that of $\frac{1}{2}$ of the lake's area?
(A)   19,000 mi²
(B)   21,000 mi²
(C)   23,000 mi²
(D)   25,000 mi²

12. The table shows items that a man bought at the grocery store. He bought at least one of each item on the list.

GROCERY LIST

Item	Price for One	Total Cost for Items
orange	$0.75	$2.25
juice	$2.50	$2.50
pear	$1.00	$6.00
candy	$0.25	$2.25

What is the total number of items the man purchased?
(A)   19
(B)   20
(C)   21
(D)   22

Go on to the next page. ➡

MA Practice Test #1

13. A student buys five items costing $4.95, $2.99, $16.75, $0.50, and $6.99. What is the estimated total cost of the student's items?
    (A)   between $20 and $25
    (B)   between $25 and $30
    (C)   between $30 and $35
    (D)   between $35 and $40

14. What is the name of a quadrilateral with no 90-degree angles, one pair of adjacent sides that are 4 cm, and another pair of adjacent sides that are 6 cm?
    (A)   square
    (B)   kite
    (C)   trapezoid
    (D)   rhombus

15. Use the diagram to answer the question.

    If one of the marbles is picked up at random, what is the chance it will be black?
    (A)   1 out of 5
    (B)   7 out of 10
    (C)   3 out of 7
    (D)   3 out of 10

16. What fraction is between $\frac{7}{10}$ and $\frac{90}{100}$?
    (A) $\frac{5}{8}$

    (B) $\frac{1}{2}$

    (C) $\frac{3}{5}$

    (D) $\frac{17}{20}$

17. RASIKA'S SCHOOL SCORES

Event 1	6.7	8.2	3.9	6.7
Event 2	9.8	8.2	6.7	6.6
Event 3	9.4	6.7	6.6	9.1
Event 4	6.7	5.8	8.2	7.0

    What is the range of the data?
    (A)   4.6
    (B)   5.5
    (C)   5.9
    (D)   6.9

18. Use the set of numbers shown to answer the question.

$$\{0, 2, 8, 9, 12, 15\}$$

    Which describes the set of numbers?
    (A)   even numbers
    (B)   whole numbers
    (C)   composite numbers
    (D)   prime numbers

19. If the area of a triangle is 40 cm², which equation can be used to determine the base of that triangle? ($A = \frac{bh}{2}$, where A = Area, b = base, and h = height.)

    (A) $b = h - 38$

    (B) $b = 38 - h$

    (C) $b = \frac{80}{h}$

    (D) $b = \frac{h}{80}$

20. What is the perimeter of a rectangle that has a length of 4 inches and a width of 7 inches? ($P = 2l + 2w$)
    (A)   11 inches
    (B)   14 inches
    (C)   22 inches
    (D)   28 inches

Go on to the next page. ➡

MA Practice Test #1

21. Use the Time Zone map to answer the question.

An airplane leaves Little Rock at 11:00 A.M. and arrives 2 hours later in Tampa. What time is it in Tampa?

(A)   1 P.M.
(B)   2 P.M.
(C)   3 P.M.
(D)   4 P.M.

22. What are the coordinates of point E below?

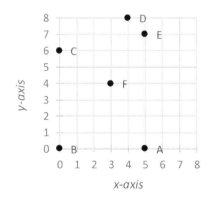

(A)   (0,0)
(B)   (4,4)
(C)   (5,0)
(D)   (5,7)

23. Use the number sequence to answer the question.

1, 2, 5, 10, 17, 26, _____

What is the next number in the sequence?

(A)   36
(B)   37
(C)   38
(D)   39

Go on to the next page. ➡

24. What is the sum of $4.4 + 1.8$?

    (A) $5\frac{2}{5}$

    (B) $5\frac{2}{10}$

    (C) $6\frac{1}{5}$

    (D) $6\frac{2}{5}$

25. Jaime has $4\frac{3}{8}$ feet of wire. He used $2\frac{1}{2}$ feet of the wire to make a lamp. How many feet of wire does he have left?

    (A) $1\frac{7}{8}$

    (B) $2\frac{1}{4}$

    (C) $2\frac{3}{8}$

    (D) $2\frac{7}{8}$

Go on to the next page. ➡

Name:

Test Site:

Room:

EXAM LEVEL
LOWER Ⓛ
MIDDLE Ⓜ
UPPER Ⓤ

FORM

⓪⓪
①①
②②
③③
④④
⑤⑤
⑥⑥
⑦⑦
⑧⑧
⑨⑨

ADMINISTRATORS ONLY

TESTING WITH ACCOMMODATIONS ◯ Yes

MARKING INSTRUCTIONS

* Use a #2 or HB pencil only on pages 1 and 2.
* Use a ballpoint pen for your essay on pages 3 and 4.
* Make dark marks that completely fill the circle.
* Erase cleanly any mark you wish to change.
* Make no stray marks on this form.
* Do not fold or crease this form.

CORRECT MARK   INCORRECT MARKS

Bubble in the first four letters of your last name.

LAST NAME

IDENTIFICATION NUMBER

❶ **VERBAL REASONING**

1 Ⓐ Ⓑ Ⓒ Ⓓ   15 Ⓐ Ⓑ Ⓒ Ⓓ   29 Ⓐ Ⓑ Ⓒ Ⓓ

2 Ⓐ Ⓑ Ⓒ Ⓓ   16 Ⓐ Ⓑ Ⓒ Ⓓ   30 Ⓐ Ⓑ Ⓒ Ⓓ

3 Ⓐ Ⓑ Ⓒ Ⓓ   17 Ⓐ Ⓑ Ⓒ Ⓓ   31 Ⓐ Ⓑ Ⓒ Ⓓ

4 Ⓐ Ⓑ Ⓒ Ⓓ   18 Ⓐ Ⓑ Ⓒ Ⓓ   32 Ⓐ Ⓑ Ⓒ Ⓓ

5 Ⓐ Ⓑ Ⓒ Ⓓ   19 Ⓐ Ⓑ Ⓒ Ⓓ   33 Ⓐ Ⓑ Ⓒ Ⓓ

6 Ⓐ Ⓑ Ⓒ Ⓓ   20 Ⓐ Ⓑ Ⓒ Ⓓ   34 Ⓐ Ⓑ Ⓒ Ⓓ

Lower Level Ends

7 Ⓐ Ⓑ Ⓒ Ⓓ   21 Ⓐ Ⓑ Ⓒ Ⓓ   35 Ⓐ Ⓑ Ⓒ Ⓓ

8 Ⓐ Ⓑ Ⓒ Ⓓ   22 Ⓐ Ⓑ Ⓒ Ⓓ   36 Ⓐ Ⓑ Ⓒ Ⓓ

9 Ⓐ Ⓑ Ⓒ Ⓓ   23 Ⓐ Ⓑ Ⓒ Ⓓ   37 Ⓐ Ⓑ Ⓒ Ⓓ

10 Ⓐ Ⓑ Ⓒ Ⓓ   24 Ⓐ Ⓑ Ⓒ Ⓓ   38 Ⓐ Ⓑ Ⓒ Ⓓ

11 Ⓐ Ⓑ Ⓒ Ⓓ   25 Ⓐ Ⓑ Ⓒ Ⓓ   39 Ⓐ Ⓑ Ⓒ Ⓓ

12 Ⓐ Ⓑ Ⓒ Ⓓ   26 Ⓐ Ⓑ Ⓒ Ⓓ   40 Ⓐ Ⓑ Ⓒ Ⓓ

Middle/Upper Level Ends

13 Ⓐ Ⓑ Ⓒ Ⓓ   27 Ⓐ Ⓑ Ⓒ Ⓓ

14 Ⓐ Ⓑ Ⓒ Ⓓ   28 Ⓐ Ⓑ Ⓒ Ⓓ

PLEASE DO NOT WRITE IN THIS AREA

❷ QUANTITATIVE REASONING

1 Ⓐ Ⓑ Ⓒ Ⓓ	15 Ⓐ Ⓑ Ⓒ Ⓓ	29 Ⓐ Ⓑ Ⓒ Ⓓ
2 Ⓐ Ⓑ Ⓒ Ⓓ	16 Ⓐ Ⓑ Ⓒ Ⓓ	30 Ⓐ Ⓑ Ⓒ Ⓓ
3 Ⓐ Ⓑ Ⓒ Ⓓ	17 Ⓐ Ⓑ Ⓒ Ⓓ	31 Ⓐ Ⓑ Ⓒ Ⓓ
4 Ⓐ Ⓑ Ⓒ Ⓓ	18 Ⓐ Ⓑ Ⓒ Ⓓ	32 Ⓐ Ⓑ Ⓒ Ⓓ
5 Ⓐ Ⓑ Ⓒ Ⓓ	19 Ⓐ Ⓑ Ⓒ Ⓓ	33 Ⓐ Ⓑ Ⓒ Ⓓ
6 Ⓐ Ⓑ Ⓒ Ⓓ	20 Ⓐ Ⓑ Ⓒ Ⓓ	34 Ⓐ Ⓑ Ⓒ Ⓓ
7 Ⓐ Ⓑ Ⓒ Ⓓ	21 Ⓐ Ⓑ Ⓒ Ⓓ	35 Ⓐ Ⓑ Ⓒ Ⓓ
8 Ⓐ Ⓑ Ⓒ Ⓓ	22 Ⓐ Ⓑ Ⓒ Ⓓ	36 Ⓐ Ⓑ Ⓒ Ⓓ
9 Ⓐ Ⓑ Ⓒ Ⓓ	23 Ⓐ Ⓑ Ⓒ Ⓓ	37 Ⓐ Ⓑ Ⓒ Ⓓ
		Middle/Upper Level Ends
10 Ⓐ Ⓑ Ⓒ Ⓓ	24 Ⓐ Ⓑ Ⓒ Ⓓ	38 Ⓐ Ⓑ Ⓒ Ⓓ
		Lower Level Ends
11 Ⓐ Ⓑ Ⓒ Ⓓ	25 Ⓐ Ⓑ Ⓒ Ⓓ	
12 Ⓐ Ⓑ Ⓒ Ⓓ	26 Ⓐ Ⓑ Ⓒ Ⓓ	
13 Ⓐ Ⓑ Ⓒ Ⓓ	27 Ⓐ Ⓑ Ⓒ Ⓓ	
14 Ⓐ Ⓑ Ⓒ Ⓓ	28 Ⓐ Ⓑ Ⓒ Ⓓ	

❸ READING COMPREHENSION

1 Ⓐ Ⓑ Ⓒ Ⓓ	15 Ⓐ Ⓑ Ⓒ Ⓓ	29 Ⓐ Ⓑ Ⓒ Ⓓ
2 Ⓐ Ⓑ Ⓒ Ⓓ	16 Ⓐ Ⓑ Ⓒ Ⓓ	30 Ⓐ Ⓑ Ⓒ Ⓓ
3 Ⓐ Ⓑ Ⓒ Ⓓ	17 Ⓐ Ⓑ Ⓒ Ⓓ	31 Ⓐ Ⓑ Ⓒ Ⓓ
4 Ⓐ Ⓑ Ⓒ Ⓓ	18 Ⓐ Ⓑ Ⓒ Ⓓ	32 Ⓐ Ⓑ Ⓒ Ⓓ
5 Ⓐ Ⓑ Ⓒ Ⓓ	19 Ⓐ Ⓑ Ⓒ Ⓓ	33 Ⓐ Ⓑ Ⓒ Ⓓ
6 Ⓐ Ⓑ Ⓒ Ⓓ	20 Ⓐ Ⓑ Ⓒ Ⓓ	34 Ⓐ Ⓑ Ⓒ Ⓓ
7 Ⓐ Ⓑ Ⓒ Ⓓ	21 Ⓐ Ⓑ Ⓒ Ⓓ	35 Ⓐ Ⓑ Ⓒ Ⓓ
8 Ⓐ Ⓑ Ⓒ Ⓓ	22 Ⓐ Ⓑ Ⓒ Ⓓ	36 Ⓐ Ⓑ Ⓒ Ⓓ
9 Ⓐ Ⓑ Ⓒ Ⓓ	23 Ⓐ Ⓑ Ⓒ Ⓓ	Middle/Upper Level Ends
10 Ⓐ Ⓑ Ⓒ Ⓓ	24 Ⓐ Ⓑ Ⓒ Ⓓ	
11 Ⓐ Ⓑ Ⓒ Ⓓ	25 Ⓐ Ⓑ Ⓒ Ⓓ	
	Lower Level Ends	
12 Ⓐ Ⓑ Ⓒ Ⓓ	26 Ⓐ Ⓑ Ⓒ Ⓓ	
13 Ⓐ Ⓑ Ⓒ Ⓓ	27 Ⓐ Ⓑ Ⓒ Ⓓ	
14 Ⓐ Ⓑ Ⓒ Ⓓ	28 Ⓐ Ⓑ Ⓒ Ⓓ	

❹ MATHEMATICS ACHIEVEMENT

1 Ⓐ Ⓑ Ⓒ Ⓓ	18 Ⓐ Ⓑ Ⓒ Ⓓ	35 Ⓐ Ⓑ Ⓒ Ⓓ
2 Ⓐ Ⓑ Ⓒ Ⓓ	19 Ⓐ Ⓑ Ⓒ Ⓓ	36 Ⓐ Ⓑ Ⓒ Ⓓ
3 Ⓐ Ⓑ Ⓒ Ⓓ	20 Ⓐ Ⓑ Ⓒ Ⓓ	37 Ⓐ Ⓑ Ⓒ Ⓓ
4 Ⓐ Ⓑ Ⓒ Ⓓ	21 Ⓐ Ⓑ Ⓒ Ⓓ	38 Ⓐ Ⓑ Ⓒ Ⓓ
5 Ⓐ Ⓑ Ⓒ Ⓓ	22 Ⓐ Ⓑ Ⓒ Ⓓ	39 Ⓐ Ⓑ Ⓒ Ⓓ
6 Ⓐ Ⓑ Ⓒ Ⓓ	23 Ⓐ Ⓑ Ⓒ Ⓓ	40 Ⓐ Ⓑ Ⓒ Ⓓ
7 Ⓐ Ⓑ Ⓒ Ⓓ	24 Ⓐ Ⓑ Ⓒ Ⓓ	41 Ⓐ Ⓑ Ⓒ Ⓓ
8 Ⓐ Ⓑ Ⓒ Ⓓ	25 Ⓐ Ⓑ Ⓒ Ⓓ	42 Ⓐ Ⓑ Ⓒ Ⓓ
9 Ⓐ Ⓑ Ⓒ Ⓓ	26 Ⓐ Ⓑ Ⓒ Ⓓ	43 Ⓐ Ⓑ Ⓒ Ⓓ
10 Ⓐ Ⓑ Ⓒ Ⓓ	27 Ⓐ Ⓑ Ⓒ Ⓓ	44 Ⓐ Ⓑ Ⓒ Ⓓ
11 Ⓐ Ⓑ Ⓒ Ⓓ	28 Ⓐ Ⓑ Ⓒ Ⓓ	45 Ⓐ Ⓑ Ⓒ Ⓓ
12 Ⓐ Ⓑ Ⓒ Ⓓ	29 Ⓐ Ⓑ Ⓒ Ⓓ	46 Ⓐ Ⓑ Ⓒ Ⓓ
13 Ⓐ Ⓑ Ⓒ Ⓓ	30 Ⓐ Ⓑ Ⓒ Ⓓ	47 Ⓐ Ⓑ Ⓒ Ⓓ
	Lower Level Ends	Middle/Upper Level Ends
14 Ⓐ Ⓑ Ⓒ Ⓓ	31 Ⓐ Ⓑ Ⓒ Ⓓ	
15 Ⓐ Ⓑ Ⓒ Ⓓ	32 Ⓐ Ⓑ Ⓒ Ⓓ	
16 Ⓐ Ⓑ Ⓒ Ⓓ	33 Ⓐ Ⓑ Ⓒ Ⓓ	
17 Ⓐ Ⓑ Ⓒ Ⓓ	34 Ⓐ Ⓑ Ⓒ Ⓓ	

PAGE 2

Chapter 7
*Quantitative Reasoning
Practice Test #2*

Section 2
Quantitative Reasoning

35 Questions	Time: 34 minutes

Each question is followed by four suggested answers. Read each question and then decide which one of the four suggested answers is best.

Find the row of spaces on your answer document that has the same answer as the question. In this row, mark the space having the same letter as the answer you have chosen. The answer document can be found after Mathematics Achievement Practice Test #2. You may write in your test booklet.

EXAMPLE 1:   <u>Sample Answer</u>

What is the value of the expression $4 + (2 \times 8) + (1 + 3)$?   Ⓐ Ⓑ ● Ⓓ

   (A)   0
   (B)   4
   (C)   8
   (D) 16

The correct answer is 8, so circle C is darkened.

STOP. Do not go on until told to do so.   **STOP**

QR Practice Test #2

1. Hugo brought some pieces of candy to school. He gave $\frac{1}{3}$ of the candy to his friend Daniel, and $\frac{1}{6}$ of the candy to his teacher. If Hugo's teacher got 3 pieces of candy from Hugo, how many pieces of candy did Daniel get?
   (A)   3
   (B)   4
   (C)   5
   (D)   6

2. Which story best fits the equation $44 \div 11 = 4$?

   (A)   I have 4 stickers, and my friend gives me 11 more stickers. How many total stickers do I have now?
   (B)   I have a sticker book. There are 4 pages, and each page has 11 stickers. How many total stickers do I have?
   (C)   I have 44 stickers, and I give exactly 11 stickers to each friend in my friend group. How many friends do I have?
   (D)   I have 44 stickers and I give 11 to a friend. How many stickers do I have left?

3. Fernanda wrote down a whole number greater than 1 and less than 4. When Antonella tried to guess the number, Fernanda told her it was greater than 2 and less than 5. What is Fernanda's number?
   (A)   1
   (B)   2
   (C)   3
   (D)   4

4. The perimeter of the triangle below is 17 centimeters. The lengths of two of the sides are shown.

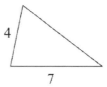

   What is the length of the third side?
   (A)   5 centimeters
   (B)   6 centimeters
   (C)   7 centimeters
   (D)   8 centimeters

5. Use the equations to answer the question.

$$3a - 5 = 25$$
$$2b + 4 = 14$$

   What is the difference of $a - b$?
   (A)   5
   (B)   10
   (C)   15
   (D)   20

6. The Venn diagram below shows what students ate for lunch today.

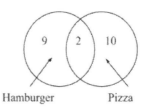

   How many students ate lunch today?
   (A)   2
   (B)   10
   (C)   19
   (D)   21

Go on to the next page. ➡

QR Practice Test #2

7. Use the diagram to answer the question.

Which piece would complete the diagram to make a square?

(A)

(B)

(C)

(D)

8. Which fraction is the least?

(A) $\frac{6}{11}$

(B) $\frac{4}{7}$

(C) $\frac{9}{19}$

(D) $\frac{8}{15}$

9. Saba and Christos were riding their bikes at the same speed on a bike path. It took Saba 15 minutes to ride 2.5 miles. How long did it take Christos to ride 7.5 miles?
   (A)   3 minutes
   (B)   6 minutes
   (C)   30 minutes
   (D)   45 minutes

10. If p can be divided by both 4 and 10 without leaving a remainder, then p can also be divided by which number without leaving a remainder?
    (A)   15
    (B)   20
    (C)   30
    (D)   44

11. Use the table to determine the rule.

Input ▲	Output ■
15	1
21	1
32	1
78	1

What is the rule for the function?
(A)   ▲ − 14 = ■
(B)   ▲ + 6 = ■
(C)   ▲ ÷ ▲ = ■
(D)   ▲ × ▲ = ■

12. The perimeter of a square is $60y$. What is the length of one side?
    (A)   15
    (B) $15y$
    (C)   30
    (D) $30y$

Go on to the next page. ➡

QR Practice Test #2

13. For a science experiment, a class put 15 fruit flies into each of three test tubes. They added a different food source to each test tube. Each day, the class counted how many fruit flies were in each test tube. The class recorded the results in the table below.

SCIENCE EXPERIMENT

	Tube 1	Tube 2	Tube 3
Start	15	15	15
Day 1	17	16	16
Day 2	19	17	18
Day 3	21	18	21
Day 4	23	19	25
Day 5	25	20	30

According to the pattern from these data, what would be the predicted number of fruit flies in Tube 3 on Day 7?
(A)   35
(B)   36
(C)   42
(D)   43

14. What is the value of z in the math equation $2z - 3 = 9$?
(A)   5
(B)   6
(C)   7
(D)   8

15. A student is selling cookies at a fundraiser.

Day	Bars Sold
Monday	4
Tuesday	11
Wednesday	18

If the pattern continues, how many cookies will the student sell on Friday?
(A)   25
(B)   27
(C)   32
(D)   33

16. The length of XY is m and the length of YZ is n.

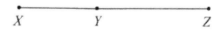

What is the length of XZ?
(A) $m - n$
(B) $m + n$
(C) $n - m$
(D) nm

17. Which diagram best represents the associative property?
(A) $\blacktriangle \times (\blacksquare + \bullet) =$
       $(\blacktriangle \times \blacksquare) + (\blacktriangle \times \bullet)$
(B) $\blacktriangle \times 1 = \blacktriangle$
(C) $\blacktriangle + \bullet = \bullet + \blacktriangle$
(D) $(\blacktriangle + \bullet) + \blacksquare = \blacktriangle + (\bullet + \blacksquare)$

Go on to the next page. ➡

18. The chart below shows the number of students in grades 8 – 12 at a school.

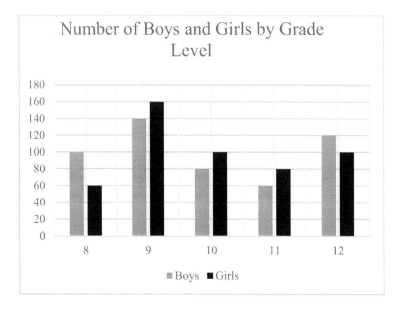

What fraction of all the boys are in 8th grade?

(A) $\frac{2}{5}$

(B) $\frac{1}{4}$

(C) $\frac{1}{5}$

(D) $\frac{100}{400}$

---

19. Wang Su had 88 music albums on his computer. If each album was 42 minutes long, which expression shows about how many minutes of music were on Wang Su's computer?
   (A) 80×30
   (B) 90×30
   (C) 80×40
   (D) 90×40

20. Use the number line below to answer the question.

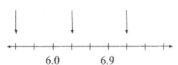

Which three numbers are the vertical arrows pointing to on the number line?
   (A)   5.8, 6.1, 7.0
   (B)   5.7, 6.3, 7.2
   (C)   5.4, 6.3, 7.2
   (D)   5.8, 6.3, 7.2

Go on to the next page. ➡

QR Practice Test #2

21. A cat had a litter of 5 kittens. Three of the kittens weighed $1\frac{1}{2}$ ounces each, 1 kitten weighed 3 ounces, and 1 kitten weighed 5 ounces. What is the mean weight of the kittens from the litter?

    (A) $1\frac{1}{2}$

    (B)   2

    (C) $2\frac{1}{2}$

    (D)   3

22. The scale on a map shows that 1.4 inches represents 20 miles. How many inches would it take to represent 50 miles?
    (A)   2.8
    (B)   3.5
    (C)   4.0
    (D)   4.2

23. Jar 1 and Jar 2 each hold 1 cup of liquid when filled to the top. The jars shown are not completely filled to the top.

    Jar 1   Jar 2

    If the liquids in the two jars are combined, approximately how many cups of liquid will there be altogether?
    (A)   1.0
    (B)   1.2
    (C)   1.5
    (D)   2.0

24. Use the pattern to help answer the question.

    $1 + 3 = 2^2$
    $1 + 3 + 5 = 3^2$
    $1 + 3 + 5 + 7 = 4^2$

    What is the solution to
    $1 + 3 + 5 + 7 + 9 + 11 + 13 + 15 + 17$?

    (A) 7^2
    (B) 9^2
    (C) 11^2
    (D) 13^2

25. In which pair of letters do both letters have an equal number of lines of symmetry?

    (A)   R A

    (B)   O C

    (C)   T M

    (D)   E F

26. A teacher put the names of all of her students into a hat. The probability that she will pull out a boy's name is 4 out of 6. There are 6 girls in the class. How many boys are in the class?
    (A)   4
    (B)   6
    (C)   12
    (D)   16

Go on to the next page. ➡

QR Practice Test #2

27. The ingredients in the recipe were evenly mixed and equally divided into 4 bags.

RECIPE
12 cups chopped chocolate pieces
6 cups of raisins
4 cups of peanuts
5 cups of pretzel sticks

Approximately how many cups of the mixture were placed in each bag?

(A)   5

(B) $6\frac{2}{8}$

(C) $6\frac{1}{2}$

(D) $6\frac{6}{8}$

28. Each side of the smaller cube is 1 ft. Each side of the larger cube is 4 ft.

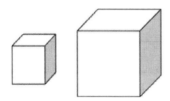

How many of the smaller cubes could fit into the larger cube?
(A)   4
(B)   16
(C)   32
(D)   64

29. Use the table to answer the question

KAITLYN'S SCHOOL SCORES

Event 1	4.7	9.0	4.7	6.7
Event 2	9.0	8.2	4.7	9.0
Event 3	9.4	4.7	6.6	9.1
Event 4	3.2	3.2	8.1	7.0

What is the mode of the data?

(A)   3.2
(B)   4.7
(C)   6.6
(D)   9.0

30. Which equation can be read as "3 less than a number divided by 7 is equal to the product of the number and 5" Let n represent the unknown number.

(A) $\frac{n}{7} - 3 = \frac{n}{5}$

(B) $\frac{n}{7} - 3 = 5n$

(C) $\frac{7}{n} - 3 = 5n$

(D) $3 - \frac{7}{n} = 5n$

31. Min-seo has a bowl of fruits: apples, oranges, bananas, and grapes. The probability of choosing a grape is 2 out of 7. What combination of fruits is possible?
(A)   2 grapes and 7 others
(B)   4 grapes and 14 others
(C)   4 grapes and 10 others
(D)   2 grapes and 9 others

Go on to the next page. ➡

32. Leon has a box shaped like a cube. He cuts some of the edges to make the box flat. Which drawing shows the flattened box?

(A)

(B)

(C)

(D)

33. A student did the problem shown on his calculator.

$$\frac{23 \times 976}{38}$$

What is a reasonable estimation for his answer?
(A)   between 400 and 600
(B)   between 600 and 800
(C)   between 800 and 1,000
(D)   between 1,000 and 1,300

34. What is the value of n in the expression

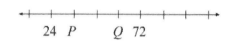

$$\frac{10(15 + 105)}{4} = n?$$

(A)   300
(B)   400
(C)   500
(D)   600

35. Use the number line below to answer the question.

24 P   Q 72

Q is the average of P and another number. What is the other number?
(A)   48
(B)   60
(C)   72
(D)   84

Go on to the next page.

Chapter 8
Mathematics Achievement
Practice Test #2

Section 4
Mathematics Achievement

| 25 Questions | Time: 25 minutes |

Each question is followed by four suggested answers. Read each question and then decide which one of the four suggested answers is best.

Find the row of spaces on your answer document that has the same answer as the question. In this row, mark the space having the same letter as the answer you have chosen. The answer document can be found after Mathematics Achievement Practice Test #2. You may write in your test booklet.

EXAMPLE 1:   Sample Answer

    What is the value of the expression $4 + (2 \times 8) \div (1 + 3)$?   Ⓐ Ⓑ ● Ⓓ

    (A) 0
    (B) 4
    (C) 8
    (D) 16

    The correct answer is 8, so circle C is darkened.

STOP. Do not go on
until told to do so. **STOP**

MA Practice Test #2

1. The figure shows a drawing of Charlie's bedroom

    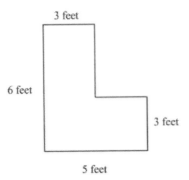

    What is the perimeter of Charlie's bedroom?
    (A)   17 feet
    (B)   22 feet
    (C)   24 feet
    (D)   30 feet

2. A total of 55 students were asked which one of four sports – basketball, soccer, tennis, or football – they preferred. If 19 students said they preferred basketball, 9 students said they preferred soccer, and 5 students said they preferred tennis, how many students said they preferred football?
    (A)   18
    (B)   22
    (C)   33
    (D)   36

3. What is the name of a quadrilateral with two pairs of opposite, parallel sides and no 90-degree angles?
    (A)   rectangle
    (B)   triangle
    (C)   trapezoid
    (D)   parallelogram

4. What is the standard form for six hundred forty two thousand ten?
    (A)   640,201
    (B)   640,210
    (C)   642,010
    (D)   642,100

5. Use the number line to answer the question

    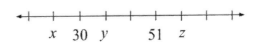

    What is the value of $z - x$?
    (A)   23
    (B)   35
    (C)   45
    (D)   58

6. What is the value of the expression $1,024 + 923$?
    (A)   101
    (B)   1,847
    (C)   1,947
    (D)   2,047

7. Which expression is equal to 6?
    (A) $4 \times (5 - 2) + (6 \div 2)$
    (B) $4 \times 2 - (5 + 6) \div 2$
    (C) $4 \times 2 - (5 + 6 \div 2)$
    (D) $(4 \times 2) - 5 + (6 \div 2)$

8. Phoebe buys five items costing $5.19, $7.99, $11.20, $3.50, and $9.25. What is the estimated total cost of Phoebe's items?
    (A)   between $35 and $40
    (B)   between $40 and $45
    (C)   between $45 and $50
    (D)   between $50 and $55

Go on to the next page. ➡

MA Practice Test #2

9. A science teacher asked his class to do an experiment. Each student placed three reactants in three separate beakers filled with different solutions. Over time, the reactants combined with the solution, leading to a decrease in the mass of reactant in each beaker. The class collected the data shown below.

SCIENCE EXPERIMENT

	Reactant 1	Reactant 2	Reactant 3
Start	50.00 mg	50.00 mg	50.00 mg
10 min	47.00 mg	49.50 mg	49.00 mg
20 min	44.00 mg	49.00 mg	47.00 mg
30 min	41.00 mg	48.50 mg	44.00 mg
40 min	38.00 mg	48.00 mg	40.00 mg
50 min	35.00 mg	47.50 mg	35.00 mg

At 40 minutes, how many more milligrams of Reactant 2 than Reactant 1 were there?
- (A) 8.00
- (B) 10.00
- (C) 12.00
- (D) 14.00

10. Which fraction is equivalent to 0.9?
- (A) $\frac{9}{90}$
- (B) $\frac{9}{100}$
- (C) $\frac{18}{20}$
- (D) $\frac{1}{9}$

11. If $4 + (☺ ÷ 6) = 7$, what number does ☺ stand for?
- (A) 12
- (B) 18
- (C) 19
- (D) 24

12. What is the value of the expression $9,050 - 645$?
- (A) 8,205
- (B) 8,305
- (C) 8,405
- (D) 9,695

13. A lake has an area of about 25,620 mi^2. Which area is closest to that of $\frac{4}{5}$ of the lake's area?
- (A) 5,000 mi^2
- (B) 10,000 mi^2
- (C) 15,000 mi^2
- (D) 20,000 mi^2

14. Use the diagram to answer the question.

If one of the blocks is picked up at random, what is the chance it will be white?
- (A) 13 out of 20
- (B) 7 out of 20
- (C) 13 out of 7
- (D) 7 out of 13

Go on to the next page. ➡

15. Cesar recorded the number of pieces of sushi 5 different students ate at lunch. Students 2 and 4 combined ate 25 more pieces of sushi than students 1 and 3 combined.

Student 1	🍣 🍣
Student 2	🍣 🍣 🍣
Student 3	🍣
Student 4	🍣 🍣 🍣 🍣 🍣
Student 5	🍣 🍣

Based on the data, how many pieces of sushi are represented by the ?

(A)   1
(B)   3
(C)   5
(D)   7

16. Use the table to answer the question

JAIME'S SCHOOL SCORES

Event 1	6.7	8.2	7.0	6.7
Event 2	3.3	8.2	6.7	9.6
Event 3	9.4	6.7	6.6	9.1
Event 4	6.7	5.8	8.2	7.0

What is the range of the data?

(A)   6.0
(B)   6.3
(C)   7.3
(D)   7.5

17. What fraction is between $\frac{1}{5}$ and $\frac{1}{2}$?

(A) $\frac{1}{6}$

(B) $\frac{3}{10}$

(C) $\frac{6}{11}$

(D) $\frac{11}{20}$

18. Use the set of numbers shown to answer the questions.

$$\{5, 13, 17, 23, 29, \ldots\}$$

Which describes this set of numbers?

(A)   even numbers
(B)   composite numbers
(C)   consecutive odd integers
(D)   prime numbers

19. What is the difference of $4.8 - 3.2$?

(A) $1\frac{1}{5}$

(B) $1\frac{3}{5}$

(C) $1\frac{6}{7}$

(D) $2\frac{6}{10}$

Go on to the next page. ➡

MA Practice Test #2

20. If the area of a rectangle is 20 cm², which equation can be used to determine the length of that rectangle? ($A = lw$ where A = Area, l = length, and h = height.)

   (A) $l = \dfrac{w}{20}$

   (B) $l = \dfrac{20}{w}$

   (C) $l = w - 20$

   (D) $l = 20 - w$

21. The rectangle below has a perimeter of 28 cm. What is the length of side x?

   (A) 4 cm
   (B) 5 cm
   (C) 7 cm
   (D) 10 cm

22. Use the coordinate grid to answer the question.

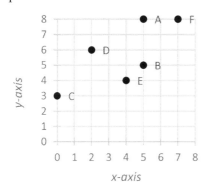

   What are the coordinates of point A in the figure?
   (A) (5,8)
   (B) (7,8)
   (C) (8,5)
   (D) (8,8)

23. Jess had $8\frac{3}{8}$ feet of wire. She used $4\frac{3}{4}$ feet of the wire to make a lamp. How many feet of wire does she have left?

   (A) $3\frac{2}{8}$

   (B) $3\frac{3}{8}$

   (C) $3\frac{4}{8}$

   (D) $3\frac{5}{8}$

24. Use the number sequence to answer the question.

$$1, 3, 9, 27, 81, \_\_\_\_$$

   What is the next number in the sequence?
   (A) 135
   (B) 162
   (C) 243
   (D) 265

25. The clocks below show the time difference between Seattle and Boston.

   Seattle   Boston

   If a plane leaves Seattle at 6:00 A.M. and arrives 4 hours later in Boston, what time will it be in Boston when the plane lands?
   (A) 10:00 A.M.
   (B) 1:00 P.M.
   (C) 2:00 P.M.
   (D) 3:00 P.M.

Go on to the next page. ➡

Name:

Test Site:

Room:

EXAM LEVEL
LOWER (L)
MIDDLE (M)
UPPER (U)

FORM

0	0
1	1
2	2
3	3
4	4
5	5
6	6
7	7
8	8
9	9

MARKING INSTRUCTIONS
- Use a #2 or HB pencil only on pages 1 and 2.
- Use a ballpoint pen for your essay on pages 3 and 4.
- Make dark marks that completely fill the circle.
- Erase cleanly any mark you wish to change.
- Make no stray marks on this form.
- Do not fold or crease this form.

CORRECT MARK   INCORRECT MARKS

ADMINISTRATORS ONLY

TESTING WITH ACCOMMODATIONS   ◯ Yes

Bubble in the first four letters of your last name.	LAST NAME	IDENTIFICATION NUMBER

① VERBAL REASONING

1 Ⓐ Ⓑ Ⓒ Ⓓ   15 Ⓐ Ⓑ Ⓒ Ⓓ   29 Ⓐ Ⓑ Ⓒ Ⓓ

2 Ⓐ Ⓑ Ⓒ Ⓓ   16 Ⓐ Ⓑ Ⓒ Ⓓ   30 Ⓐ Ⓑ Ⓒ Ⓓ

3 Ⓐ Ⓑ Ⓒ Ⓓ   17 Ⓐ Ⓑ Ⓒ Ⓓ   31 Ⓐ Ⓑ Ⓒ Ⓓ

4 Ⓐ Ⓑ Ⓒ Ⓓ   18 Ⓐ Ⓑ Ⓒ Ⓓ   32 Ⓐ Ⓑ Ⓒ Ⓓ

5 Ⓐ Ⓑ Ⓒ Ⓓ   19 Ⓐ Ⓑ Ⓒ Ⓓ   33 Ⓐ Ⓑ Ⓒ Ⓓ

6 Ⓐ Ⓑ Ⓒ Ⓓ   20 Ⓐ Ⓑ Ⓒ Ⓓ   34 Ⓐ Ⓑ Ⓒ Ⓓ
                                     Lower Level Ends

7 Ⓐ Ⓑ Ⓒ Ⓓ   21 Ⓐ Ⓑ Ⓒ Ⓓ   35 Ⓐ Ⓑ Ⓒ Ⓓ

8 Ⓐ Ⓑ Ⓒ Ⓓ   22 Ⓐ Ⓑ Ⓒ Ⓓ   36 Ⓐ Ⓑ Ⓒ Ⓓ

9 Ⓐ Ⓑ Ⓒ Ⓓ   23 Ⓐ Ⓑ Ⓒ Ⓓ   37 Ⓐ Ⓑ Ⓒ Ⓓ

10 Ⓐ Ⓑ Ⓒ Ⓓ   24 Ⓐ Ⓑ Ⓒ Ⓓ   38 Ⓐ Ⓑ Ⓒ Ⓓ

11 Ⓐ Ⓑ Ⓒ Ⓓ   25 Ⓐ Ⓑ Ⓒ Ⓓ   39 Ⓐ Ⓑ Ⓒ Ⓓ

12 Ⓐ Ⓑ Ⓒ Ⓓ   26 Ⓐ Ⓑ Ⓒ Ⓓ   40 Ⓐ Ⓑ Ⓒ Ⓓ
                                     Middle/Upper Level Ends

13 Ⓐ Ⓑ Ⓒ Ⓓ   27 Ⓐ Ⓑ Ⓒ Ⓓ

14 Ⓐ Ⓑ Ⓒ Ⓓ   28 Ⓐ Ⓑ Ⓒ Ⓓ

PLEASE DO NOT WRITE IN THIS AREA

2 QUANTITATIVE REASONING

1 Ⓐ Ⓑ Ⓒ Ⓓ	15 Ⓐ Ⓑ Ⓒ Ⓓ	29 Ⓐ Ⓑ Ⓒ Ⓓ
2 Ⓐ Ⓑ Ⓒ Ⓓ	16 Ⓐ Ⓑ Ⓒ Ⓓ	30 Ⓐ Ⓑ Ⓒ Ⓓ
3 Ⓐ Ⓑ Ⓒ Ⓓ	17 Ⓐ Ⓑ Ⓒ Ⓓ	31 Ⓐ Ⓑ Ⓒ Ⓓ
4 Ⓐ Ⓑ Ⓒ Ⓓ	18 Ⓐ Ⓑ Ⓒ Ⓓ	32 Ⓐ Ⓑ Ⓒ Ⓓ
5 Ⓐ Ⓑ Ⓒ Ⓓ	19 Ⓐ Ⓑ Ⓒ Ⓓ	33 Ⓐ Ⓑ Ⓒ Ⓓ
6 Ⓐ Ⓑ Ⓒ Ⓓ	20 Ⓐ Ⓑ Ⓒ Ⓓ	34 Ⓐ Ⓑ Ⓒ Ⓓ
7 Ⓐ Ⓑ Ⓒ Ⓓ	21 Ⓐ Ⓑ Ⓒ Ⓓ	35 Ⓐ Ⓑ Ⓒ Ⓓ
8 Ⓐ Ⓑ Ⓒ Ⓓ	22 Ⓐ Ⓑ Ⓒ Ⓓ	36 Ⓐ Ⓑ Ⓒ Ⓓ
9 Ⓐ Ⓑ Ⓒ Ⓓ	23 Ⓐ Ⓑ Ⓒ Ⓓ	37 Ⓐ Ⓑ Ⓒ Ⓓ
		Middle/Upper Level Ends
10 Ⓐ Ⓑ Ⓒ Ⓓ	24 Ⓐ Ⓑ Ⓒ Ⓓ	38 Ⓐ Ⓑ Ⓒ Ⓓ
		Lower Level Ends
11 Ⓐ Ⓑ Ⓒ Ⓓ	25 Ⓐ Ⓑ Ⓒ Ⓓ	
12 Ⓐ Ⓑ Ⓒ Ⓓ	26 Ⓐ Ⓑ Ⓒ Ⓓ	
13 Ⓐ Ⓑ Ⓒ Ⓓ	27 Ⓐ Ⓑ Ⓒ Ⓓ	
14 Ⓐ Ⓑ Ⓒ Ⓓ	28 Ⓐ Ⓑ Ⓒ Ⓓ	

4 MATHEMATICS ACHIEVEMENT

1 Ⓐ Ⓑ Ⓒ Ⓓ	18 Ⓐ Ⓑ Ⓒ Ⓓ	35 Ⓐ Ⓑ Ⓒ Ⓓ
2 Ⓐ Ⓑ Ⓒ Ⓓ	19 Ⓐ Ⓑ Ⓒ Ⓓ	36 Ⓐ Ⓑ Ⓒ Ⓓ
3 Ⓐ Ⓑ Ⓒ Ⓓ	20 Ⓐ Ⓑ Ⓒ Ⓓ	37 Ⓐ Ⓑ Ⓒ Ⓓ
4 Ⓐ Ⓑ Ⓒ Ⓓ	21 Ⓐ Ⓑ Ⓒ Ⓓ	38 Ⓐ Ⓑ Ⓒ Ⓓ
5 Ⓐ Ⓑ Ⓒ Ⓓ	22 Ⓐ Ⓑ Ⓒ Ⓓ	39 Ⓐ Ⓑ Ⓒ Ⓓ
6 Ⓐ Ⓑ Ⓒ Ⓓ	23 Ⓐ Ⓑ Ⓒ Ⓓ	40 Ⓐ Ⓑ Ⓒ Ⓓ
7 Ⓐ Ⓑ Ⓒ Ⓓ	24 Ⓐ Ⓑ Ⓒ Ⓓ	41 Ⓐ Ⓑ Ⓒ Ⓓ
8 Ⓐ Ⓑ Ⓒ Ⓓ	25 Ⓐ Ⓑ Ⓒ Ⓓ	42 Ⓐ Ⓑ Ⓒ Ⓓ
9 Ⓐ Ⓑ Ⓒ Ⓓ	26 Ⓐ Ⓑ Ⓒ Ⓓ	43 Ⓐ Ⓑ Ⓒ Ⓓ
10 Ⓐ Ⓑ Ⓒ Ⓓ	27 Ⓐ Ⓑ Ⓒ Ⓓ	44 Ⓐ Ⓑ Ⓒ Ⓓ
11 Ⓐ Ⓑ Ⓒ Ⓓ	28 Ⓐ Ⓑ Ⓒ Ⓓ	45 Ⓐ Ⓑ Ⓒ Ⓓ
12 Ⓐ Ⓑ Ⓒ Ⓓ	29 Ⓐ Ⓑ Ⓒ Ⓓ	46 Ⓐ Ⓑ Ⓒ Ⓓ
13 Ⓐ Ⓑ Ⓒ Ⓓ	30 Ⓐ Ⓑ Ⓒ Ⓓ	47 Ⓐ Ⓑ Ⓒ Ⓓ
	Lower Level Ends	Middle/Upper Level Ends
14 Ⓐ Ⓑ Ⓒ Ⓓ	31 Ⓐ Ⓑ Ⓒ Ⓓ	
15 Ⓐ Ⓑ Ⓒ Ⓓ	32 Ⓐ Ⓑ Ⓒ Ⓓ	
16 Ⓐ Ⓑ Ⓒ Ⓓ	33 Ⓐ Ⓑ Ⓒ Ⓓ	
17 Ⓐ Ⓑ Ⓒ Ⓓ	34 Ⓐ Ⓑ Ⓒ Ⓓ	

3 READING COMPREHENSION

1 Ⓐ Ⓑ Ⓒ Ⓓ	15 Ⓐ Ⓑ Ⓒ Ⓓ	29 Ⓐ Ⓑ Ⓒ Ⓓ
2 Ⓐ Ⓑ Ⓒ Ⓓ	16 Ⓐ Ⓑ Ⓒ Ⓓ	30 Ⓐ Ⓑ Ⓒ Ⓓ
3 Ⓐ Ⓑ Ⓒ Ⓓ	17 Ⓐ Ⓑ Ⓒ Ⓓ	31 Ⓐ Ⓑ Ⓒ Ⓓ
4 Ⓐ Ⓑ Ⓒ Ⓓ	18 Ⓐ Ⓑ Ⓒ Ⓓ	32 Ⓐ Ⓑ Ⓒ Ⓓ
5 Ⓐ Ⓑ Ⓒ Ⓓ	19 Ⓐ Ⓑ Ⓒ Ⓓ	33 Ⓐ Ⓑ Ⓒ Ⓓ
6 Ⓐ Ⓑ Ⓒ Ⓓ	20 Ⓐ Ⓑ Ⓒ Ⓓ	34 Ⓐ Ⓑ Ⓒ Ⓓ
7 Ⓐ Ⓑ Ⓒ Ⓓ	21 Ⓐ Ⓑ Ⓒ Ⓓ	35 Ⓐ Ⓑ Ⓒ Ⓓ
8 Ⓐ Ⓑ Ⓒ Ⓓ	22 Ⓐ Ⓑ Ⓒ Ⓓ	36 Ⓐ Ⓑ Ⓒ Ⓓ
		Middle/Upper Level Ends
9 Ⓐ Ⓑ Ⓒ Ⓓ	23 Ⓐ Ⓑ Ⓒ Ⓓ	
10 Ⓐ Ⓑ Ⓒ Ⓓ	24 Ⓐ Ⓑ Ⓒ Ⓓ	
11 Ⓐ Ⓑ Ⓒ Ⓓ	25 Ⓐ Ⓑ Ⓒ Ⓓ	
	Lower Level Ends	
12 Ⓐ Ⓑ Ⓒ Ⓓ	26 Ⓐ Ⓑ Ⓒ Ⓓ	
13 Ⓐ Ⓑ Ⓒ Ⓓ	27 Ⓐ Ⓑ Ⓒ Ⓓ	
14 Ⓐ Ⓑ Ⓒ Ⓓ	28 Ⓐ Ⓑ Ⓒ Ⓓ	

PAGE 2

Part VI
*Answer Keys &
Interpreting Your Results*

Chapter 9
Answer Keys

Quantitative Reasoning Answer Key – 35 Items
Practice Test #1

Item	Key	Your Answer	+ If Correct	*Type
1	B			ND
2	C			NW
3	B			NW
4	A			M
5	D			A
6	B			G
7	B			NW
8	C			ND
9	B			A
10	A			D
11	C			D
12	A			A
13	D			M
14	B			A
15	B			A
16	A			ND
17	B			D
18	D			ND
19	D			A
20	A			A
21	B			NW
22	B			M
23	B			ND
24	C			A
25	D			G
26	D			ND
27	C			D
28	B			A
29	A			G
30	B			D
31	A			A
32	A			D
33	A			NW
34	B			NW
35	A			A

*Key to Type of Item

NW = Numbers and Operations (Whole Numbers)
ND = Numbers and Operations (Decimals, Percents, Fractions)
A = Algebraic Concepts
G = Geometry
M = Measurement
D = Data Analysis and Probability

Quantitative Reasoning Answer Explanations – 35 Items
Practice Test #1

1. (B)   8 out of 16 total squares are shaded in, so the fraction should be $\frac{8}{16}$. This is not an option,

   so you must find an equivalent fraction. The only possible answer is $\frac{4}{8}$

2. (C)   (A) represents addition, (B) represents division, and (D) represents subtraction.
          (C) is the only correct answer.

3. (B)   If the number is greater than 23 and less than 27, the number could be 24, 25, or 26. The
          number is not 26, so the final answer must be 24 or 25. Noam told Weiwei that the
          number is greater than 24, which leaves 25 as the only possible answer.

4. (A) $36 - 14 - 12 = 10$.

5. (D) $x = 3$ and $y = 5$. $5 + 3 = 8$. (A) represents $5 - 3$, while (B) and (C) represent the values of
          x and y, respectively. Be careful not to choose trick answers!

6. (B)   (B) is the only option that fits into the given diagram.

7. (B)   There are a few ways to do this question. One way is to figure out how long it takes Peter
          and Jessie to hike 1 mile, then multiply that answer by 11. If it takes 32 minutes to hike 2
          miles, then it takes 16 minutes to hike 1 mile, because 1 is half of 2, and 16 is half of 32.
          $16 \times 11 = 176$. You can also set up a ratio, cross multiply, and solve. $\frac{32}{2} = \frac{x}{11}$. After cross
          multiplying, you get $2x = 352$. $2 \times 176 = 352$, so 176 is the answer.

8. (C)   If the numerator of several fractions is the same, the fractions become larger as the
          numerator becomes larger. All of the fractions in this question have 1 as their numerator.
          (C) has the smallest denominator and is therefore the largest fraction.

9. (B)   First, ask yourself what number is the smallest number that is divisible by both 5 and 8.
          The answer is 40. Then, look at the answer choices and see which one is divisible by 40.
          $40 \div 20 = 2$, so (B) is the only possible answer.

10. (A) The numbers in the shaded region will be **both** multiples of 3 and **even** numbers. 3, 5, 21,
          and 33 are odd, so those won't work. Out of 6, 12, 14, and 30, 14 is the only number not
          divisible by 3. That leaves 3 numbers: 6, 12, and 30.

Quantitative Reasoning Answer Explanations – 35 Items
Practice Test #1

11. (C) There is a lot of information in this table, so don't waste your time focusing on irrelevant data. You are only asked about Reactant 1, so focus your efforts on that column. The amount of reactant remaining in column 1 goes down by 3 every 10 minutes. At 60 minutes, there will be 35.00 – 3.00 = 32.00 mg remaining. At 70 minutes, there will be 32.00 – 3.00 = 29.00 mg remaining. At 80 minutes, there will be 29.00 – 3.00 = 26.00 mg remaining.

12. (A) Remember your order of operations. $5 \times 3 - 7 = 8$, $9 \times 3 - 7 = 20$, and $10 \times 3 - 7 = 23$. It's usually unnecessary to check all four inputs.

13. (D) Each side of a square has an equal length. $40y \div 4 = 10y$.

14. (B) You can work backwards on this question. $4(8) + 9 = 32 + 9 = 41$.

15. (B) In Row 1, the answer is 2^2. In Row 2, the answer is 3^2. In Row 3, the answer is 4^2. As you can see, for each row, the base of the answer will be the row number + 1. Therefore, in row 10, the answer will be $10 + 1 = 11$. The exponent is always 2.

16. (A) Cookies and cream $= \frac{1}{2}$ of the pie chart, and mint $= \frac{1}{4}$ of the pie chart. Chocolate chip and vanilla are both smaller than mint. The only fraction smaller than $\frac{1}{4}$ is $\frac{1}{8}$. You can also divide the pie into 8 equal pieces to see that chocolate chip and vanilla $= \frac{1}{8}$, mint $= \frac{2}{8}$, and cookies and cream $= \frac{4}{8}$

17. (B) Mean = average. Add up all of the numbers and divide by the total number of numbers. $4\frac{1}{2} + 4\frac{1}{2} + 2 + 5 = 16$. $16 \div 4 = 4$.

18. (D) Find the difference between the labeled tick marks on the number line. $2.9 - 0.5 = 2.4$. Then, divide by the number of spaces between the two numbers. $2.4 \div 4 = 0.6$. Therefore, each tick mark represents an increase of 0.6. The value of the tick mark immediately to the right of 0.5 is $0.5 + 0.6 = 1.1$. You can eliminate (A) and (B). The value of the tick mark under the second arrow is $1.1 + 0.6 + 0.6 = 2.3$. (D) is the only possible answer.

19. (D) The first row has 1 triangle, the second row has 3 triangles, and the third row has 5 triangles. The number of triangles increases by 2 in each row. Therefore, the fourth row will have 7 triangles, the fifth row will have 9 triangles, and the sixth row will have 11 triangles.

Quantitative Reasoning Answer Explanations – 35 Items
Practice Test #1

20. (A)   You can use real numbers here. If $HJ = 10$ and $IJ = 6$, you would do $10 - 6$ to find the length of HI. Therefore, $HI = x - y$.

21. (B)   14 rounds up to 15 and 33 rounds down to 30.

22. (B)   The length, width, and height of a cube are all equal to one another. $6 \times 6 \times 6 = 216$.

23. (B)   Jar 1 is $\frac{1}{3}$ full, and Jar 2 is $\frac{1}{2}$ full. $\frac{1}{3} + \frac{1}{2} = \frac{2}{6} + \frac{3}{6} = \frac{5}{6}$. $\frac{5}{6}$ is greater than $\frac{1}{2}$ but less than 1, so the answer must be 0.8

24. (C)   The equation for triangle area is $\frac{bh}{2}$. Fill in with the given information and solve. $\frac{(9)(10)}{2} = \frac{90}{2} = 45$.

25. (D)   Focus on the upper left semicircle. If you flip it over line w, it will then be on the same side of line w as the semicircle on the bottom right. Then, if you flip it over line y, it will land on top of the other semicircle.

26. (D)   This question is asking you to find the average amount of mixture in each bag. Add up the numbers and divide by the number of bags. $\frac{1 + 2 + 4 + 6 + 1}{3} = \frac{14}{3} = 4\frac{2}{3}$

27. (C)   If the probability of pulling a girl's name is 7 out of 9, the probability of pulling a boy's name is 2 out of 9. Since there are actually 14 boys in the class, that means the multiplier is 7, because $2 \times 7 = 14$. $7 \times 7 = 49$, so there must be 49 girls and 14 boys in the class.

28. (B)   1 sphere + 7 spheres + 10 spheres = 18 spheres. 18 spheres = 36 grams, which means 1 sphere equals 2 grams. Therefore, the pyramid weighs $7 \times 2 = 14$ grams, and the cube weighs $10 \times 2 = 20$ grams. You can then add these values to confirm you did everything correctly: $2 + 14 + 20 = 36$. (A) and (C) are trick answers.

29. (A)   Draw a line from L to the other vertices in the pentagon. Three triangles will be formed. You can also remember that in these question types, the number of triangles formed will always be two fewer than the number of sides in the shape.

Quantitative Reasoning Answer Explanations – 35 Items
Practice Test #1

30. (B)   Jimmy watched 30 minutes and Latoya watched 20, so (A) is incorrect. The range is 30 – 10 = 20, and Latoya watched 20 minutes, so the range is equal to, not greater than, the number of minutes Latoya watched. Carl and Ahmed watched 10 + 15 = 25 minutes, which is more than Latoya watched. By process of elimination, (B) must be the correct answer. Remember that finding the mean is always more time consuming than finding the median, mode, and range, so only find the mean when you absolutely have to.

31. (A)   "5 times a number" = $5 \times n$. "2 more than" = $+ 2$, so you can eliminate (D). "4 divided by that number" = $\frac{4}{n}$. "8 less than" = $- 8$. When you put everything together, is looks like this: $(5 \times n) + 2 = \frac{4}{n} - 8$

32. (A)   If there is a 9 out of 20 chance of choosing a chocolate filled with vanilla, that means there is an 11 out of 20 chance of choosing something else. Therefore, Vanilla chocolates much be in multiples of 9, and other chocolates must be in multiples of 11. (A) is the only answer that works.

33. (A)   The question asks for an estimate, so you should not try to do this question as written. Rewrite $\frac{578 \times 111}{52}$ as $\frac{600 \times 100}{50}$. You may be able to do 600×100 in your head: just add 2 zeros to 600 to get 60,000. Otherwise, you'll have to write out the multiplication. $60,000 \div 50 = 1,200$. (A) is the best answer. If you used a calculator, you'd get 1,233.81, which is pretty close to the answer you got by estimating.

34. (B)   You can't estimate on this question; you'll actually have to do the work. Remember your order of operations. $\frac{15(10 + 60)}{5} = \frac{15(70)}{5} = \frac{1,050}{5} = 210$.

35. (A)   First, fill in the missing tick marks on the number line. $50 – 10 = 40$. There are 4 blank spaces between 10 and 50. $\frac{40}{4} = 10$, so each tick mark represents $+10$. Therefore, $M = 30$ and $N = 60$. If M is the average of N and another number, then $\frac{60 + x}{2} = 30$. Then, work backwards using the answer choices. $\frac{60 + 0}{2} = 30$, so (A) is the correct answer.

Mathematics Achievement Answer Key – 25 Items
Practice Test #1

Item	Key	Your Answer	+ If Correct	*Type
1	D			B
2	B			D
3	C			G
4	A			NW
5	C			G
6	A			A
7	B			ND
8	A			D
9	B			NW
10	D			A
11	A			NW
12	A			ND
13	C			ND
14	B			G
15	D			D
16	D			ND
17	C			D
18	B			NW
19	C			A
20	C			M
21	B			M
22	D			G
23	B			A
24	C			ND
25	A			ND

*Key to Type of Item

NW = Numbers and Operations (Whole Numbers)
ND = Numbers and Operations (Decimals, Percents, Fractions)
A = Algebraic Concepts
G = Geometry
M = Measurement
D = Data Analysis and Probability

Mathematics Achievement Answer Explanations – 25 Items
Practice Test #1

1. (D) $5 + 9 + 10 = 24$.

2. (B) $33 - 14 - 6 = 13$.

3. (C)   Squares have 4 equal sides, so (A) is incorrect. Rectangles have *opposite* sides that are equal, not *adjacent* sides, so (B) is incorrect. Pentagons have 5 sides, so (D) is incorrect. (C) is the only possible answer.

4. (A)   See the *Standard Form* section in Part III if you do not understand how to do this question.

5. (C)   Plot the points:

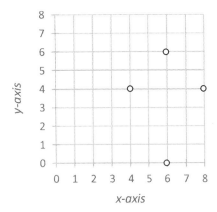

The shape that is formed has 2 pairs of adjacent sides that are the same length and no right angles. The only shape that matches this description is a kite.

6. (A) $(6 \times 6) + 2 - 8 = 36 + 2 - 8 = 38 - 8 = 30$.

7. (B) $0.2 = \frac{20}{100}$. This is not an option, so reduce the fraction. $\frac{20 \div 20}{100 \div 20} = \frac{1}{5}$

8. (A)   On Day 5, there were 45 flies in Tube 3 and 40 flies in Tube 2. $45 - 40 = 5$.

9. (B)   You should review basic subtraction if you are unsure of how to do this question.

10. (D)   Work backwards. $4 \times (4 + 6) = 4 \times (10) = 40$.

11. (A)   Round 38,150 down to 38,000. $\frac{1}{2}$ of 38,000 is 19,000.

Mathematics Achievement Answer Explanations – 25 Items
Practice Test #1

---

12. (A)   The man bought 3 oranges (3 × $0.75 = $2.25), 1 juice, 6 pears (6 × $1.00 = $6.00) and 9 candies (9 × $0.25 = $2.25). 3 + 1 + 6 + 9 = 19.

13. (C)   This question asks you to estimate. $4.95 rounds up to $5.00, $2.99 rounds up to $3.00, $16.75 rounds up to $17.00, $0.50 can stay the same, and $6.99 rounds up to $7.00. 5 + 3 + 17 + 0.5 + 7 = $32.50, which is between $30 and $35.

14. (B)   Square have four 90-degree angles, so (A) is wrong. Trapezoids must have 1 pair of parallel sides, which is not the case here, so (C) is wrong. Rhombi have 4 sides that are all the same length, so (D) is wrong. (B) is the only possible answer.

15. (D)   There are 3 black marbles out of 10 marbles total. The probability of choosing a black marble is 3 out of 10.

16. (D)   Convert $\frac{7}{10}$ to $\frac{70}{100}$ to make the two fractions easier to compare. You can't make $\frac{5}{8}$ have 100 in the denominator, so ignore (A) for now. $\frac{1 \times 50}{2 \times 50} = \frac{50}{100}$, which is too small. $\frac{3 \times 20}{5 \times 20} = \frac{60}{100}$, which is also too small. $\frac{17 \times 5}{20 \times 5} = \frac{85}{100}$, which is in the middle of the two fractions. You don't have to check (A). (D) must be the correct answer.

17. (C)   Range is the difference between the largest and smallest number in a data set. The largest number in this data set is 9.8, and the smallest number is 3.9. 9.8 – 3.9 = 5.9.

18. (B)   9 and 15 are odd, so (A) is wrong. 2 is prime, not composite, so (C) is wrong. Several of the numbers are not prime, so (D) is wrong. Whole numbers are positive integers and 0, so (B) is the correct answer.

19. (C)   Input the given information and then rearrange the equation to solve. $40 = \frac{bh}{2}$. Multiply both sides by 2 to get $80 = bh$. Divide both sides by h to get $\frac{80}{h} = b$. (C) is the correct answer.

20. (C)   2(4) + 2(7) = 8 + 14 = 22.

21. (B)   Flying for two hours from Little Rock results in 11:00 A.M. + 2 hours = 1:00 P.M. Tampa is 1 hour ahead of Little Rock, so you must add on 1 more hour to get 2:00 P.M.

Mathematics Achievement Answer Explanations – 25 Items
Practice Test #1

22. (D)   To get to point E, you must move 5 spaces right and 7 spaces up.

23. (B)   The pattern is $+1, +3, +5, +7, +9$. $26 + 11 = 37$.

24. (C) $4.4 + 1.8 = 6.2$. $0.2 = \frac{20}{100}$, which reduces to $\frac{1}{5}$. The final answer is $6\frac{1}{5}$

25. (A)   First, convert $\frac{1}{2}$ to $\frac{4}{8}$. $4\frac{3}{8} = \frac{35}{8}$. $2\frac{4}{8} = \frac{20}{8}$. $\frac{35}{8} - \frac{20}{8} = \frac{15}{8}$. $\frac{15}{8} = 1\frac{7}{8}$

Quantitative Reasoning Answer Key – 35 Items
Practice Test #2

Item	Key	Your Answer	+ If Correct	*Type
1	D			ND
2	C			NW
3	C			NW
4	B			M
5	A			A
6	D			D
7	D			G
8	C			ND
9	D			NW
10	B			A
11	C			A
12	B			M
13	D			D
14	B			A
15	C			A
16	B			A
17	D			NW
18	C			ND
19	D			NW
20	C			ND
21	C			D
22	B			ND
23	B			ND
24	B			A
25	C			G
26	C			D
27	D			ND
28	D			M
29	B			D
30	B			A
31	C			D
32	B			G
33	A			NW
34	A			NW
35	D			A

*Key to Type of Item

NW = Numbers and Operations (Whole Numbers)
ND = Numbers and Operations (Decimals, Percents, Fractions)
A = Algebraic Concepts
G = Geometry
M = Measurement
D = Data Analysis and Probability

Quantitative Reasoning Answer Explanations – 35 Items
Practice Test #2

1. (D)   Hugo's teacher received 3 pieces of candy, which is $\frac{1}{6}$ of Hugo's total candy. 3 is $\frac{1}{6}$ of 18, which means Hugo started with 18 pieces of candy. Daniel received $\frac{1}{3}$ of the total number of pieces of candy. $\frac{1}{3}$ of 18 is 6, so Daniel received 6 pieces of candy.

2. (C)   (A) represents addition, (B) represents multiplication, and (D) represents subtraction. (C) is the only correct answer.

3. (C)   If the number is greater than 1 and less than 4, it could either be 2 or 3. The number is also greater than 2 and less than 5, which means it cannot be equal to 2. The only possible number is 3.

4. (B) $17 - 7 - 4 = 6$.

5. (A) $a = 10$ and $b = 5$. $10 - 5 = 5$.

6. (D)   9 students ate only hamburgers, 10 ate only pizza, and 2 ate both. $9 + 10 + 2 = 21$.

7. (D)   The top row of the missing piece is 4 boxes across, the second and third rows are each 1 box across, and the bottom row is 4 boxes across. (D) is the only piece that fits this description.

8. (C)   (A), (B), and (D) are all greater than $\frac{1}{2}$. (C) is the only fraction that is less than $\frac{1}{2}$.

9. (D)   7.5 is 3 times as much as 2.5. Therefore, it would take 3 times as long for Christos to ride that far. $15 \times 3 = 45$.

10. (B)   Think of a number that 4 and 10 both go into. That number could be 20, 40, 60, 80, etc. All 4 of those examples are divisible by 20.

11. (C)   Any number divided by itself is 1 (with the exception of 0, because $0 \div 0$ is undefined). (C) represents each number in the Input column being divided by itself.

12. (B)   The lengths of each side of a square are equal. $60y \div 4 = 15y$.

Quantitative Reasoning Answer Explanations – 35 Items
Practice Test #2

---

13. (D)   In Tube 3, from Start to Day 1 the number of fruit flies increased by 1; from Day 1 to Day 2, the number of fruit flies increased by 2, from Day 2 to Day 3 the number of fruit flies increased by 3, etc. From Day 5 to Day 6, the number of fruit flies will increase by 6 to 36. From Day 6 to Day 7, the number of fruit flies will increase by 7 to 43.

14. (B)   You can work backwards on this question. $2(6) - 3 = 12 - 3 = 9$.

15. (C)   The student sells 7 more cookies on each successive day. On Thursday, the student will sell $18 + 7 = 25$ cookies. On Friday, the student will sell $25 + 7 = 32$ cookies.

16. (B)   You can use real numbers here. If $XY = 4$ and $YZ = 5$, you would do $4 + 5$ to find the length of XZ. Therefore, $XZ = m + n$.

17. (D)   The *associative property* states that when adding or multiplying, the sum or product will be the same regardless of how the numbers are grouped. An example of the associative property is $(2 + 7) + 5 = 2 + (7 + 5)$. The only answer that matches this example is (D).

18. (C)   Add up the total number of boys: $100 + 140 + 80 + 60 + 120 = 500$. There are 100 boys in 8$^\text{th}$ grade. $\frac{100}{500} = \frac{1}{5}$

19. (D)   88 rounds up to 90, and 42 rounds down to 40.

20. (C)   Find the difference between the labeled tick marks on the number line. $6.9 - 6.0 = 0.9$. Then, divide by the number of spaces between the two numbers. $0.9 \div 3 = 0.3$. Therefore, each tick mark represents an increase of 0.3. The value of the tick mark immediately to the right of 6.0 is 6.3. The value of the tick mark two to the left of 6.0 is $6.0 - 0.3 - 0.3 = 5.4$. (C) is the only possible answer.

21. (C)   Mean = average. Add up all of the numbers and divide by the total number of numbers. $1\frac{1}{2} + 1\frac{1}{2} + 1\frac{1}{2} + 3 + 5 = 12\frac{1}{2}$. $12\frac{1}{2} \div 5 = \frac{25}{2} \div \frac{5}{1} = \frac{25}{2} \times \frac{1}{5} = \frac{25}{10} = 2\frac{5}{10} = 2\frac{1}{2}$

22. (B)   50 is $2\frac{1}{2}$ times as large as 20. Therefore, you must multiply 1.4 by $2\frac{1}{2}$. $1.4 \times 2.5 = 3.5$.

23. (B)   Jar 1 is $\frac{5}{6}$ full. Jar 2 is $\frac{1}{3}$ full. $\frac{5}{6} + \frac{1}{3} = \frac{5}{6} + \frac{2}{6} = \frac{7}{6}$, which is slightly larger than 1. (B) is the best answer.

Quantitative Reasoning Answer Explanations – 35 Items
Practice Test #2

24. (B)   In Row 1, the sum of 2 numbers is 2^2. In Row 2, the sum of 3 numbers is 3^2. The base of the exponent will always be equal to the number of integers added together. There are 9 integers in the example, so the answer will be 9^2.

25. (C) R has zero lines of symmetry, and A has one line of symmetry. O has infinite lines of symmetry, and C has one line of symmetry. E has one line of symmetry, and F has zero lines of symmetry. T has one line of symmetry, and M has one line of symmetry. (C) is the correct answer.

26. (C)   If the probability of pulling out a boy's name is 4 out of 6, then the probability of pulling out a girl's name is 2 out of 6. There are actually 6 girls in the class, which means the multiplier is 3. The chance of pulling out a boy's name is 4 out of 6. $4 \times 3 = 12$. There are 12 boys and 6 girls in the class.

27. (D) $12 + 6 + 4 + 5 = 27$. 27 cups will be equally divided into 4 bags. $\frac{27}{4} = 6\frac{3}{4}$. This is not an answer choice. However, $6\frac{3}{4} = 6\frac{6}{8}$. (D) is the correct answer.

28. (D)   You must find the volume of each cube. The volume of the smaller cube is $1 \times 1 \times 1 = 1$ ft^3. The volume of the larger cube is $4 \times 4 \times 4 = 64$ ft^3. $64 \div 1 = 64$.

29. (B)   **Mo**de means **mo**st. 3.2 appears 2 times, 4.7 appears 4 times, 6.6 appears 1 time, and 9.0 appears 3 times. 4.7 appears more than any other number, so it is the mode.

30. (B)   "A number divided by 7" $= \frac{n}{7}$. "3 less than a number" $= -3$, so you can eliminate (D). "The product of the number and 5" $= 5n$. When you put everything together, it looks like this: $\frac{n}{7} - 3 = 5n$.

31. (C)   If there is a 2 out of 7 chance of choosing a grape, that means there is a 5 out of 7 chance of choosing something else. Therefore, grapes must be in multiples of 2, and the other fruits must be in multiples of 5. (C) is the only answer choice that works.

32. (B)   To fold the flattened boxes into a cube, there must be four squares in a row. You can eliminate (A) and (D). (C) will not form a cube. (B) is the only correct answer.

Quantitative Reasoning Answer Explanations – 35 Items
Practice Test #2

33. (A)   The question asks for an estimate. Rewrite $\frac{23 \times 976}{38}$ as $\frac{20 \times 1,000}{40}$. You may be able to do

$20 \times 1,000$ in your head: just add 3 zeros to 20 to get 20,000. Otherwise, you'll have to

write out the multiplication. $20,000 \div 40 = 500$. (A) is the best answer. If you used a

calculator, you'd get 590.7, which is pretty close to the answer you got by estimating.

34. (A)   You can't estimate on this question; you'll actually have to do the work. Remember your

order of operations: $\frac{10(15 + 105)}{4} = \frac{10(120)}{4} = \frac{1,200}{4} = 300$.

35. (D)   First, fill in the missing tick marks on the number line. $72 - 24 = 48$. There are 4 blank

spaces between 24 and 72. $\frac{48}{4} = 12$, so each tick mark represents $+12$. Therefore, $P = 36$

and $Q = 60$. If Q is the average of P and another number, then $\frac{36 + x}{2} = 60$. Then, work

backwards using the answer choices. $\frac{36 + 84}{2} = 60$, so (D) is the correct answer.

Mathematics Achievement Answer Key – 25 Items
Practice Test #2

Item	Key	Your Answer	+ If Correct	*Type
1	B			M
2	B			D
3	D			G
4	C			NW
5	B			NW
6	C			NW
7	D			A
8	A			ND
9	B			D
10	C			ND
11	B			A
12	C			NW
13	D			NW
14	A			D
15	C			D
16	B			D
17	B			ND
18	D			NW
19	B			ND
20	B			A
21	D			M
22	A			G
23	D			ND
24	C			A
25	B			M

*Key to Type of Item

NW = Numbers and Operations (Whole Numbers)
ND = Numbers and Operations (Decimals, Percents, Fractions)
A = Algebraic Concepts
G = Geometry
M = Measurement
D = Data Analysis and Probability

Mathematics Achievement Answer Explanations – 25 Items
Practice Test #2

---

1. (B)   The missing horizontal side is $5 - 3 = 2$ feet. The missing vertical side is $6 - 3 = 3$ feet. Now, add all the sides together. $6 + 3 + 3 + 2 + 3 + 5 = 22$.

2. (B) $55 - 19 - 9 - 5 = 22$.

3. (D)   A rectangle has four 90-degree angles, so (A) is incorrect. Triangles only have three sides, so (B) is incorrect. Trapezoids only have one pair of parallel sides, so (C) is incorrect. Parallelograms have two pairs of parallel sides, and they have either no 90-degree angles or four 90-degree angles. (D) is the correct answer.

4. (C)   See the *Standard Form* section in Chapter III if you do not understand how to do this question.

5. (B)   First, find the value of the tick marks. $51 - 30 = 21$. There are three blank spaces between 30 and 51. $21 \div 3 = 7$. Each tick mark represents $+7$. Therefore, $x = 30 - 7 = 23$. $Z = 51 + 7 = 58$. $58 - 23 = 35$.

6. (C)   You should review basic addition if you are unsure of how to do this problem.

7. (D) $4 \times (5 - 2) + (6 \div 2) = 4 \times (3) + (3) = 12 + 3 = 15$
$4 \times 2 - (5 + 6) \div 2 = 8 - (11) \div 2 = 8 - \frac{11}{2} = 8 - 5\frac{1}{2} = 2\frac{1}{2}$
$4 \times 2 - (5 + 6 \div 2) = 8 - (5 + 3) = 8 - 8 = 0$
$(4 \times 2) - 5 + (6 \div 2) = 8 - 5 + (3) = 3 + 3 = \mathbf{6}$. (D) is correct.

8. (A)   Estimate: $5 + 8 + 11 + 3.50 + 9 = 36.50$. This falls between 35 and 40.

9. (B)   At 40 minutes, there were 48.00 mg of Reactant 2 and 38.00 mg of Reactant 1. $48 - 38 = 10$.

10. (C) $0.90 = \frac{90}{100}$. $\frac{90 \div 5}{100 \div 5} = \frac{18}{20}$.

11. (B)   Work backwards. $4 + (18 \div 6) = 4 + 3 = 7$.

12. (C)   You should review basic subtraction if you are unsure of how to do this problem.

13. (D)   Round 25,620 down to 25,000. $\frac{4}{5}$ of 25,000 is 20,000.

14. (A)   There are 13 white blocks out of 20 total blocks, so the chance of picking a white block is 13 out of 20.

Mathematics Achievement Answer Explanations – 25 Items
Practice Test #2

15. (C)   On the graph, Students 2 and 4 ate 8 total pieces of sushi, and Students 1 and 3 ate 3 total pieces of sushi. $8 - 3 = 5$. Ask yourself, "what times $5 = 25$?" The answer is 5. Students 2 and 4 actually ate 40 total pieces of sushi, and Students 1 and 3 actually ate 15 total pieces of sushi. $40 - 15 = 25$, so you know you have found the correct answer.

16. (B)   The largest number on the table is 9.6 and the smallest number is 3.3. Range = largest number – smallest number. $9.6 - 3.3 = 6.3$.

17. (B)   Convert the given fractions so they have the same denominator. $\frac{1}{5} = \frac{2}{10}$, and $\frac{1}{2} = \frac{5}{10}$. $\frac{3}{10}$ is between these two fractions, so (B) is the correct answer.

18. (D)   All of the numbers are odd, so (A) is incorrect. None of the numbers are composite, so (B) is incorrect. There are no consecutive odd integers, so (C) is incorrect. All of the numbers are prime, so (D) is correct.

19. (B) $4.8 - 3.2 = 1.6$. $0.6 = \frac{60}{100}$. Then, reduce the fraction. $\frac{60 \div 20}{100 \div 20} = \frac{3}{5}$. The correct answer is $1\frac{3}{5}$

20. (B) $20 = lw$. Divide both sides by w to get $l = \frac{20}{w}$

21. (D)   The two vertical sides are both 4 cm long. $28 - 4 - 4 = 20$. The combined length of the two horizontal sides is 20 cm. $\frac{20}{2} = 10$.

22. (A)   From $(0,0)$, move 5 spaces to the right and 8 spaces up. The coordinates of Point A are $(5,8)$.

23. (D)   Convert the mixed numbers to improper fractions. $\frac{67}{8} - \frac{19}{4} = \frac{67}{8} - \frac{38}{8} = \frac{29}{8} = 3\frac{5}{8}$

24. (C)   Each number in the sequence is multiplied by 3. $81 \times 3 = 243$.

25. (B)   Boston is 3 hours ahead of Seattle. If the flight leaves at 6:00 A.M. and takes 4 hours, it lands at 10:00 A.M. Seattle time. Then, add 3 hours to account for the time zone change.

Chapter 10
Interpreting Your Results

Interpreting Your Results

Once you've completed a practice test, check your answers using the answer key. Place a "+" next to each correct answer to determine your raw score (the total number of questions you answered correctly). Then, look at the Conversion Table to find your Reported Range. Using your Reported Range, look at the appropriate grade level on the Scaled Score Quartiles chart. Finally, use your quartile to determine your stanine.

Example: A student applying to 5th grade answers 27 questions correctly on the Quantitative Reasoning test. This gives the student a reported range of 851 to 881. A score of 861 puts a student applying to 5th grade in the 75th percentile of students taking the test. The lowest end of this student's range is a bit below the 75th percentile, while the highest end would put the student above the 75th percentile. A percentile rank of 75 would convert to a stanine of 6. Because this is the lowest range of the student's scores, he or she would receive a stanine score of approximately 6 to 8.

Quantitative Reasoning Conversion Table – Lower Level ISEE

Raw Score	Reported Range	
35	877	907
34	874	904
33	870	900
32	867	897
31	864	894
30	861	891
29	858	888
28	854	884
27	851	881
26	848	878
25	845	875
24	841	871
23	838	868
22	835	865
21	832	862
20	829	859
19	826	856
18	822	852
17	819	849
16	816	846
15	813	843
14	810	840
13	806	836
12	803	833
11	800	830
10	797	827
9	793	823
8	790	820
7	787	817
6	784	814
5	780	810
4	777	807
3	774	804
2	771	801
1	768	798
0	764	794

2018 ISEE Practice Tests Scaled Score Ranges (Min. = 764 and Max. = 907)

Comparative Data Scaled Score Quartiles Based on 2017-2018 ISEE Norms			
Applicants to GRADE	75th	50th	25th
5	861	845	829
6	874	858	843

Percentile Rank	Stanine
1-3	1
4-10	2
11-22	3
23-39	4
40-59	5
60-76	6
77-88	7
89-95	8
96-99	9

*Minimum reported range is 30 points wide

281

Mathematics Achievement Conversion Table – Lower Level ISEE

2018 ISEE Practice Tests Scaled Score Ranges (Min. = 781 and Max. = 904)		
Raw Score	**Reported Range**	
25	874	904
24	870	900
23	866	896
22	862	892
21	859	889
20	855	885
19	851	881
18	847	877
17	844	874
16	840	870
15	836	866
14	833	863
13	829	859
12	825	855
11	822	852
10	818	848
9	814	844
8	811	841
7	807	837
6	803	833
5	800	830
4	796	826
3	792	822
2	788	818
1	785	815
0	781	811

*Minimum reported range is 30 points wide

Comparative Data Scaled Score Quartiles Based on 2017-2018 ISEE Norms			
Applicants to GRADE	**75th**	**50th**	**25th**
5	865	850	834
6	876	864	849

Percentile Rank	Stanine
1-3	1
4-10	2
11-22	3
23-39	4
40-59	5
60-76	6
77-88	7
89-95	8
96-99	9

Made in the USA
Middletown, DE
10 October 2023

40534796R00157